OBJECTS OF CHANGE

SMITHSONIAN SERIES IN ARCHAEOLOGICAL INQUIRY

Robert McC. Adams and Bruce D. Smith, Series Editors

The Smithsonian Series in Archaeological Inquiry presents original case studies that address important general research problems and demonstrate the values of particular theoretical and/or methodological approaches. Titles include well-focused, edited collections as well as works by individual authors. The series is open to all subject areas, geographical regions, and theoretical modes.

OBJECTS OF CHANGE

The Archaeology and History of Arikara Contact with Europeans

J. DANIEL ROGERS

Smithsonian Institution Press
Washington and London

Cover and title page: A drawing taken from the robe of Bloody Knife, a noted Arikara scout and warrior. Courtesy of the National Anthropological Archives.

Printed in the United States of America.

Editor, Robin A. Gould
Designer, Linda McKnight

Library of Congress
Cataloging-in-Publication Data
Rogers, J. Daniel.
Objects of Change: the archaeology and history of Arikara contact
with Europeans / by J. Daniel Rogers
p. cm. — (Smithsonian series in archaeolgical inquiry)
Includes bibliographical references.
ISBN 0-87474-840-2
1. Arikara Indians—History. 2. Arikara Indians—First contact
with Occidental civilization. 3. Arikara Indians—Antiquities.
4. Great Plains—
Antiquities. I. Title. II. Series.
E99.A8R64 1990
303.48'2'089975—dc20 89-600382

97 96 95 94 93 92 91 90 5 4 3 2 1

♾The paper used in this publication meets the minimum requirements of the American National Standard for Permanence of Paper for Printed Library Materials Z39.48—1984.

TO THE ARIKARA PEOPLE

CONTENTS

LIST OF FIGURES

LIST OF TABLES

ACKNOWLEDGMENTS

In 1982 I completed my M.A. thesis at the University of Oklahoma and decided that I would seek a complementary yet different experience for the continuation of my graduate studies. With this goal in mind I attended the University of Chicago where I had the good fortune to study with Raymond D. Fogelson, Marshall Sahlins, Don S. Rice, Leslie G. Freeman, Robert McC. Adams, and Karl W. Butzer and where I also had the opportunity to take courses at nearby Northwestern University with James A. Brown, Jane E. Buikstra, Christopher S. Peebles, and Mark S. Aldenderfer. My studies at Chicago have had a major impact on my research interests and I thank each of my teachers for their major and minor contributions to the content and scope of this volume. I also acknowledge the contributions of fellow students, friends, and colleagues who gave freely of their time and consideration during the formative stages of this study and later by commenting on various drafts; those individuals include Randi Korn, Garry F. Rogers, Marianne D. Carr, Carla M. Sinopoli, Samuel M. Wilson, David Jessup, Douglas R. Parks, Jack L. Hofman, Carlyle S. Smith, Charles E. Orser, Jr., and Stanley A. Ahler. My wife, Randi Korn, has rendered special assistance, not only by commenting on the study, but in a number of more subtle, yet equally important ways. I also offer special thanks to Craig M. Johnson for his generous assistance in helping to sort out the complexities of Arikara site chronologies.

Several agencies, institutions, and individuals made it possible to collect the information necessary to complete this study. I thank the National Science Foundation for the award of a grant (#BNS-8518547) and the American Museum of Natural History for the award of a Lounsbery Research Grant to conduct archival studies at various institutions. Research data were collected at the National Anthropological Archives at the Smithsonian Institution, the Nebraska State Museum, the Nebraska Historical Society, the University of Nebraska, the Missouri Historical Society, and the Department of Anthropology at the University of Tennessee. I thank all of the individuals at each of the institutions who facilitated access to the necessary information. At the University of Tennessee, special thanks go to William M. Bass and Patrick S. Willey, not only for their permission to examine field records on Arikara excavations, but also for their active interest in this project.

Computer assistance for the Q-Analysis, discussed in Chapter 8, was generously provided by Larry Gorenflo, who also contributed valuable commentary on this portion of the study. The analysis was run on the computer facilities at Open University, Milton Keynes, Great Britain, with software developed by J. H. Johnson.

During the preparation of this volume I had the good fortune to spend a year at the School of American Research in Santa Fe. This was an opportunity of immeasurable value and I thank the entire staff of the School, with special gratitude to Douglas W. Schwartz, President, Jonathan Haas, former Director of Research, and the other fellows, Thomas W. Killion, Timothy A. Kohler, Harold Littlebird, and Carla M. Sinopoli.

1

INTRODUCTION

From their first contact with Europeans, the Arikaras, like so many other Indian groups on the Great Plains, underwent a series of drastic changes that would forever redefine their world. Many of these changes were associated with the introduction of new diseases, new tools and weapons, and new patterns of social interaction. The Arikaras were reduced in number by the diseases; the gun and other metal tools replaced more traditional stone and bone counterparts; and a myriad of new social pressures helped complete the transformation to a new way of life. Some inevitability to this general trend exists, but the process is neither standardized nor prescribed. As Edward Spicer (1961:537–543) and his colleagues point out, multiple and varied stages shape the process of acculturation. In some perspectives on processes of culture change, however, only a limited variety of interactions are viewed as taking place in the context of culture contact, and the role of individual cultural variation and local history is obscured. Because individual cultures are in fact constituted differently, and may be expected to respond in a variety of ways to European contact, duration, proximity, or intensity of contact can not alone define interaction. While these factors may work to order the contact experience on the most general of levels, they also leave an entire host of phenomena unexplained. This can, in many ways, be corrected by considering cultures in social and material contexts.

OBJECTIVES

This study has two primary objectives: (1) to explore the Arikara contact experience as an interactive process conditioned by the cultural values and logic of the Arikaras as well as the Euro-Americans, and (2) to examine the extent to which changes in the Arikara material record are associated with changes in known historical events and processes. Both objectives are considered as part of a study of the restructuring of Arikara modes of adaptation to Euro-American contact with primary emphasis on changes in the material system.

In recent years many studies, under the heading of ethnoarchaeology, have sought a more thorough understanding of the processes of change by closely examining the factors responsible for shaping the material record (David 1972; R. Gould 1978, 1980; Kramer 1979, 1982; Peterson 1971, 1973; White 1967; Yellen 1977). Although these studies and many others have made important contributions, few have dealt specifically with the fundamental question of the relationship of material culture to other aspects of the cultural system (important exceptions include studies by Hayden and Cannon [1984] and Miller [1982]), especially under circumstances of change. Although not a typical ethnoarchaeological project, the study undertaken here, of the contact period Arikaras, is designed to examine changes in material culture over a specified period of time, while working within a known historical frame of reference. This essentially allows a diachronic investigation of the material correlates of historical change.

Although many factors affect change in the early historic period (drought, warfare, and depopulation), one of the most important was the introduction by Euro-Americans of vastly different and, at the same time, similar material technologies. The goods introduced by the Euro-Americans were certainly exotic, but not all of these items were conceptually unfamiliar to the Arikaras: after all, beads were for wearing whether they were made of bone or glass, and knives were for cutting whether they were stone or iron.

Arikara participation, with the Euro-Americans, in an international trading system dealing in furs and other commodities had a profound influence on every aspect of Arikara life. This influence, however, was not unidirectional, nor did it operate only from a Euro-American perspective. Arikara interaction with the world economy did not, at least initially, result in the development of a new mode of production but, instead, resulted in an intensification of the preinteraction mode of production.

Relatively few studies of the early historic period have attempted to describe the processes associated with the incorporation of Euro-American trade goods into native cultures and the subsequent changes in the local artifact inventories (Fitzhugh 1985:2). Some works have, however, dealt with various aspects of the interaction issue (Baerreis 1983; Fitting 1976; Orser 1984a; Ray 1978; Toom 1979). In many cases, as pointed out by Brown (1979:225) and Pollack and Henderson (1983), it is simply assumed that the availability of Euro-American trade goods caused a rapid and almost total shift away from traditional implements. It is also too readily assumed that Indians everywhere interacted with Euro-Americans in the same way and that the results of this interaction produced similar effects on Indians, "irrespective of geography, native culture type, and the specific nature of the European group—its size, composition, national and cultural origin, religious denomination, economic orientation, and general motivation" (Fitzhugh 1985:6). This perspective in essence supports the eurocentric view that native peoples did not act but were only acted upon by the white intruders (Wolf 1982:x). Any group of people experiencing contact with a foreign and powerful cultural system must develop ways of dealing with the potential effects of that contact. Among various groups, trade goods introduced by Europeans were often adopted selectively (Abel 1939:72; Fitzgerald 1986; Hamell 1983; Washburn 1967; Wolf 1982:4), and to some extent this process can be considered as part of innovation acceptance (Hugill and Dickson 1988; Rogers 1983). Rather than rely on the investigative orientation established in innovation and diffusion studies, the objective here is to develop a more encompassing cultural view of the interaction process (e.g., Osborn 1988).

In the long run, the interaction strategies used by both Euro-Americans and natives resulted in the transformation of peoples and their material culture, but the results were often different and the process almost never the same. The single overriding fact of all contact situations is that each culture operates according to its own set of expectations and works to maintain a viable system. Even if Euro-American trade goods were in high demand by Northern Plains groups (Ewers 1955:13, 1968:24; Innis 1970:82; Jablow 1951:16–17; Mandelbaum 1940:176; Masson 1960:379; Phillips 1961:590) ample evidence exists to illustrate that the process of trade good introduction was neither simple nor one-sided (e.g., Abel 1939:72, 171; Denig 1961:51). Some examples of the variability of the interaction process, especially as it relates to the introduction of trade goods, will be discussed in Chapter 2. While it is important to recognize variability in culture contact, the focus of this analysis will be on identifying systematic relationships that can be used as a basis for processual analysis.

Using archaeological and ethnohistorical evidence this study examines the ways in which trade goods became part of the Arikara system of material expression over a period of approximately 180 years, from 1680 to 1862. This is the period extending from the first direct contact with Europeans to the time of Arikara incorporation with the Mandans and Hidatsas at Like-A-Fishhook village (United States 1863:162–163). When combined with an analysis of the ethnohistorical records from the contact period, it will be possible to develop a view of the role of a changing artifact inventory and how this inventory was interactively redefined in relation to a changing history.

NATURE OF THE INFORMATION

In several ways the Arikaras represent an excellent opportunity to address contact period social interactions and the relationship of historical events and social trends to changing patterns of artifact usage (Rogers 1987). First, the Arikaras were located in an area of North America that did not undergo extensive Euro-American contact until the beginning of the nineteenth century (Fig. 1). Change, although drastic, occurred at a slower, and thus more manageable rate, than in other areas of North America (e.g., Wilson 1986). Change in the early historic period also occurred in the absence of any real missionizing influences. It was not until the 1860s that Christian teachings became a routine part of Arikara life. Because of the late arrival of missionaries, "traditional" belief systems remained intact until a relatively late date (Dorsey 1904a; Gilmore 1929). This simplifies the analytic process by limiting the sources of outside influence.

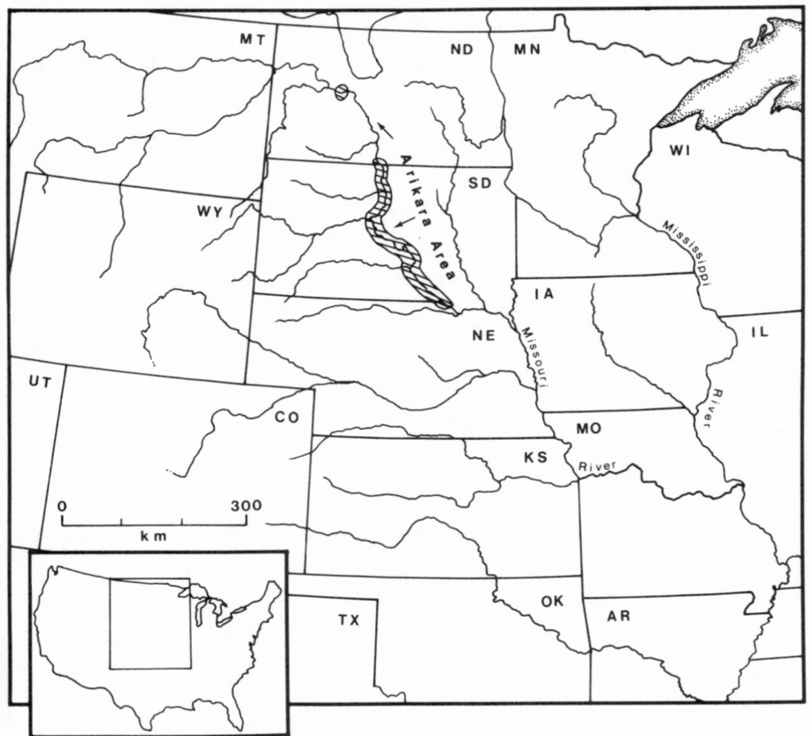

Fig. 1. The Missouri Basin and the location of Arikara sites.

Ethnohistorical information documenting the contact period in the Missouri River Valley is extensive. Although the Arikaras are not the most thoroughly discussed group in the region, many texts are available relating to particular aspects of the contact period and the fur trade (Cuthbertson and Ewers 1939:103–114; Ewers 1954; Phillips 1961; Sunder 1965; Wishart 1979). Many of the most useful journals and letters have been published (Abel 1939; Denig 1961; Nasatir 1952). Other important documents, such as price lists and inventories of goods traded to Indians on the Missouri River, are available at archives such as the Missouri Historical Society (Missouri Historical Society 1822, 1826, 1829). In addition to fur trade records, many materials describe the comings and goings of other Euro-Americans, including explorers (Brackenridge 1962; Coues 1893; Dale 1918; Gass 1958), military men (Robinson 1902), naturalists (Thwaites 1906a), and artists (Curtis 1970).

A third factor that makes the Arikara case especially appropriate for the study of change is the availability of extensive archaeological information. A number of excavated sites with reasonably good chronological control are available for each segment of the early historic period (Krause 1967:192; Lehmer 1971:131–179). While some ambiguities do exist, the sheer number of sites, the extensive nature of the excavations, the available chronological controls (radiocarbon, dendrochronology, detailed ceramic seriations, dating of historic artifacts, and direct historical observation), and the diachronic distribution of sites make the Arikaras a laboratory for the study of change, remarkable for its completeness.

THE INVESTIGATIVE PROCESS

The investigation of the relationship between social and material change will be undertaken as a three-part process. In the first part (Chapter 2), I take the theoretical position that views change as the reformulation of attitudes in conjunction with important economic, social, and demographic constraints. Coupled with this is a consideration of goods in the trade process as interactive agents of change—communicators of social and symbolic relations.

Following the development of this theoretical perspective, a historical outline for the Arikara/Euro-American culture contact process is presented. The objective in describing this historical framework is to interpret the nature of the interactions and to develop a model of historical change to be examined in the archaeological record. The construction of the historical outline is divided into three major parts: first, Arikara social, cosmological, and economic systems are described (Chapter 3); second, Arikara cultural perspectives are considered in relation to the logic of interaction with Euro-Americans (Chapter 4); and third, the historical chronology is constructed, taking into consideration major political, social, and economic changes affecting the interaction process in the context of trade on the Missouri River (Chapter 5).

The third and final part of the study focuses on the construction and evaluation of a series of hypotheses about the relationship of the historical outline to changes in the material record, specifically with reference to the Arikara archaeological data (Chapter 6). Included in this part is a review of the archaeological data and the specific analysis of changing material patterns represented in Arikara domestic earthlodges, ceremonial earthlodges, and burials (Chapters 7 and 8). Finally, conclusions and discussion are presented to evaluate the significance of the study in relation to larger themes of social and cultural change and the archaeological correlates of these changes (Chapter 9).

2

MATERIAL SYSTEMS AND CULTURE CONTACT

Metaphor is largely in use among these Peoples; unless you accustom yourself to it, you will understand nothing.

REVEREND FATHER PAUL LE JEUNE,
NEW FRANCE 1636

To explore the nature of the relationship between sociocultural variables and material systems in the early historic period, it is important to define the relevance of certain criteria. First, and foremost, is the role of cultural systems in determining the orientation of the interaction process; and second, the relevance of objects as markers of cultural categories, in this case as mediators of interaction. In culture contact, diversity expressed in each instance of trade good acceptance or rejection is structured by the varied juxtaposition of cultural systems.

CULTURAL RELEVANCE

Cultural relations operate in a number of ways to structure the sorts of processes that take place under circumstances of culture contact. For

The epigraph that appears above is from Thwaites 1896–1901:219.

the Arikaras, the first two centuries of contact with Euro-Americans were closely bound to the process of trade. The interactions associated with trade were conditioned not only by the objectives of the Euro-Americans, but also by the goals of the Arikaras. Arikara goals were not determined solely by the immediate utility of a new item (e.g., Bailey 1937:47), as in the simple replacement of iron for stone (White 1983:318), nor by its apparent economic importance (Washburn 1967:50). No simple idea of the technological superiority of Euro-American goods over native items (Lewis 1977:147) can offer a complete explanation of the process of adoption or rejection of a newly introduced technology. Rather than overwhelming Euro-American technological superiority, it may be argued that native technologies were initially superior, in at least some cases. Waselkov and Paul (1981:311) have illustrated this point by reference to some of the first colonization attempts in North America, in which native foods and farming techniques were substituted for inappropriate Old World techniques, including the substitution of the hoe for the plow (Carrier 1957:31; Lewis 1975:153). Regardless of the clash of technologies, other issues are at stake, especially the conceptual framework within which goods are used.

Linton (1940:470) states,

> Because of the value system of our own culture, European investigators are prone to think of the acceptance of new culture elements as conditioned primarily by considerations of immediate utility, yet we know that this does not hold even within the narrow frame of our own culture and society.

Martin (1978:8) describes his view of the typical interpretation of Indian participation in the fur trade in much the same way; "European hardware and other trade items were immediately perceived by the Stone Age Indian as being far superior in their utility to his primitive technology and general material culture." He states further that "The Indian's position in the Canadian fur trade has rarely been explained in any 'language,' i.e., conceptual mode, other than that of the Western bourgeois economist" (1978:10). An economic interpretation alone is inadequate to understand Arikara choices. Choices were determined also by a native world view carrying an inherent set of connotations, determining the value and role of an object within the Arikara cultural system. It may not be assumed that native peoples automatically want to acquire the technologically exotic Euro-American trade goods ([Elkin 1951:164] or, for that matter, accept the self-proclaimed superiority of European customs [Goodenough 1963:62]). This perspective does not deny the relevance of economic relations nor the perceived value of trade goods; instead, such relations are viewed as an inseparable part of the cultural ideology.

The coming together of Euro-Americans and Arikaras in the early historic period was an event unique in content but not in form. The Arikaras recognized the form of this encounter from an Arikara perspective that acknowledged and made use of mythically based notions within an Arikara tradition of proper action. "The event thus enters culture as an instance of a received category, the worldly token of a presupposed type" (Sahlins 1981:7). A particular event or set of events and their encounter with the cosmologically based structures of a cultural system form the nexus of history and structure—termed by Marshall Sahlins, the "structure of the conjuncture." This phrase implies that historically based events are not merely unique occurrences, simply to be described, but are in fact part of a set of relations open to analysis. Recognizing and investigating a structured set of relations, under conditions of culture contact, should encompass a consideration of cultural constraints, attitudes, and motivations of the actors. The incorporation of cultural factors in the analysis should not, however, be viewed as an attempt to reduce behavior to a series of mental abstracts. Factors structuring change exist both externally and internally.

The incorporation of cultural and historical explanatory factors, however, is largely denied by a functional empiricist framework. Yet, history is one of the basic means of describing or comparing development of the interrelationships of society (Lévi-Strauss 1963:12), but more than this, history is a way of reincorporating the role of native culture and by so doing, expanding interpretation. The interpretation rests not only on structure but also on defining events in historical time, which form and transform structure (Cohn 1981:247), just as structure forms and transforms events. As Sahlins (1985:vii) indicates,

> History is culturally ordered, differently so in different societies, according to meaningful schemes of things. The converse is also true: cultural schemes are historically ordered, since to a greater or lesser extent the meanings are revalued as they are practically enacted.

History is a way of developing the importance of both cultural and material context. The events that constitute history provide an opportunity to examine more than an elitist past or a past built only on economic relationships. Events can be used to show how cultures respond to different situations as a function of their own view of that situation. This can be examined for the Arikaras by reference to ethnohistorical documentation and Euro-American trade goods in the archaeological record.

The historicity of the Arikara encounter with Euro-Americans is a good example of the bringing together of cultural events and historical processes. For the Arikaras, Euro-Americans were often regarded as special beings with special powers, and many of the objects they brought were often in great demand. Yet it must be remembered that trade goods had entered the native stream of consciousness, by way of other Indian groups, long before the Arikaras, or any other people on the Upper Missouri, had come in direct contact with the light-skinned strangers. The reality of contact, at first, was in the white man's calling cards—disease and trade goods. The reality of this early phase of physical encounter was recognized largely through a native system of material usage, as yet only marginally affected by the expanding reach of the fur trade. With the advent of the fur trade and its special brand of economics and interaction, Arikara systems of artifact preference and usage acquired new dimensions unlike any previous system. Within the framework of contact that developed with Euro-Americans, there were reformulations of the dialectic of interaction—key to understanding the role of changing systems of material usage. These reformulations in one sense are only aspects of a sequence of historical events relating to changing attitudes and economics, however, they are also important guidelines for charting the relationship of object to event. The term reformulation is used here as a means of expressing the existence of a recognizable disjuncture in praxis.

MATERIAL RELEVANCE

Objects, whatever they may be, cannot be defined without reference to a culturally derived system of concepts, known to vary between cultures (Bruner et al. 1956; Goodenough 1957). As Frake (1969:28) points out, "Even with reference to quite obvious kinds of material objects, it has long been noted that many people do not see 'things' quite the way we do." The noncomparable ways that cultures view objects is especially apparent in culture contact situations and necessitates a consideration of how meaning is differentially attached to objects, if changes in the use and distribution of objects are to be analyzed. To accept an object in trade implies an incorporation of the object into the existing cultural system and that the object is given meaning and value. Beyond mere subsistence and competitive display it may be assumed that objects make "visible and stable the categories of culture" (Douglas and Isherwood 1979:59) and, by so doing, serve to structure and restructure social relations. Objects are naturally also significant at the level of the individual—contributing to a delineation of the self. As Csikszentmihalyi and Rochberg-Halton note (1981:16),

> The material objects we use are not just tools we can pick up and discard at our convenience; they constitute the framework of experience that gives order to our otherwise shapeless selves.

Yet, whether at the level of the culture or the self, the value and meaning attached to objects is transitory and subject to change within the ever-fluctuating context of social relations.

The cultural meaning and value of objects is often expressed in symbolic terms. Symbolism plays a major role in forming and transforming notions about cosmological order, ritual functioning, and social relations in general. These factors are represented in almost every facet of material culture, from the nonrandom distribution of trash deposits near a building (Moore 1982), to houses (Cunningham 1973; Donley 1982; Kuper 1980), villages (Adams 1973; Douglas 1972; Fritz 1978), and to the patterning of ceremonial centers (Isbell 1976; Knight 1981). Although symbolic relations are expressed in material remains, this, however, does not imply that the meaning of a particular symbolic element can be determined (Korn 1978:163). If symbolic grammars do exist, it is probably less as a language of meaning than as a context for meaning development. Because archaeology deals with objects and the relationship between objects, the form of symbolic systems is seldom examined, but as Edmund Leach (1977:167) points out:

> Ideas are more important than things; creative imagination is deeply entangled with the formulation of verbal concepts; archaeologists need to appreciate that the material objects revealed by their excavations are not "things in themselves," nor are they just artifacts—things made by men—they are representations of ideas.

The representation of ideas in artifacts is clearly a symbolic and metaphorical process, and if meaning is to be attached, then it will depend, to a large extent, on defining the relevant cultural basis through a consideration of cosmology, myth, and sociocultural relations in general. Munn (1974:605) points out that symbolism works as a "mobilization of shared life meanings" through the communal linkages developed within ritual. Symbols may become part of life meanings through processes of focalization and evocation (Sperber 1975:119). The former channels the direction of attention, while the latter brings certain memories to the realm of consciousness. The evocative aspect operates through the empirical relationship between the symbolic item and experience (Turner 1969:43).

Because of the complex manner in which meaning becomes part of the system of symbols (Sperber 1975:4–5), as in the multivocal (or polysemic) aspects of many symbols (Turner 1977:186, 190), no necessarily obvious correlation exists between the object and the referent. However, Turner (1977:187) notes that a positional element can exist in the selection of particular symbolic theme assemblages, "that is, of the manner in which the object or activity assigned symbolic value is placed or arranged vis-à-vis similar objects or activities." Munn (1974:581) adds support to this perspective by stating

> Different ritual messages can be created through various reformulations or coinages of the same code elements, as for instance in the case of different rituals that draw on the same or similar selections of the cultural lexicon.

The existence of a positional aspect of symbols within a ritual context is an element of the communicative power of ritual and the ability of context to work as a restructuring mechanism in meaning development. The pattern of symbols is, in effect, the basis for interpretation of the ritual structure (Douglas 1970:11), although it must be remembered that "the referential determination of the sign is not a simple expression of the 'true' nature of things" (Sahlins 1981:70). Symbols, as manipulated by people, do not simply restate social "concerns" but may in fact transform, integrate, or otherwise manipulate content to reformulate the message being expressed.

As symbols are constructed in various ways, so are contexts, whether they be ritual or secular in nature. Context, as used here, refers to the framework in which processes, interactions, and relations are defined as part of the relevance of an object or social entity within a particular social or material setting. Context, as a locus of interactions, is not merely a background to action but is also part of the process of structuring the interactions. Meaning, in a social sense, is part of this structuring and is at least partially context specific, which simply indicates that different contexts often elicit different social responses. Although context is integral to every social and material set of relations, it is possible to separate the social and material aspects for heuristic purposes. In fact, it is also possible to recognize that the social context may change rapidly in relation to a single material context. An example can be cited from a linguistically related group located far to the south of the Arikaras. The death-related ritual of the Hasinai Caddos of east Texas (Swanton 1942:203–210) illustrates the differential treatment accorded the corpse depending on whether the soul is believed to still be present or to have already departed. In either case the material context is the same, but the cultural importance and meaning of the corpse is vastly different.

Among the Arikaras other simple examples may be cited to illustrate the differential meaning attached to objects depending on physical context. In past times the Arikaras dedicated a small shrine to Mother Corn in each household (Gilmore 1925). The shrine was not elaborate, consisting of two ears of corn and a braid of sweetgrass held in a buffalo skin bag. The ears of corn were considered sacred representations of Mother Corn, and were prayed to, "incensed," and offered veneration. However, in another context, corn was something to be eaten, hardly considered a sacred object in the same sense. Although the connection with Mother Corn was never ignored completely, corn used in daily meals did not have the same connotations as the corn that became part of the sacred shrines.

As another example, the contrast in meaning attached to sacred cedar trees by the Arikaras and the neighboring Mandans may be cited. Both the Arikaras and the Mandans included a cedar tree as an important sacred element in major ceremonies. Among the Mandans the cedar tree was a symbol of Lone Man, a supernatural figure that played an important role in the origin myth (Chalfant 1951:47). Among the Arikaras, however, the cedar tree was emblematic of Mother Corn, also an important mythical figure, but with decidedly different connotations compared to those of Lone Man (Dorsey 1904a:12–44).

No shortage of other Arikara examples exist that show how ordinary objects, such as corn, can have different meanings depending on their context. Meaning, in this way, is somewhat context specific. But metaphorical connections between contextualized meaning are always present at a number of levels, and there is no easy way to derive meaning from the physical context in the absence of native exegesis. Evans-Pritchard (1940:89) described objects in material culture as "chains along which social relationships run, and the more simple is the material culture, the more numerous are the relationships expressed through it." By implication, as objects may have complex multiple meanings, so may contexts.

DIVERSITY IN CONTACT

The foregoing discussion has presented some basic ideas about the relevance of different cultural systems in contact situations and about the role of objects in making cultural categories visible and stable. This section illustrates some of the themes presented in the previous discussion by providing examples of the diverse ways in which cultural considerations affect the exchange of goods in the contact environment and how introduced goods may drastically and catastrophically restructure social relations.

Probably one of the most thoroughly described and poignant examples of the effects of a single introduced type of item into a native culture is the case of steel axes and the Yir Yoronts, an Australian group living on the west coast of Cape York Peninsula (Sharp 1934a, 1934b, 1939, 1952). One of the most essential tools the Yir Yoronts possessed was the short-handled stone axe. The stone used in making the axe head was acquired through a complex series of male trading partner relations from sources far to the south. The axes were in relatively short supply and their value was high. Stone axes belonged to men, as part of a male dominated society in which "Every active relationship . . . involved a definite and accepted status of superordination or subordination" (Sharp 1952:76). Sharp (1952:77) indicates the important social role of the stone axe,

> It can be seen that repeated and widespread conduct centering on the axe helped to generalize and standardize throughout the society these sex, age, and kinship roles, both in their normal benevolent and in exceptional malevolent aspects, and helped to build up expectancies regarding the conduct of others defined as having a particular status.

In the Yir Yoront view, the present was a reflection of cosmological order, in which each part of the environment and each object of totemic value had mythic and ancestral connections.

> There was thus in Yir Yoront ideology a nice balance in which the mythical world was adjusted in part to the real world, the real world in part to the ideal preexisting mythical world, the adjustments occurring to maintain a fundamental tenet of native faith that the present must be a mirror of the past [Sharp 1952:80–81].

The Yir Yoronts readily accepted the new steel axes. But the steel axes did not come from traditional trading partners and even worse, the Europeans seemed to be unconcerned about who received the steel axes. Women and children acquired axes, and older adult males quickly lost their monopoly over access to this once scarce resource.

The missionary intent in providing the axes was to allow for technological progress, but the new axes held few advantages over the stone axes (Sharp 1952:82). The result was instead a drastic disruption of social relations that was a major factor in the eventual demise of the Yir Yoront way of life. "All this led to a revolutionary confusion of sex, age, and kinship roles, with a major gain in independence and loss of subordination on the part of those able now to acquire steel axes" (Sharp 1952:84). By the 1930s Yir Yoront society was trying to cope by incorporating European introduced phenomena into the ideological system, including the creation of myth to justify totemic relations. The result was less than satisfactory and only temporarily abated the continued erosion of basic values.

Axes were a valuable item in precontact Yir Yoront society and it is easy to see why they were readily adopted when new sources were made available. Other kinds of items would probably have been less acceptable to the Yir Yoronts, at least initially. For instance, the Yir Yoronts have no canoes, even though it would be an advantage to have them. Their neighbors have canoes and the materials necessary to build canoes are easily available within Yir Yoronts' territory. But the mythical ancestors of the Yir Yoronts *did not* have canoes, consequently canoes were not appropriate additions to the material inventory. The

Yir Yoronts would have been uninterested in canoes brought by Europeans or by any other source.

In other areas of the Pacific, exposure to Europeans and European trade goods did not signal social collapse. In fact, on the island of Erromango, European goods were rejected entirely. On the Isle of Pines, Europeans were asked to leave after the outbreak of disease. The chief said he had enough trade goods (Marshall Sahlins, personal communication 1982).

In situations in which European goods were accepted, there was much variation in the types of items in demand. Hawaii and the Northwest Coast groups provide an interesting contrastive example. In Hawaii, chiefs generally controlled access to trade, however chiefs did not participate in the world economy through attempts to increase basic production. Consequently, after Vancouver's time (1790s), chiefly demand for implements of production vanished. The trade, instead, centered on variety expressed in luxury goods as indicators of status among the Hawaiian aristocracy (Sahlins 1985:141). Storehouses were filled with exotic goods to be owned, but not used.

On the Northwest Coast of North America the various groups participated in the world economy through the fur trade (Fisher 1977; Gunther 1972). Access to European goods seems to have been related to an increase in ranking among the Kwakiutl through potlatching and increased ceremonial activity, partly expressed through more totem poles. Unlike the Hawaiian system, in which status was related to the accumulation of luxury goods, Northwest Coast wealth went into acquisition of thousands of blankets and "trifles" in huge quantities. Status was enhanced by giving away or destroying this raw wealth. In Hawaii it was important to acquire everything that was different; in contrast, on the Northwest Coast it was important to acquire everything that was the same.

In other parts of North America, specific Indian choices were also determined by a native ideology carrying an inherent set of connotations determining the value and role of trade goods. Hamell (1983) illustrated this effectively through analysis of trade bead preferences by Siouan, Algonquian, and Iroquoian peoples of the Northeastern Woodlands. His study points to the metaphorical connection between light as a domain for the expression of important cosmological concepts and the ritualized use of shell, crystal, and native copper. "They are reflective substances, literally and figuratively, and substances in which native ideological and aesthetic interests are one" (Hamell 1983:5).

The traditional sources of shell, crystal, and native copper are the Under World Grandfathers who may bestow precious gifts associated with well-being and success. In a ritual context these materials are "metaphors for light, mind, knowledge and/or greatest being" (Hamell 1983:6). These concepts are themselves considered prerequisite to life. This metaphorical relationship was in turn, key to understanding why the Northeast Woodland Indians expressed, at least initially, a particular interest in obtaining such goods as glass, copper, brass, or other "shiny" materials. Often these preferences were expressed to the exclusion of objects made of iron. The relationship between light as an ideological concept, and certain shiny objects may not be unique to the Northeast Woodlands, but its particular expression, as part of the interaction with Europeans, is.

The Northeast was, in general, an area of intense contact and decided Christian influence, but native systems of material usage in burials, for instance, continued well into the Colonial period (Biglow 1830:15–16; Chapin 1927). In the Southeast, Creek women continued to make traditional ceramics after all other objects had been replaced by Euro-American goods (Fairbanks 1962). Another example of differential acceptance and use of trade goods is illustrated by the Timucua of Florida who seemed to incorporate new objects only as each generation grew to adulthood, having known of the items since they were children (Milanich 1978:84).

Among the Arikaras, ceramic manufacture and the use of the bison scapula hoe continued long after metal counterparts were available and even preferred by neighboring groups such as the Mandans and Hidatsas (Denig 1961:51; Lehmer 1971:76, 152; Wilson 1917:12). At least as late as 1879 Arikara women were still making their own pottery (Hall 1879). With the Arikaras and many other groups, it can even be said that little or no initial interest existed in the trade goods offered by Euro-Americans (Orser 1980a:166). The fur trader Tabeau wrote (Abel 1939:72)

> It is evident that with the bow and arrow the Savages of the Upper Missouri can easily do without our trade, which becomes necessary to them only after it has created the needs.

It so happens that Tabeau and others made their trade felt in many ways on the Upper Missouri.

Although it is possible to cite numerous additional examples of native responses to European contact, the point to be made here is that the contact experience is diverse and complex in nature. Formal economic relationships alone can not determine how and where trade items may become part of the archaeological record. Instead, it is necessary to examine a particular instance of contact as the bringing together of a diverse set of relationships within a specific frame of reference.

Because objects carry meaning within a cultural context, it is important to define the parameters of this context and to consider the varying world views and modes of social reproduction involved. For an analysis of changing artifact patterns in the early historic period on the Upper Missouri it is necessary to consider Arikara perspectives and motivations as well as those of the various Euro-American groups involved. Changes in the attitudes held by each group regarding the interaction process serve as a useful criteria for examining historical change.

3

THE ARIKARAS IN CONTEXT

> Three things . . . will keep you right: Corn, the office of Chief, and the secrets that were revealed in the lodge. These three things you must preserve always.
>
> THE SUPREME DEITY NESANU,
> SPEAKING TO THE ARIKARAS

An important aspect of comprehending Arikara attitudes, motivations, and goals in their interactions with Euro-Americans is understanding something of the character of Arikara culture. Beginning with the cosmological "top" and ending with the economic and historical/event "base," this chapter provides a general context in which to consider those sociocultural aspects relevant to the interaction process. To do this, the following discussion begins by describing cosmology and ritual as a means of exploring some of the themes of social concern that form the Arikara world view. In the absence of any significant source of Arikara self-explication of their system of beliefs and perceptions in the eighteenth and nineteenth centuries, available descriptions of rituals and myth transcribed by white observers become crucial for understanding this important time period.

The Arikaras were a settled agricultural group who occupied the

---

The epigraph that appears above is from Curtis 1970:85.

middle portion of the Missouri River Valley in late prehistoric and historic times. In general the Arikaras were organized in roughly the same way as their close relatives the Skiri Pawnees (Dorsey 1904b; Grinnell 1891:279; Weltfish 1965:20) and, indeed, shared many characteristics with the neighboring Mandans and Hidatsas. Linguistically the Arikaras represent the northernmost extension of the Caddoan language family (Chafe 1973:1167). Arikara is closely related to Pawnee, probably having separated sometime after A.D. 1400 (Blakeslee 1981:99; Hollow and Parks 1980:77, 80). This fact lends support to oral traditions, archaeological findings, and physical anthropological research indicating a common central Plains ancestry for the Pawnees and Arikaras (Jantz et al. 1978:153; Lehmer 1954b:143–145; Wedel 1961:182–183; Ubelaker and Jantz 1979:256).

COSMOLOGY

All aspects of Arikara life are tied together in a framework of belief and meaning, incorporating the religious and secular in one stream of prescribed action. Much of what is presented here holds a close resemblance to the cosmology and ceremonial organization of the Skiri Pawnees (Parks 1981), but also bears the imprint of the Siouan neighbors of the Arikaras and of general Plains belief systems. To conceptualize the religion of the Arikaras and other Caddoan speaking groups, Holder (1970:51) noted the dualistic nature of the forces that played important roles. The dualism was in the form of a dialectic of natural and cultural processes. "There were and must be forces of reproduction and disintegration, elements of construction and destruction, magic powers of life and of death" (Holder 1970:51). This dialectic was expressed in such things as the concept of two seasons—one of growth and one of dormancy. The contrastive character of natural forces was also evident in the powers of the doctors, derived from worldly sources, as opposed to the power of the priests, sanctioned by heavenly authority.

The best way to introduce and understand the basic principles that serve to organize the Arikara outlook on the world around them is to consider the actors and actions that play a part in the Arikara origin myth. This myth describes the emergence of the Arikaras from a dark underworld and how the people were shown the will of god. George Dorsey (1904a:12–44) recorded ten versions of this myth around the turn of the twentieth century. Versions similar to those recorded by Dorsey were described by Curtis (1970:80–86) and Gilmore (1926b, 1929). In the basic story, the Arikaras and all living things are held within the earth, yet the people long to be free. God (Nesanu) sends Mother Corn to lead the people to the surface. With the assistance of the badger, the mole, and the long-nosed mouse, the people reach the surface of the earth. The people begin an arduous journey during which they face many obstacles. In finding their way through a dense forest, some people are trapped and transformed into forest-dwelling creatures; in attempting to cross a lake some people do not make it and remain behind to become fish. In this way the animals of the water, earth, and sky are created and always remain kin of the Arikaras. Mother Corn gave the people corn to plant, but the people still had no rules and did not know how to behave. Nesanu saw this and sent Mother Corn again, this time with a man, to inform the people of the proper ways to act. The man told the people that they must have a chief, whom they will call Nesanu. The man also taught about raiding and gaining prestige through taking scalps, and he instructed the doctors (or medicine men). Mother Corn made the medicine bundle, songs, and ceremonies that the people used to remember the teachings of Nesanu and to offer homage to all the gods. When the people had learned the proper ways of acting, Mother Corn turned into a cedar tree and became known as Wonderful Grandmother. The man who came with her became a stone and is known as Wonderful Grandfather. In one version of the myth the Grandfather Stone fell to earth as Big-Black-Meteoric Star. This star is mentioned among the Skiri Pawnees (who are close relatives of the Arikaras) as a powerful god who gave knowledge to the people (Parks 1981:39). Finally, the people reached a place where they could live along the banks of the Missouri—the holy river. This was their residence when first encountered by whites.

The origin myth includes some of the most important themes in Arikara religion. Nesanu is the principal god and is the ultimate source of Arikara well being. If the Arikaras follow the teachings given to them by Mother Corn and Grandfather Stone, they will receive the blessings of god. If, however, the Arikaras fail to observe the prescribed ceremonies and make the proper offerings, then they may expect trouble. In many ways, the calamities of epidemics, warfare, and other social stress that affected the Arikaras in the eighteenth and nineteenth centuries were seen as punishment sent by Nesanu for improper behavior. One of the Arikara responses to these threats to their existence was to intensify ceremonial activity (Meyer 1977:79) with the hope of appeasing Nesanu and the other gods.

Nesanu was not alone in the sky; he had as assistants the four semicardinal directions (Gilmore 1929:104–105). Each of the directions had specific connotations and powers. The southeast was associated with the sunrise and vegetation; the southwest was identified with thunder and animals; the northwest was associated with wind and the forms of life that flew (including birds and insects); and the northeast was connected with night and Mother Corn. Other lesser supernatural spirits and powers also inhabited certain places or were part of animals and plants. In his journal of the Lewis and Clark expedition, Coues (1893:165–166, 175) noted two rock formations held in deep veneration by the Arikaras, apparently as oracles. A large oak tree standing alone on the prairie was considered a source of power and could help a man become braver.

As noted above, the word of Nesanu was given to the Arikaras through Mother Corn and the man who became the Grandfather Stone. Of the two, Mother Corn was clearly the most important. Her goodwill was a necessary ingredient for a successful harvest and she played the major role in the most important ceremonies (Gilmore 1926a:256). It was also through her that the most sacred elements of the religion had been transmitted.

As the origin myth indicates, the Arikaras were closely allied with animals. In fact, many Arikaras were transformed into animals. This formed a kinship bond with the animals, who were themselves important sources of supernatural power. One very important exception to the ties uniting humans and animals was that of the buffalo. The buffalo did not come from the underground with the people, but instead attempted to destroy the people during their initial journey (Dorsey 1904a:37–44). The leader of the buffalo was a huge, horned monster that rose from a lake as the Arikaras passed. This monster's name was Cut Nose and he and the other buffalo killed many Arikaras. Only by praying to Mother Corn were the Arikaras finally saved from the buffalo. Through the divine promise of Mother Corn, buffalo became the primary gift of the animal world.

The foregoing discussion has reviewed some of the basic themes of Arikara social concern by considering them within their mythic context. In order for the Arikaras to live in harmony with their surroundings, they had to follow the ceremonies given by Mother Corn. This would insure that propitiation for good harvests and good hunts were heard by Nesanu. It was also important to maintain the office of chief as a means of maintaining order in society. The attainment of personal power and prestige had their basis in more earthly sources. The power held by the doctors was derived from plants and animals or purchased from other men. Other individuals might win prestige on the battlefield or receive supernatural power from an earthly origin revealed in a dream. Vision quests, practiced by many other groups on the Plains, were not a significant part of the Arikara approach to personal power. Although vision quests, as such, were not a routine part of Arikara life, the myths recorded by Dorsey do point to the importance of dreams as a source of supernatural information (1904a).

Man's attainment of earthly power and prestige was but a prelude to a more substantial cosmic connection. Little is recorded in the ethnohistorical sources about Arikara conceptions of the soul and afterlife, however some basic facts are known. Death seldom, if ever, occurred by natural causes, especially if the person was relatively young; a supernatural source of the malady was ascribed, usually a spell cast by a doctor (Abel 1932:203). The burial of Arikara individuals observed by early travelers provides some clues about the nature of the soul. Because burials are used as a source of information in a later portion of this study, the available accounts of early Arikara burial practices are presented here in some detail. More thorough reviews of information on Arikara burial practices are presented in Orser (1980a, 1980b).

The various individuals who witnessed Arikara burial ritual generally reported direct interment. Brackenridge, during his trip up the Missouri River in 1811, noted that the Arikaras did not practice scaffolding, like the other groups of the Upper Missouri (Thwaites

1904b:141–142). A few years earlier (between 1795 and 1805), Tabeau (Abel 1939:201–202) wrote that "the corpses are often exposed and placed upon a scaffold upon trees where the open air leaves a beautiful space for a promenade." Culbertson, writing in 1850 (1851:117), noted that the Arikaras had abandoned the past practice of scaffold burial. Recent studies of fly puparia and beetle remains found in association with Arikara skeletons, suggest that bodies were often exposed in an open air environment for an extended period of time before interment (Gilbert and Bass 1967; Orser 1980b; Ubelaker and Willey 1978). Although in limited cases, fly larvae or even adults may burrow or crawl below surface into a shallow grave, the Arikara evidence is extensive enough to strongly favor the open air scenario (Rodriguez and Bass 1985:845, 848). This, however, does not necessarily imply scaffolding, only that some type of secondary burial processing was involved. Such processing was not recorded by any of the historical sources, although the bioarchaeological evidence is strong. One possible explanation for the biological evidence is described in a story recorded by Dorsey (1904a:162). In the beginning of the story, a boy's father dies and is placed in the ground, but is not covered with soil. Instead,

> The people had stuck two forks in the ground and placed a pole across the forks. Then some poles were placed on the sides, and instead of piling stones and dirt over the grave a buffalo robe was spread over it, so that there was no dirt. Stones were placed on the robe where it touched the ground.

Such a burial procedure as this would explain the open air exposure of the body without the use of scaffolding. Today, the Arikaras have no memory of scaffold use (Douglas Parks, personal communication 1986).

In the nineteenth century, direct interment was the general rule. In 1833, Maximilian, Prince of Wied-Neuwied (Thwaites 1906a, vol. 23:394) noted:

> The Arikkaras affirm that God said to them that they were made of earth, and must return to earth; on which account they bury their

> dead in the ground. Various things are sometimes cast into the graves of eminent men; the corpse is dressed in the best clothes, the face painted red, and sometimes a good horse is killed on the grave. If the deceased has left a son, he receives his father's medicine apparatus; if not, it is buried with him in the grave.

Gilmore (1927:349) also notes that it is conceivable that bundles (or "medicine apparatus" as in the above quote) were buried with their custodians if no one remained alive who knew the ceremonies of the bundle. In 1862, Morgan (1959:162) visited Fort Clark and observed that

> Just out of the village is the burying ground. The Arickarees did not scaffold the dead but buried them in the ground. The most of the graves, and there were hundreds of them visible, are on the segment of a great circle. Others are grouped together. They wrapped up the body, dug a grave, and put it either in a sitting posture or doubled it up. I do not know which. I saw the size of some of the graves. They could not have extended the body and I could not tell whether it was an empty grave and timbered roof like the Omaha, or the earth was placed upon the body.
>
> The best or most conspicuous grave was that of an Arickaree chief who was killed by the Sioux a few years ago. A large mound was raised over the grave about four feet high and oblong six or eight feet. There was another grave close beside it and mound over it. On the top of the chief's grave were two bull buffalo skins, side and side, their horns wound with red bands, and the forehead of one spotted with vermilion. The soil or sod was cleared off for a space of five feet around the mound and lined with a circle of buffalo skulls of which I counted 17. They made about two thirds of a circle and were on the side of the chief's mound and to show that they were placed there for him, and not for the adjoining mound.

Curtis (1970:63) outlines the actual burial process.

> The dead were dressed and painted by the parents and other close relations, and if no appropriate clothing had been left by the

> deceased they furnished it. The moment life had passed, the family hired some old woman to dig the grave, and at mid-forenoon of the following day her relations placed the body on a buffalo-robe and carried it to the grave, where it was laid on its back wrapped in a robe, the head toward the east and resting on a pillow. The old woman threw a handful of earth into the grave, with the words: 'This man has gone to a happy place. This is a bad place, but he has gone where everything is good.' Then the grave was quickly filled. In later times the body of an adult was usually carried on a travois. A gathering of relations and friends followed, and the parents and the bereaved spouse remained by the grave, crying and wailing until sunset, the mourning women usually cutting and gashing their legs. A man in mourning cut the tips of his hair-braids and placed them in the robe with the corpse. The fourth day after death, food and water were placed beside the grave, for the spirit was now to begin its journey, and must be made strong after the debilitating illness of the body. Weapons were never buried, nor were horses sacrificed at the grave. It was simply said of a dead man, *Wetikaish*—'He has gone home.'

Curtis notes that horses were not sacrificed and weapons were not placed in the grave. These observations go against earlier accounts, but rather than representing a contradiction, Curtis's remarks probably illustrate changing practices through time or his own assumption that the observation of one or a few instances were characteristic of the entire burial program, which they were almost certainly not.

Little is known about the afterlife or the soul of the individual, except that, "When a man dies, they say, he has not even his wives with him in the land of the dead, so that those who fight and kill each other for women are fools and mad men" (Beauregard 1912:30). Curtis (1970:63–64) comments directly about the soul,

> The soul, called *sishu,* is responsible for all the acts of a man during life; it resides in the breast, and appears in the spoken work, in the look of the eye, in the movement of the muscles. It is *sishu* that rattles in the throat of the dying in its attempt to escape. The shadow *nanokaatu* is vaguely identified with the soul. All animals have *sishu,* but not trees or other inanimate objects.

The missionary C. L. Hall (1879:21–22) reported,

> The Rees believe in God in a sense Personal; but they also consider natural elements as sacred and eternal, as not created and perishable, as the trees, animals, and man are. The earth, heavens and the wind for example are very sacred. The wind is the source of life, and at death the breath goes back to the wind again. . . . Nacituk [God] said that the planted corn would spring up and bear new seed, which they were carefully to preserve and plant again, and again a new plant would appear beautiful and perfect as before. So the body of the departed soul, buried in the earth, would be renewed again, and the soul that had gone to the wind, would once more find a bodily home. So the sacred men comfort bereaved ones, and tell them not to cut themselves, nor weap [sic] over much, for the dead are well off, and will live again in the Ressurection [sic].
>
> In the meantime the ghosts of the departed find amusement and occupation o'nights, when the Rees have all laid down, by coming to the village, and whistling, as the wind does for those with whom they wished to communicate. In open day, you can often detect the motions of these ghosts. When you see a little whirl of dust on a windy day, you may know that a Ree spirit is assending [sic] heavenward.

Reverend Hall's mention of the Resurrection obviously reflects Christian influences. In a brief story recorded by Dorsey (1904a:152–153), a man describes how he died and visited the land of the dead and eventually returned to the land of the living. When he died, he saw a path leading to the east. He followed this path and went through a small hole. On the other side of the hole he saw the village of the dead and a lodge, in which the dead were calling to their living relatives to come and join them in the land of the dead. The man did not enter this lodge and was able to return to the living.

The story of the visit to the world of the dead suggests that the souls traveled east to a land similar to that of the living. It is interesting to note that east is the direction from which the Arikaras came in their original journey from the underworld. Also, in the above quote from Curtis, it was said of the dead man that "he has gone home" (1970:63). The dead held a malicious intent for their living relatives, wishing upon them sickness, so that they too would come to the land of the dead. The souls of the dead were to be feared and avoided and hopefully sent on their eastern journey without trouble.

CEREMONY

The Arikaras expressed their relationship to the gods through a complex series of ceremonies that together formed an expressive ideology of symbolic action. Every aspect of life was dominated by the necessity of symbolically performing, and thus acknowledging, the proper ways of acting through rituals, both large and small. Some aspects of ritual were described in the previous section, in the context of man's relationship to the supernatural powers that govern the world. However, in this section the focus will be on the major ceremonies receiving villagewide participation that served to punctuate the yearly cycles of planting, harvesting, and hunting. The available information for the period under study (approximately 1675–1862) does not present a complete picture of Arikara ritual life, in fact only a few ceremonies are known in any detail. Those that are known in a more or less complete and "traditional" form were generally recorded after the 1860s. By comparison with the Pawnees, close linguistic and cultural relatives of the Arikaras, it may be inferred that the Arikara ceremonial cycle was considerably more complex than the early accounts would indicate. It has been suggested that the Pawnees had one of the most complex ritual cycles of any group in North America (Parks 1981), and it is reasonable to conclude that this applies equally to the Arikaras (Will 1928:51).

Before proceeding with a discussion of particular ceremonies, certain spatiosymbolic facets should be mentioned. The dialectical forces of the universe and the organization of the cosmos, as mentioned previously, were codified in Arikara thought within all levels of society, providing a constant reminder of man's relationship to the world around him. Nesanu, the supreme deity, and his four assistants, the semicardinal directions, formed a model for ordering many social and material aspects of life. At a basic level, the domestic dwelling, usually occupied by more than one extended family, reminded its inhabitants of the basic organization of the cosmos. The Arikara earthlodge was constructed with four large interior posts providing the support for the earth covered, dome-shaped roof, representative of the sky above (Chalfant 1951:16). In the center of the lodge was a hearth with a smoke hole above, leading through the roof (Reid 1930). The hearth was representative of Nesanu, and each of the interior support posts represented one of his assistants. The numerical theme of one and four was even more complete in the village ceremonial earthlodge, in which the symbolism also extended to the seating arrangements of the chiefs and the medicine societies (Gilmore 1930). Other symbolic connections with the cosmological organization are mentioned in the following discussion of some of the important rituals and the subsequent section on social organization.

The priests and the doctors were the primary groups involved in the performance of the major ritual activities. Although these individuals were mutually concerned with control of the supernatural, their approaches and sources of power differed considerably. Some researchers have failed to distinguish between priests and doctors, although the contrasts are very important (Chalfant 1951; Will 1930). The priests were sanctioned by the gods and dealt primarily with issues of group concern, such as control of natural phenomena by propitiation to the gods. The Arikara sacred bundles were an integral part of rituals conducted by the priests. One of the main functions of the priests was the custodianship of the sacred village bundles, including a thorough knowledge of associated rituals. It was the duty of the priests to live a blameless life and to be kind and temperate in all things (Gilmore 1931:37). By contrast, the doctors derived their powers from the earthly spirits of animals and plants or from other men (Curtis 1970:64). Doctors used their powers to cure the sick or inflict harm on the enemies of their clients or their personal adversaries. As the trader Tabeau put it (Abel 1939:183–184):

> among the Sioux and still more among the Ricaras, there prevails no natural sickness, as all illness is either the result of the vengeance of some angry spirit or a succession of evil deeds of a magician, diviners are the only recourse. They are called *medicine men,* which signifies supernatural power. These charlatans are here in their midst, admired and feared with the most stupid crudity. [emphasis in original]

Doctors were organized into a series of eight societies, according to Gilmore (1931:46–47) and Will (1928:53–54), or nine societies, according to Curtis (1970:64–65). The number of societies noted by these two sources does not represent an actual discrepancy, in that Curtis includes the "Principal Medicine" (i.e., the apparent overall leadership of the medicine societies) in his list. The only apparent discrepancy exists in the inclusion of a society called Mother Night or Young Dog in the Curtis list and a society called the Sioux in the Gilmore list or Dakota and Rabbit, in the Will list. It is probable that these are all names for the same group. In other respects the lists are comparable. The Principal Medicine, noted by Curtis (1970:65), consisted of four men representing Beaver, Otter, Muskrat, and Swamp-owl. When all the societies came together in the ceremonial earth-lodge, these four men took their places on the altar at the rear of the lodge. The seating arrangement described by Curtis is presented in Figure 2. According to Gilmore, there were originally four societies: the Ghost, the Buffalo, the Owl, and the Bear. An initiation ceremony for the Bear Society is described by Howard and Woolworth (1954) for the early 1950s. Four more societies were added later: the Deer, the Cormorant, the Duck, and the Sioux. These groups, however, were not as powerful as the first four. The two groups of four societies again reiterate the cosmological organization reflected in god's four assistants—the semicardinal directions.

Parallel to the medicine societies were a series of secular (dance) societies (Lowie 1915). Some of the secular societies were associated with prowess in warfare or had special duties such as taking care of the poor or homeless. They also served purely social functions as support groups for their own members. The medicine societies differed from

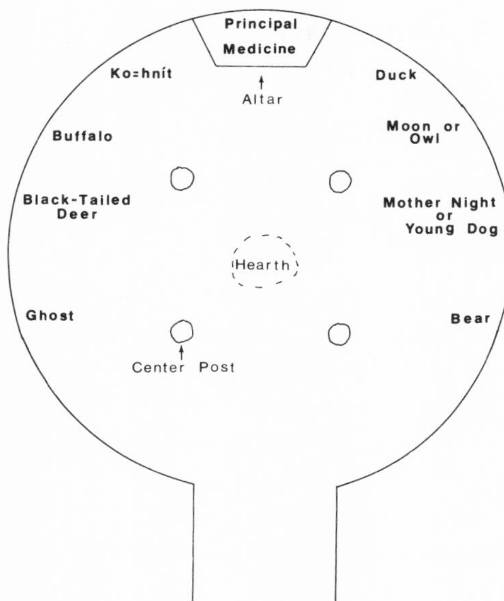

Fig. 2. Seating arrangement of the medicine societies in the ceremonial earthlodge. According to Will (1928:54) the Mother Night or Young Dog Society was also called the Dakota or Rabbit Society. Adapted from Curtis (1970, facing page 64).

the secular in that their function was primarily curing and the maintenance of specialized knowledge (Curtis 1970:69). Younger members of the medicine societies acquired knowledge, through payment, from older members.

The priests were not organized into societies like the doctors. Instead, a priest presided over each of the Sacred Village Bundles. There was also an overall group priest who had four assistants (Gilmore 1931:37). Although information is lacking, it may be presumed that each of the assistant priests was drawn from the group of villages associated with each of the four semicardinal directions. The priesthood was hereditary in certain families, assuming of course that the candidate was capable (Gilmore 1931:35).

The practitioners who gained access to special powers from both cosmic and earthly sources participated as ritual intermediaries between the supernatural and the people. Of the various ceremonies recorded, three, in particular, can be considered as playing an important role in the yearly cycle; the First Fruits Ceremony, the Mother Corn Ceremony, and the Doctor's Ceremony. The first of these ceremonies is not known in any detail, although Maximilian, in 1833–34, mentioned it as one of the most important ceremonies, occurring as soon as the first squash is ripe (Thwaites 1906a, vol. 23:392). The Mother Corn and Doctor's ceremonies have been described to varying degrees by Curtis (1970:65–69, 70–76), Hoffman (1884:528–532), Tabeau (Abel 1939:187–189, 216), and Will (1928; 1930:259–265). The most complete descriptions are by Curtis in 1908 and Will for the early 1920s. The Mother Corn Ceremony was held in the late summer as the corn became ready for harvest. The ceremony was on the theme of world renewal and involved the opening of sacred bundles, and the offering of prayers for a successful harvest through Mother Corn as an intermediary with God. A cedar tree, representing Mother Corn, was cut in the forest and brought to the ceremonial earthlodge. The bringing of the cedar tree was actually part of the Medicine Ceremony that formed a prelude to the Mother Corn Ceremony. The cedar tree was planted in front of the lodge near the Grandfather Stone. Inside the lodge, dances were held in which women imitated the process of planting and cultivating crops. In a later phase of the dancing, the women cover themselves with buffalo robes and are symbolically tracked and killed by a hunter. In this way the two important themes of agriculture and the hunting of buffalo are represented in the same ritual. Near the close of the proceedings, offerings made in the lodge are distributed to the priests and the other officials present. Finally, a corn plant used to represent Mother Corn in the lodge is taken to the Missouri River and allowed to float downstream to inform the ancestors that the ceremony has been completed.

The Doctor's Ceremony contrasts sharply in theme and scope with that of the Mother Corn Ceremony. The primary objective of the Doctor's Ceremony is to illustrate the powers of the doctors, especially their abilities to cure, through the performance of numerous magical acts (Will 1928:65). An extensive review of the various sources of information on the Doctor's Ceremony is provided by Howard (1974). Each of the eight medicine societies sang songs during the course of the ceremony, and each night was devoted to the performance of a particular set of magical feats (Curtis 1970:65–66). This ceremony was held in the fall and lasted about a month (Dorsey 1904a:161). In general character, the Arikara Doctor's Ceremony was very similar to the Thirty Day Ceremony of the Skiri Pawnee doctors (Parks 1981:170–176). In addition to the relatively extensive observations made by Curtis (1970:65–69) and Will (1928), the ceremony was first observed and recorded by Truteau between 1795 and 1805 (Abel 1939:187–189), but was also commented on by Brackenridge in 1811 (Thwaites 1904b:125), Maximilian in 1834 (Thwaites 1906a, vol. 23:393), De Smet between 1847 and 1859 (Thwaites 1906b:187–188), and Trobriand in 1867 (1941:95–98). Although the various observers were skeptical of the powers of the doctors, they performed some feats of legerdemain that could not easily be explained away.

An important physical element in all of the major ceremonies was the sacred bundle. Bundles were mnemonic devices containing sacred objects relating to events of social and symbolic importance. The objects in a bundle referred to a symbolism of core ideas—as such the objects were integrated with the ideas, not only in the context of the bundle, but in other contexts as well. Gilmore (1931) describes four classes of bundles: village, society, household and home affairs, and personal. The village bundles were the most important. The objects in the village bundles

> give an account of the origin and development and mutual interdependence of all living creatures, both plant and animal, and of man's place in that living world as a partner and companion with all other living things on earth. [Gilmore 1931:35]

Gilmore (1926d:92) quotes an Arikara priest regarding the meaning of the bundles.

> The Sacred Bundle is the thing which binds the people together. It did so in the ancient time and it does so now . . . . In the ancient days the keepers of the Sacred Bundle were jealous in imparting the teachings to those who earnestly sought them, and the people were faithful to the teaching. Then the people were strong and healthy, of good courage and high spirit. And so should it be with us now. Our people should be united and devoted to the good teachings which we have had from Mother Corn from the ancient

days. Mother Corn will keep her promise to us forever, if we do our part.

Typically the village bundles contained a pipe and tobacco, a mussel shell to hold the tobacco, four ears of corn, a bison scapula hoe, and various other objects, such as bird and mammal skins, scalps, enemy arrows, feathers, fish skins, and other objects. The bundle was normally wrapped in a buffalo skin and tied with a thong. On the outside of the bundle was a wooden bar with five gourd rattles attached to it. The five rattles were symbolic of God (Nesanu) and his four assistants. One village (Hukawirat) bundle also had attached to the outside a sheaf of thirty-four sandbar willow sticks (Gilmore 1927:338). When the bundle was opened these sticks were placed in a circular arrangement around the fireplace, each stick representing an important element in the origin myth (Gilmore 1929:97; see Fig. 3). An Arikara bundle of this type, probably the same bundle, is in the collection of the Field Museum of Natural History in Chicago.

A very unusual bundle or "bird case" was described by Maximilian in 1833–34 (Thwaites 1906a, vol. 23:391). This bundle was made of a four-cornered parchment case and was six or seven feet long with seven rattles attached to the outside. Inside the case were stuffed bird skins and a large, "very celebrated medicine pipe which is smoked only on extraordinary occasions and great festivals." A bundle of such proportions as this is not mentioned by any of the later observers; it may have been the overall Arikara group bundle.

A second class of bundles were those belonging to the doctors' societies (Gilmore 1931:46–49; see also Howard 1974). These bundles contained objects symbolic of the particular society and representative of the powers of the society. For instance, among other things, the Owl Society bundle contained a stuffed owl, bracelets made of owl skin, owl and eagle plumes used as headdresses, and the head and neck of an owl, used in magical performances. Attached to the bundle were four deer hide rattles, each containing five pieces of gravel. The gravel represented the four most important societies plus the altar group.

A third type of bundle was the domestic or household shrine to Mother Corn (Gilmore 1925, 1931:49–50). These were very simple

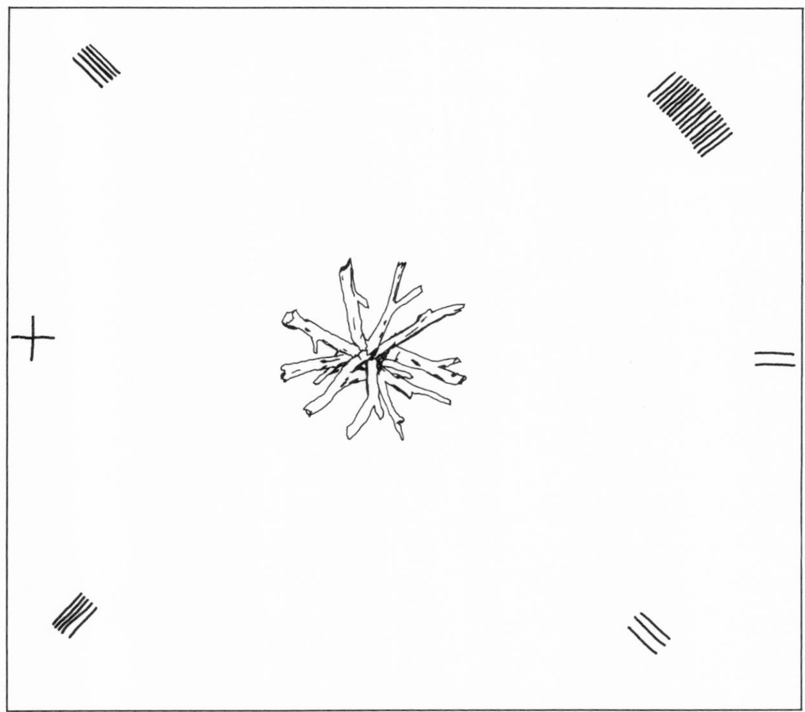

Fig. 3. Placement of 34 bundle sticks used to represent important aspects of the origin myth. North is at top of figure. Adapted from Gilmore (1929:99).

buffalo skin bags containing a perfect ear of flour corn and a braid of sweet grass (*Savastana odorata*). These bundles were kept in the home and were used periodically to offer prayers to Mother Corn. The sweet grass was used as incense.

The fourth and final type of bundle was of a personal nature. These bundles were small and contained objects revealed through dreams as being significant to the individual. In 1811, Brackenridge (Thwaites 1904b:126) noted

> every one has his private magic in his lodge, or about his person. Anything curious is immediately made an amulet, or a talisman; and is considered as devoted or consecrated.

Maximilian, in 1833–34, observed that "maize is one of the principal medicines of the Arikkaras" and an ear of maize was worn around the neck of warriors going on raiding expeditions (Thwaites 1906a, vol. 23:391). Bundles, whether personal or group, provided an object-based connection with powers that were beyond the realm of everyday life, but which were needed to exist in the everyday world. The rituals, of which bundles were usually a part, provided the physical, social, and action context to encompass the role of the bundle and complete the link with the supernatural.

SOCIAL ORGANIZATION

Before the 1860s the Arikaras consisted of a number of loosely organized subgroups, each occupying a separate village (Fletcher 1906:86). At the time of the earliest European knowledge of the Arikaras, 43 or more villages may have been located on the lower reaches of the middle Missouri River in present-day South Dakota (Villiers 1925:62). The most complete information on social organization comes from material collected by Gilmore in the 1920s (1927, 1928). By that time, Gilmore's informants had knowledge of only 12 named villages that had existed in early times. Although this number fits well with Gilmore's overall organizational scheme, there were certainly more than 12 villages in the early eighteenth century.

Arikara villages were semiautonomous, each having a head chief and three or four subchiefs (Curtis 1970:149). There was also an overall chief who usually came from the Awa'hu band (Gilmore 1927:332–345). Chieftainship tended to run in family lines, although increased rank could be acquired by gaining prestige (O'Shea 1978:72). Brackenridge (Thwaites 1904b:123) noted that "Their government is oligarchical, but great respect is paid to popular opinion." Several myths recount the stories of individuals who received special powers, obtained war honors, and eventually became chiefs in recognition of their special deeds (Dorsey 1904a:61, 136, 151). The office of chief, however, was generally hereditary and, in fact, sanctioned by heavenly authority, or as Holder (1970:51) puts it, "the chiefs were sky figures come to earth." It is also appropriate to note that the same word, Nesanu, is the name for the supreme deity and for chiefs. Possibly the myths collected by Dorsey, describing the attainment of chieftainship through personal exploits, reflect the influences of the Mandans and Hidatsas with whom the Arikaras had been living in Like-A-Fishhook for some 30 years before Dorsey's visit. It is also apparent that the status of "war chief" might be gained through personal valor, however, the hereditary chiefly positions were still separate and above the acquired positions (Holder 1958:214). The chief who served as the overall group chief was elected from the ranks of the hereditary chiefs by the four highest "classes" of the populace (Gilmore 1928). Arikara villages were organized into four subgroups; each subgroup was represented in the overall group council by a subgroup head chief and four assistants (in Gilmore's reckoning, one from each village). In councils, held in the ceremonial earthlodge, subgroup head chiefs and the villages they represented were associated with a particular semicardinal direction, which dictated the location of their seating.

According to Gilmore (1928), the Arikaras were organized into several distinct "classes" (see also Holder 1958). The highest class was that of the chiefs and consisted of the head chief, his four assistants, and the chiefs representing each of the villages. Chiefs were afforded special considerations, including the placement of their lodges towards the center of the village (Hoffman 1884:529; Holder 1970:60), where the ceremonial earthlodge and plaza were normally located (Gilmore 1930:48). The elites (chiefs and well-to-do families) spoke a different dialect or "better language" than the rest of the populace (Thwaites 1904b:128). Through the medium of the fur trade, it is also apparent that the wealth of the chiefs was increasing (Holder 1970:62–63), although greater wealth was far from the ideal of the chief as a noble man of self-sacrificing proportions (Thwaites 1904a:176). Next in rank was a civic order consisting of men and women (probably including priests and doctors) who were initiated in consideration of their "excellence of character" (Gilmore 1928:411). A third group of the population consisted of men who had received war honors. A fourth group included all men who had served honorably as soldiers, whether they had received honors or not. A fifth group, not mentioned by Gilmore, must have consisted of the remainder of the people, constituting the bulk of the population.

The kinship structure of the Arikaras in the eighteenth and nineteenth centuries is known only in general outline. The Arikaras tended to be matrilineal (Abel 1939:181–182) with matrilocal residence (Curtis 1970:63). In the absence of clans, the social and medicine societies tended to organize and regulate intragroup activities. Deetz (1965:30–37) has argued that Arikara social organization was undergoing rapid change, including a shift to a generational, rather than lineage, type of arrangement, based on the increasingly less sedentary nature of Arikara settlements, presumably a characteristic of societies with generational systems (Eggan 1955:93). Deetz also argued that because of population decline, village agglomeration, and general reductions in earthlodge size through time, residence patterns were probably shifting away from the matrilocal ideal. Although Deetz's ideas are plausible, and probably correct, no real documentary evidence exits to support these interpretations.

SUBSISTENCE AND ECONOMIC ORGANIZATION

As expressed in the origin myth and aspects of Arikara ceremonial organization, agriculture and hunting were two primary subsistence activities, although the collecting of roots, nuts, berries, and other naturally occurring resources formed an important supplement (Gilmore 1919). Corn was the principal crop, although beans, squash, sunflowers, and tobacco were also grown (Thwaites 1904a:175; Catlin 1842:224). Denig (1961:44), who resided on the Upper Missouri from 1833 to 1856, noted that

> These Indians cultivate small patches of land on the Missouri bottom, each family working from a half to one and a half acres, which are separated from each other by brush and pole fences of rude construction. The land is wrought entirely by hoes, the work done altogether by the women, and the vegetables raised are Indian corn, pumpkins, and squashes of several kinds.

Chiefs decided on the distribution of land for gardening amongst the various households. The larger households and those of higher rank received more land. In each household the "woman-founder" controlled the land (Holder 1958:214–215).

Denig (1961:44–45) described Arikara corn as having a stalk 2.5 to 3 ft high and producing small cobs with small, hard grains. Will and Hyde (1964:299–300) provide a list of 11 varieties of corn cultivated by the Arikaras. Some of these varieties were apparently the same as those grown by the neighboring Mandans and Hidatsas. Denig (1961:44–45) estimated that production was usually about 20 bushels per acre. After the Arikaras were incorporated with the Mandans and Hidatsas at Like-A-Fishhook in 1862, several reports of crop production were available. The reports, however, were for all three groups combined. In 1867, De Smet (1905:885) reports that the three groups were cultivating a total of about 1,200 acres and had added potatoes to their list of crops. In August of 1878, the Indian agent at Fort Berthold (United States 1878:32) noted 800 acres under cultivation and

> More than half of this they have prepared with hoes [the other half was plowed]. This has been as nicely planted and as cleanly kept as any farms in Minnesota. I estimate that they will raise 15,000 bushels of corn and 5,000 bushels of potatoes, besides a large amount of squashes, beans, turnips, onions, etc.

The acreage estimate by the Indian agent is probably more accurate than De Smet's estimate. If anything, De Smet's estimate should be lower than the later estimate (after the introduction of the plow). With 800 acres being cultivated and a combined production of 20,000 bushels, the per acre production of corn and potatoes would be about 25 bushels. This figure is within the general range suggested by the earlier figure of 20 bushels per acre, estimated by Denig for the Arikaras alone.

Planting took place between about the middle of April and the first of May. Harvesting was done in August. Crops were stored in cache pits for winter and spring use (Denig 1961:46). In some years plentiful harvests were obtained, but frequent droughts, floods, grasshopper plagues, and other natural disasters were constant obstacles. For example, in 1803 the crops were destroyed by flood and by the next spring the people were in a state of starvation. Virtually the entire population (except the old people) went on a bison hunt—one that proved to be largely unsuccessful. The three Arikara villages were forced to survive on next to nothing until the young squash was edible (Abel 1939:74, 149).

Fields for cultivation were irregular in shape. No fertilizer was used, and the fields were periodically abandoned and new ones cleared. "Sometimes after a few years of rest they would resume the cultivation of an old field that was quite near the village, for proximity lent some value to the land" (Matthews 1877:11).

In good years crop surpluses were traded to the nomadic groups and to the Euro-American traders. The role of the Arikaras, and the other village groups on the Middle Missouri, as middlemen in a far-flung trade network is well known (Berry 1978; Blakesley 1975). The Cheyennes traded flour made from prairie turnip for corn (Abel 1939:98). Various Sioux groups were also important trading partners, although the Arikaras often fared poorly in their exchanges with their numerous and powerful neighbors. To the Sioux the Arikaras were "a certain kind of serf, who cultivates for them and who, as they say, takes, for them, the place of women" (Abel 1939:130). Products of the hunt were exchanged for those of the field.

> the Sioux come from all parts loaded with dried meat, with fat, with dressed leather, and some merchandise. They fix, as they wish, the price of that which belongs to them and obtain, in exchange, a quantity of corn, tobacco, beans, and pumpkins that they demand.

The Arikaras also carried on a trade in agricultural products with the Euro-Americans (see Beauregard 1912:27). This subject will be examined more closely in other parts of this study.

Through the nineteenth century, the Arikaras were often forced to move their villages owing to pressure from the Sioux or the scarcity of resources. As a consequence, the Arikaras relied less and less on agriculture and more on hunting. By the time the Arikaras came into close association with the Indian agents, game had become scarce (1860s), and the Arikaras were forced to count on the annuities provided by the government to supplement what they themselves could produce or catch. Obviously, considering the above account by the Indian agent, agriculture was being practiced, and attempts were made to expand production. Even so, the weather was often uncooperative and social circumstances had placed the Arikaras in a difficult position. Successful harvests tended to be the exception rather than the rule.

The agricultural pursuits of the Arikaras were but one part of the subsistence picture; hunting was also of prime importance. The Arikaras hunted buffalo and other game species throughout the year, but concentrated much of their efforts on a winter bison hunt (Boller 1959:348; Denig 1961:48). During this hunt virtually the entire village moved to temporary winter camps consisting of skin covered tepees, usually south of the permanent habitations. At times when buffalo were scarce, buffalo skulls were positioned on surrounding bluffs with *Artemisia* placed in the eye and nose cavities, with the objective of appeasing the buffalo spirit and hence drawing the herds nearer (Thwaites 1904a:141). Another major source of buffalo were the carcasses found floating in the Missouri River during the spring thaw. In the winter herds of buffalo crossed the Missouri, if the ice was thin the animals fell through and drowned. The drowned buffalo could be easily collected as they floated down river in the spring. Although the animals were often in an advanced state of decay, the Arikaras ate parts of the meat raw—a sight the European observers could not reconcile with their own tastes (to put it mildly) (Denig 1961:49; Abel 1939:74–75).

Deer and antelope were hunted. Large numbers of antelope could be killed as the herds crossed the Missouri in the spring and fall (Abel 1939:76–77). The Arikaras were also good fishermen and made traps constructed of sandbar willow stakes placed in a penlike arrangement in the eddies of the river (Denig 1961:48; Gilmore 1924b). Construction and use of the trap was controlled by ritual sanctions and could only be undertaken by an individual who had purchased the authority to do so. A recent study of faunal remains from the Mobridge site (A.D.

1675–1780) noted the presence of at least 36 different animal species (Parmalee 1979). In terms of the proportion of meat production within the sample of species represented, bison ranked first (82 percent); pronghorn and deer were also represented in significant amounts, as were dog bones. Catfish bones and a number of bones of different bird species were present. The bird bones represented in the sample suggested that the avifauna was being hunted largely for plumage.

FIRST ENCOUNTERS

The ceremonial, social, and economic life of the Arikaras is part of the framework for making sense of the interactions that took place with Euro-Americans.

The beginning of the eighteenth century marked the inception of a period of European exploration of the Missouri River region. In the late 1600s French explorers and traders had visited the Missouri region and some of the groups residing on the lower reaches of the river, but no attempts had yet been made to reach the Upper Missouri (Nasatir 1952:5). The date of the first encounter between the Arikaras and Europeans is not known. It is, however, almost certain that before direct contact was made, the Arikaras had received access to Euro-goods through other Indian intermediaries (Ewers 1954:436). In 1702, French knowledge of the Missouri region included only groups from the Lower Missouri, but by 1714 Bourgmont's description of the Missouri noted the presence of the Arikara villages. One account suggests that Bourgmont had actually visited the Arikara villages (Giraud 1953:330–333). In 1719, information indicated that the Osages and Missouris may have been raiding the Arikaras for slaves (Nasatir 1952:13, 19). Bienville (Nasatir 1952:25), the French governor in New Orleans, learned in 1734 that a Frenchman had visited the Arikaras,

> who inhabit the upper part of this same river [Missouri] and who had not yet seen any Frenchman, [and] found in that district many silver mines which appeared to him to be very rich.

Such reports as this did much to increase French interests in the Upper Missouri. About 1738 La Verendrye visited the Mandans, who resided above the Arikaras. In 1742 La Verendrye's sons visited the Mandan villages again, as well as the Arikaras, on their return to St. Louis (Nasatir 1952:32–33). Before the French had made a concerted effort to explore the Upper Missouri from St. Louis, a treaty was signed with Spain ending the Seven Years War. By this treaty, Spain acquired the Missouri region from France in 1763, but did not take possession until about 1774. Not until the 1790s did Spain make a concerted effort to continue the exploration of the Upper Missouri. In the meantime British-Canadian trading interests established an overland route from the northeast and had a well-situated trading enterprise at the Mandan villages.

Until the 1790s information on the Arikaras is sketchy and includes only such things as their general location and perhaps the number of villages. However, in the 1790s the Spanish authorities in St. Louis authorized several privately funded expeditions to the Upper Missouri. Each of the expeditions had primarily economic goals, but also had the objective of defending Spanish territory from British encroachment. These expeditions ultimately hoped to reach the Pacific Ocean, although none succeeded. In 1790, Jacques D'Eglise obtained a license to trade on the Missouri and managed to make his way to the Mandans. In 1793, D'Eglise made a second trip up the Missouri to attempt to reach the Mandans, but was turned back by hostile Sioux and Arikaras (Nasatir 1952:83). In his first visit to the Mandans, D'Eglise met a Frenchman who had resided in the region for 14 years. The first major expedition under government authorization left St. Louis in the spring of 1794 under the leadership of Jean Baptiste Trudeau (or Truteau). Trudeau is the author of a journal that is the first major source on the Arikaras (Beauregard 1912). A second expedition followed in 1795 and a third shortly thereafter.

The official expeditions are the best documented. However, it is also clear that unofficial trade was taking place with the Arikaras, carried on by various individual and small-scale traders who left no record of their activities (Nasatir 1952:93). From at least the mid-1700s until the 1790s, a small number of Europeans (perhaps only one or two at a time) were living in the Arikara villages or in the villages of the neighboring Mandans. In many ways this type of encounter with Europeans did not represent a drastic departure from what the Arikaras had come to expect from the steady stream of visitors wishing to trade their goods at their villages. The stable villages of the agricultural groups on the Upper Missouri had been known for centuries as trading centers in a network reaching well beyond the margins of the Plains (Berry 1978; Blakeslee 1975; Ewers 1954:436; Jablow 1951:29; Wood 1974:11–13). Although the small number of Europeans who first visited the Arikaras could be seen within the conditions of aboriginal trade, it was equally true that the Europeans and their goods had a bold and fascinating strangeness to them, one that placed Europeans within a new frame of reference (Chapter 4 considers specific Arikara impressions of Euro-Americans). In such small-scale encounters as those in the eighteenth century, the European traders were clearly at the mercy of their hosts (Nasatir 1952:264). This type of contact with Europeans also placed the settled agricultural groups in an enviable position for controlling trade with the surrounding nomadic groups. This situation was eventually to reverse itself, with the decline in the population of the village groups and the steady increase in the number of Europeans and Americans.

In 1803 the Missouri region was sold by France to the United States as part of the Louisiana Purchase. This event and the subsequent explorations by Lewis and Clark began an era of expanded trade and contact with the Indians of the Upper Missouri. The corps of discovery under the leadership of Lewis and Clark made important contributions to knowledge about the Indians and to the economic potential of resources in the region, especially furs. Lewis and Clark estimated that with an annual investment of $2,500, a return of $6,000 could be expected from trade with the Arikaras (Thwaites 1904–05, vol. 6:80–98). Lewis and Clark made similar estimates for the other groups on the Upper Missouri. After Lewis and Clark, a flood of Euro-Americans made their way up the Missouri to trade and also to observe the customs and manners of the inhabitants of the region. The dominant context of contact, however, continued to be one of trade in furs. It was not until the 1870s that missionaries and government officials became part of the everyday existence.

4

ATTITUDES AND TRADE

> You must now be careful not to take the new things that he has, but you shall take the old things. Take the old weapons.
>
> THE MOON ADVISES NO-TONGUE
> —FROM AN ARIKARA MYTH

From a cultural and historical perspective, many factors structured the capacity for change that was a part of the interaction process on the Upper Missouri. This chapter will discuss and characterize those factors that played critical roles in the eighteenth and nineteenth centuries. In particular, there are three aspects of the culture contact process, ranging from the abstract to the concrete, relevant to a balanced view of Arikara historical dynamics. First, the attitudes and perspectives held by the Arikaras and Euro-Americans towards each other are presented. As argued in Chapters 1 and 2, the sociocultural context is an important aspect of interaction, and considering that the history of contact on the Upper Missouri during the study period was largely structured by trading objectives, it is likewise important to understand how the participants in this process viewed each other and pursued their often contradictory goals. Second, by noting the changing physical settings of exchange (i.e., villages or forts), power relations can be investigated

---

The epigraph that appears above is from Dorsey 1904a:61.

as a further aspect of altered economic patterns and cultural perceptions. Third, trade objects are discussed in conjunction with exchange networks that existed prior to and after Euro-American arrival. The items bartered and the routes utilized offer additional insights into the trading behavior and motivations of all participants.

ARIKARA PERSPECTIVES

The objects brought to the Missouri River region by Euro-American traders were not viewed by the Arikaras as simply interchangeable elements in their own material systems. Euro-goods were almost always made of strange materials, even if they were conceptually similar to existing artifact categories. But what is even more important is that Euro-goods had their origins in a context that largely fell outside of accepted notions of trade or, for that matter, contact with other groups in general. Euro-Americans and their goods were often accorded a symbolically charged marginal role that had to be integrated in some way with sets of cultural categories in existence long before contact and interaction with the white traders. The Arikaras interpreted the new trade goods within an Arikara frame of reference. The power of the Europeans, from the Arikara point of view, was closely associated with objects, because in other ways the Europeans were generally detestable and hardly worth serious social consideration or emulation.

To the Arikaras (and undoubtedly many other native peoples), Euro-Americans represented a mass of social contradictions. Euro-Americans were undoubtedly powerful beings and the owners of fantastic and powerful objects, but they were also sources of trouble and unparalleled disaster (e.g., epidemics rightly attributed by Indians to Euro-Americans). Euro-Americans were ignorant beings, often behaving in ways contrary to Arikara notions of proper action. Even more so, Euro-Americans, or at least the traders, were considered greedy, evil, and often socially wrong in their behavior. The power held by Euro-Americans was not unyielding or monolithic, it could be acquired by Arikara individuals. The powers inherently associated with Euro-Americans could be purchased, bargained for, exchanged as gifts, or acquired by women through means of their own. As already suggested, the power held by Euro-Americans was transferred largely through trade goods or items given as presents.

An Arikara notion that fits in well with the powerful nature of Euro-Americans as traders selling powerful objects is the idea of purchasing knowledge as a route to power. Among the Arikaras, individuals gained access to, or increased their standing within various social groups (e.g., medicine and secular societies) by purchasing access to knowledge (Holder 1958:214; Lowie 1915). For instance, novices within the medicine societies achieved higher levels of participation by purchasing the secrets of the society from the highly respected older practitioners. Often, these secrets to power were bartered reluctantly by the leading doctors. Likewise, the Euro-Americans exacted a high price for their exotic and powerful goods. The connection between goods, knowledge, and power was recognized by the Arikaras as an integral part of interaction with Euro-Americans.

The specifics of Arikara attitudes towards Euro-Americans were occasionally mentioned in trader journals. A trader named Trudeau (Beauregard 1912:24) wrote in the 1790s that "The Panis Ricaras are a rather gentle nature; they respect and defer to the White Men." Trudeau (Beauregard 1912:24) also notes that, "the Indians of this country do not know any distinction between the French, Spanish, English, etc., calling them all indifferently White Men or Spirits." Trudeau states further:

> It is said that formerly the Ricara nation held us in such great veneration that they gave us a sort of worship, having certain festivals at which they offered us the choicest morsels, and even threw into the river robes which had been dyed, and dressed skins decorated with feathers, as a sacrifice to the White Man. I have been assured that the Cheyennes and other more distant nations still practice this custom; while the Ricaras, through having for so many years associated with the Sioux and the Panis Mahas have changed the ideas which they had inherited from their ancestors in regard to the White Men whom they regarded as divinities.

A trader named Pierre-Antoine Tabeau, speaking of the Arikaras in the first decade of the nineteenth century (Abel 1939:200-201), wrote:

> It is only a little while since the Ricaras deified the French, who unhappily, have only too well disabused them by their conduct and their talk. Thus they have passed today from one extreme to the other and we are, indeed, nothing in their eyes. They worshipped the very vehicles which they brought into their villages to make sacrifices and feasts to them. All the furniture and instruments, the art of which is beyond their conception, are today objects still of superstitious respect. Few men are likely to touch my metal thermometer. The quadrant, phosphorus, and the magnet were regarded at the Captains' [Lewis and Clark] as medicine; that is to say as supernatural and powerful.

Tabeau also states (Abel 1939:134):

> This nation, having already wasted great quantities, is accustomed to receive gratuitously. It looks upon the whites as beneficent spirits who ought, since they can, to supply all its needs and it looks upon the merchandise, brought to the village, as if destined for it and belonging to it.

Although some traders saw a decline in the level of respect held by the Arikaras for Euro-Americans, it is also clear that Euro-Americans were still seen as having spiritlike qualities and were the owners of objects of supernatural power. An example of how the Arikaras appropriated the power of Euro-American objects can be illustrated by their use of certain "official" gifts within ceremonial contexts. Trudeau, in 1794 (Beauregard 1912:39–40), noted that:

> The following day on the 7th of the month he [the Arikara chief Crazy Bear] bade all of the Chiefs and *consideres* to his Cabin, he placed the flag before the door and placed his medal around his neck. At the furtherest [sic] end of the hut, exposed on a mat, the letter patent which his Spanish Father [in the 1790s the Upper Missouri was still under Spanish authority] had sent him by me, having had placed before it some live coals on which was burned a certain kind of dried grass the smoke of which produces a very strong odor, and which they use as we use incense. They hold such things as medals, flags, and letters in such deep veneration that

> whenever these are taken from their wrappings, they are smoked and hold the most important place at their feasts.

The use of Euro-goods in this way parallels traditional systems of bundle use. Among the Arikaras, bundles are discrete collections of sacred objects having special powers and serving as mnemonic devices to recount important mythical, cosmological, and historical events and concepts (Gilmore 1931). Bundles also worked as a means of legitimating the access of various individuals to sacred knowledge (see Chapter 3 for a further discussion of bundles). In this regard it is interesting to note that such things as flags, medals, and letters were almost always given to village or tribal chiefs. Only a few years after the time of Trudeau, Lewis and Clark visited the Arikara villages and, in their terms, "made or acknowledged three chiefs" (Coues 1893:160) by presenting them with a series of official gifts. The gifts included, "a flag, a medal, a red coat, a cocked hat and feather, also some goods, paint and tobacco." Some of the smaller gifts were apparently distributed by the chiefs to other individuals. If chiefs were the owners of the major items, then the above Trudeau quote may suggest that they were manipulating these objects without the assistance of priests, thus circumventing normal practice and perhaps enhancing the role and authority of chiefs through an Arikara interpretation extending beyond the notion of the gift itself.

Among a neighboring village group, the Hidatsas (and probably the Mandans, also), conflict over power arose late in the nineteenth century between those individuals owning tribal bundles and those owning personal bundles (Bowers 1950:250). The result of this conflict was a split in the Hidatsa community. Control and access to power through bundles was obviously a critical issue. As suggested above, the Arikaras may also have been experiencing a restructuring of traditional authority relations with regard to the power of bundles. Yet, instead of resulting in factionalism, chiefly attempts to amass additional sources of power may have helped solidify social networks. Ultimately, such approaches to social solidarity were unequal to the opposing forces of social disruption. Population decline, in particular, resulting in the conflation of villages and the bringing together of chiefs from several villages into one village, caused internal strife among the leadership (e.g., Denig 1961:61–62; Abel 1939:130).

If the Arikara chiefs were using Euro-goods to capture and express notions of power, it clearly indicates that these objects had special potency and were being integrated by the Arikaras into their own ritual systems. In another instance Trudeau (Beauregard 1912:47) describes the generally held belief in the power of at least certain Euro-goods:

> the great Spanish father had also given a flag, a medal, and a letter to a young Cheyenne who was named as "the great Chief of their Nation" . . . he turned out to be wicked and had not kept his promise of peace. . . . That without doubt the medal, the flag and the letter, who were great spirits, had become angry, for three of his children had died, and what is more, lightning had struck the hut of his own brother who, with his wives, children, dogs and horses tied before the door, had been reduced to ashes . . . [this] confirmed anew their belief that the White Men were great spirits and all powerful . . . this occurrence gave them [the Arikaras] much to think about.

The preceding quote illustrates how Euro-goods themselves held the power of retribution, but it was also recognized that Euro-Americans had some of the same powers as the medicine men (i.e., doctors) among the Arikaras.

A myth recounted by Dorsey (1904a:105–106) illustrates the symbolic connection the Arikaras made between at least certain Euro-goods (in this case the gun), and the power of the medicine men. In this myth all the animals who possessed special powers went to a lodge to perform their magic, as in the Doctor's Ceremony of the Arikaras. Among them was an old woman (Witch-Woman) who performed her magic also. She was holding a strange object (Dorsey 1904a:106).

> The old woman had a buffalo robe over her shoulders, and she held in her hands a mysterious looking thing dotted with spots of white clay and painted in black. At the top of it were red feathers. The object was a gun, a thing to kill with, to shoot medicine. Now, at this time, the old woman wanted to show the power of this mysterious object.

In conjunction with the gun the woman gave birth to a child, "who was to become a great medicine-man among the people and a leader in the medicine dance" (Dorsey 1904a:106). The relationships implied here are very significant. Euro-Americans and objects of Euro-American origin are mentioned very rarely in any of the Arikara myths, suggesting that they do not play an important part in defining long-standing symbolic relationships. In this myth, the gun appears in a covering of black paint and white dots, which may be viewed as a way of incorporating the strangeness of this object within known symbolic relationships, and consequently removing it from the culture of Euro-Americans. Even so, the process of symbolic incorporation does not alter the truly strange medicine-powers of the gun. The gun remains as an object outside the bounds of normal things. The gun was an object associated with the power of medicine-men (and even their creation) and Euro-Americans.

Certain Euro-Americans were also specifically identified as medicine men. For instance the naturalist, Bradbury, visited the upper Arikara village (a part of the Leavenworth site) in 1811 and was mistaken for a medicine man because he had been collecting plants. An Arikara medicine man greeted Bradbury and displayed the contents of his bundle (Thwaites 1904a:133). Euro-Americans, like medicine men, were believed to be able to cause the death of an individual. Tabeau (Abel 1939:203) wrote:

> Death itself, especially when it is premature, is a source of superstition. In it is always found some supernatural cause and, if there is in the camp a Frenchman supplied with merchandise, it is unusual for him not to suffer for it. Either suspicions really fall upon him or spitefulness and the hope of presents under the guise of credulity have the greater share in the accusation.

As with most traders, Tabeau saw Indian actions as little more than the hope for material gain, but this was not the sole motivation. Euro-Americans were spirits and, like medicine men, were capable of controlling supernatural powers.

Not only could Euro-Americans cause the death of an individual, they could bring disaster to entire villages by causing epidemics. By the 1830s, and probably earlier, the Arikaras and other village groups on the Upper Missouri were consistently blaming Euro-Americans for the diseases that were taking such a heavy toll. In 1837 a devastating smallpox epidemic hit all of the village groups. The Hidatsas blamed the trader Chardon, stationed at Fort Clark, and the Arikaras blamed whites in general (Abel 1932:124, 127). Chardon (Abel 1932:127) reported:

> The Rees are Making Medicine for their sickness. Some of them have made dreams, that they talked to the Sun, others to the Moon, several articles has [sic] been sacrifised [sic] to them both.

Washington Matthews (1877:16) reported that it was difficult to obtain accurate population estimates for the Arikaras and the other village groups because earlier censuses had been linked to the outbreak of disease. As late as 1879 there was opposition to attending the missionary schools, especially because it meant giving names in order to be enrolled. The general belief was that: "The sacred white man has only to speak their name, and desire it, and they will die" (Hall 1879:66).

In 1851, a severe cholera epidemic was attributed to the painter Rudolph Kurz, and was specifically believed to result from his attempts to paint Indian portraits. It was remembered that the epidemic of 1837 had closely followed the visits of the painters Karl Bodmer and George Catlin, thus confirming the evil power of Kurz's portraiture (Hewitt 1937:72–73, 76–77, 95; Meyer 1977:104). In 1857, a trader was killed to avenge epidemic-induced Arikara deaths (United States 1857:127). The evil powers that the Euro-Americans too often supposedly used contrasted sharply with Indian beliefs in the curing powers of the Euro-Americans. Chardon (in Abel 1932:132) observed that "the confidence that an Indian has in the Medicine of the whites, is half the cure." In effect, this completes the Indian view of at least some Euro-Americans as having the characteristics of medicine men—the ability to cure or kill.

There was little question of the many powers of the Euro-Americans. Another method, less material than strict purchase or gift, for the acquisition of Euro-American power and goods was through the sexual favors given by Arikara women to the traders and explorers (Thwaites 1904a:134, 140–41; 1904b:129–130). Trudeau (Beauregard 1912:31) noted of the women that

> there is not one whose modesty is proof against a bit of vermillion [sic] or a few strands of blue glass beads; what is more, the fathers, brothers and even the husbands offer and take the youngest and most beautiful daughters, sisters and wives to the White Men for their diversion, in exchange for the few trifles which they receive.

Tabeau (Abel 1939:180) states:

> A Savage regards the infidelity of his wife in favor of a white man less of a sin, in that she is won by the allurement of gain and he does not dream that this rival presumes to think that he is preferred to himself.

Lewis and Clark (Coues 1893:164) likewise note the availability of women given with the full consent of their husbands or brothers. Of special interest is the case of Captain Clark's black servant, York, "instead of inspiring any prejudice, his color seemed to procure him additional advantages from the Indians, who desired to preserve among them some memorial of this wonderful stranger" (Coues 1893:164). Arikara interest in York was also noted by Tabeau (Abel 1939:201). Clearly, if Arikara women were drawn to York because of his uniqueness, then there is little basis in concluding that they were only interested in material gain.

The sexual liaisons of Arikara women with Euro-Americans can be interpreted as a means for Arikara women, as well as men, to acquire Euro-American power; either through the acquisition of goods or of physical life force directly. Undoubtedly some of the items received for sexual favors were given by the women to their male relatives, but women who became pregnant held this transferred power of the Euro-Americans exclusively. Sexual relations between Arikara women and Euro-Americans were in actuality no more than an extension of a practice already common among the Arikaras. Trudeau (Nasatir

1952:258) observed further, "that many of them take a pride in treating some of the considerable men among them with their youngest and handsomest women." This practice was probably part of the "walking" ceremonies—in which the power held by older men was transferred to younger men through the wives of the latter (Meyer 1977:80).

In contrast to the "loose" character of the women noted by most Euro-American observers, Brackenridge (Thwaites 1904b:131) remarked on a ceremony in which young women who had preserved their chastity might touch the sacred cedar tree (representative of Mother Corn) and also receive gifts. The contradiction that exists between condoned sexual promiscuity and an ideal of chastity may indicate that there were notions and ways of behavior associated with different Arikara social groups. In Arikara society, those with the most to gain from close association with Europeans were members of the lower status categories. The chiefly and priestly groups in society may have been less concerned with the sexual acquisition of Euro-American power and goods, and more concerned with maintenance of cultural ideals. Consequently, the young women who righteously touched the cedar tree most likely were members of the higher ranking status categories.

Although powerful, Euro-Americans often did not behave in ways understandable to the Arikaras. Through time the Arikaras saw the Euro-Americans in an increasingly less favorable way for three major reasons: first, the trading behavior of the Euro-Americans did not match accepted practice; second, fluctuations in Arikara access to fur resources often left the Arikaras with nothing to exchange; and third, the disastrous epidemics made it painfully clear to the Arikaras that whites were of no value in the long run. The first of these reasons is of primary concern here. The trading behavior of the Euro-Americans was based on the accumulation of furs for the sake of profit. Although the Arikaras had a notion of the accumulation of wealth, it was based on a different set of concepts. The notion of trade, or more generally, exchange, was based on a native view of social obligations combined with, and not separate from, the acquisition of materials. The Arikaras, for instance, could not understand why the trader Tabeau had more or wanted more than he could actually use. Tabeau wrote (Abel 1939:134–135):

> Besides, their minds not grasping our ideas of interest and acquisition beyond what is necessary, it is a principle with them that he who has divides with him who has not. 'You are foolish,' said one of the most intelligent seriously to me. 'Why do you wish to make all this powder and these balls since you do not hunt? Of what use are all these knives to you? Is not one enough with which to cut the meat? It is only your wicked heart that prevents you from giving them to us. Do you not see that the village has none? I will give you a robe myself, when you want it, but you already have more robes than are necessary to cover you.'

The Arikaras also did not like the high prices Tabeau set, and even less, his refusal to give the proper gifts (Abel 1939:136).

> I made few presents beyond the ordinary and I even aspired to free myself from making them to villages that had nothing to offer in return. I refused to establish in my lodge a public smoking-room, an abuse consecrated by its age and expensive as it is tiresome. I did not pay back invitations with feasts, still less the dishes brought with interested designs.

Tabeau was staying in the lodge of the Arikara chief (Kakawita or Kakawissassa), but he made every effort to separate himself from the social obligations of the domestic setting by building a partition of upright stakes to enclose his part of the lodge from the other households residing there. "This innovation at first caused murmuring. I was a miser, a hard man, a glutton; but time caused their claims gradually to be forgotten" (Abel 1939:145). The trader Trudeau tried to keep gift giving to a minimum while also recognizing that under some circumstances it was necessary to give gifts (Beauregard 1912:44). These examples suggest that traders often behaved in socially inappropriate ways.

The social nature of the Arikara view of exchange is also expressed in an incident recorded by Bradbury in 1794 (Thwaites 1904a:178–179):

> two men, Jones and Carson, . . . remained with the Aricaras during the winter, and on our return, Carson was desirous of

> rewarding the Indian with whom he had boarded during that period. For that purpose he obtained some articles from Mr. Hunt, and offered them to the *savage,* who refused to accept them, and as a reason for it, observed, that *'Carson was poorer than himself'* [Bradbury's italics].

Considering the high Arikara demand for at least some kinds of trade goods, the refusal to accept goods from whites implies a social view of exchange, and especially the giving of gifts. Clearly the transfer of goods is more than just economic—functioning as well from a cultural perspective of proper action (e.g., Orser 1984a:101, 106). At least in the 1790s, the Arikaras were following an accepted social etiquette of exchange.

Although the traders often saw Arikara gift giving as an attempt to acquire goods in excess of the gift's value, which may have been true, it was also, however, part of the process of establishing social links. By avoiding participation in the full network of social obligations, the Euro-Americans helped to enhance their own separateness. Even traders such as Chardon, who married Indian women, managed to remain distinctly outside of local Indian society (Abel 1932:109, 160). Trader reluctance to participate in gift giving also suggested a disregard for accepted practices of establishing social obligations and validating or increasing social standing. Yet, in spite of disregard for proper action, it was clear that Euro-Americans held high social standing among the Arikaras. This social standing, however, was constructed in piece-meal fashion from the outside-in participation of Euro-Americans in Arikara culture.

In addition to the overall disjuncture between Arikara and Euro-American views of trade, there were other characteristics of the Euro-Americans that made them socially unacceptable. Two brief examples may be cited. During the visit of Lewis and Clark, alcohol was offered to the Arikaras, which greatly surprised them. They responded, "that they were surprised that their father should present to them a liquor which would make them fools" (Coues 1893:160). The Arikaras had previously told Tabeau "that no man could be their friend who tried to lead them into such follies" (Coues 1893:160). In another incident, an

Arikara chief was much disturbed and cried openly when he witnessed the punishment lashes received by a soldier being court martialed (Coues 1893:167). The chief said that "his nation never whipped even children from their birth" (Coues 1893:168). Although powerful, Euro-Americans obviously did not know how to behave properly.

By considering Arikara attitudes towards Euro-American traders and the trade process in general, it is possible to more accurately assess Arikara actions beyond strictly economic motivations. Arikara attitudes were not the same as those of the traders and consequently can not be adequately understood outside of their own cultural context. Based on the imperfect correspondence between the cultural logic of two contrasting societies, the Arikaras molded a composite, if somewhat disjointed, view of the Euro-Americans.

EURO-AMERICAN PERSPECTIVES

In contrast to the few observations that may be gleaned or surmised from the ethnohistorical sources regarding Arikara perspectives on Euro-Americans, there is no corresponding scarcity of information characterizing Euro-American attitudes towards the Arikaras. Throughout previous discussions Euro-Americans have been considered largely as a single group with a single motivation. This outlook is far from the truth. There were, in fact, a variety of Euro-American attitudes and perspectives on the Arikaras that changed through time depending on the ethnic or national groups involved. But even more than this, the objectives of particular Euro-American groups structured their interactions with the Arikaras. Even as Arikara perspectives differed, depending on the social and temporal context of the individual, so did the perspectives of the Euro-Americans differ based on their grounds for being on the Upper Missouri.

It is not the intention of this discussion to provide a comprehensive background to Euro-American views of the natives of North America. The task of understanding the larger themes, attitudes, and motivations of Euro-Americans in relation to American Indians has been extensively examined by numerous other studies (e.g., Bernheimer

1952; Chiapelli et al. 1976; Elliot 1970; Jaenen 1976). There are, however, some general ideas that should be noted, as a means of considering the nature of Euro-American attitudes towards the Arikaras.

By the time people of European origin came into contact with the Arikaras and other groups on the Upper Missouri, Euro-Americans already had a perspective on Indians, developed over several hundred years. In many ways it was a view that saw Indians as a collective entity, having similar characteristics regardless of the obvious differences. The numerous groups and divisions defined by the Indians themselves and the myriad languages spoken were certainly of interest, but did not seriously alter the basic "Indianness" of all the peoples in North America. Berkhofer (1978:25–26) cites some fundamental Euro-American perspectives on Indians. He characterizes Euro-American interpretations as

> (1) generalizing from one tribe's society and culture to all Indians, (2) conceiving of Indians in terms of their deficiencies according to white ideals rather than in terms of their own various cultures, and (3) using moral evaluation as description of Indians.

The outlooks that generally describe Euro-American views of Indians certainly pertain to whites who visited the Upper Missouri, but there are more specific orientations that apply to the particular visitors who came to the Arikara villages.

Until the late 1860s most Euro-American contact with the Arikaras was by traders, interested primarily in acquiring furs. A second major group of visitors, before the 1860s, were the explorers, painters, and naturalists who traveled the Missouri with increasing frequency after the sojourn of the Lewis and Clark party. By all accounts, however, the traders had the greatest impact on the Arikaras during the first 150 years of contact with Euro-Americans.

As mentioned earlier, the traders were, without doubt, businessmen, who lived in a frontier environment they saw as inhospitable and lonely. The traders' motivation was profit, and even those who became "amateur savages" (Matthews 1877:30) seldom, if ever, completely severed their ties and allegiances to the outside white "civilization." The traders who left the best accounts of their experiences were usually employed by one of the large trading companies, such as the American Fur Company in St. Louis. There were also many independent traders operating with fewer goods on a lower profit margin, who left virtually no record of their presence. For instance, the Lewis and Clark expedition encountered several Frenchmen, including Tabeau, who were living with the Arikaras. One of the Frenchmen (Gravelines) spoke Arikara (Coues 1893:158).

The profit motivation of the traders, whether they left accounts of their stays with the Arikaras or not, meant that they must extract the most favorable exchange rates possible and they must keep gift giving to a minimum. Both of these practices were a mystery to the Arikaras, and a constant source of ill will. The traders also actively attempted to manipulate the trade situation by creating a need for their goods (Abel 1939:43). Tabeau (Abel 1939:163), speaking of all the groups on the Upper Missouri, observed that

> None of these nations values our merchandise highly and, if we except some iron implements, they have more liking for their skins, white as alabaster, which they work upon and ornament in different ways and which are, throughout the Upper Missouri, the foremost fancy goods.

Tabeau states further (Abel 1939:166), "the idea of luxury will give birth among the Savages to new needs; and the necessity of enjoying will produce the activity required to procure the means for them." Brackenridge (Thwaites 1904b:129) in 1811, related his views of the results of whites trading with Indians.

> It is true that an intercourse with the whites, never fails to render these people much worse than before; this is not by imparting any new vices, but by presenting temptations which easily overcome those good qualities, which 'sit so loosely about them.'

For the most part, the traders maintained a very negative view of the Arikaras. The trader Tabeau (circa 1804), a man of few positive insights, considered the Arikaras lazy and intractable in nature. He saw Arikara women as dirty and unattractive (Abel 1939:150, 172, 174). Ten years earlier the trader Trudeau described the Arikaras as gentle, easy to get along with, and harboring no malice towards Euro-Americans (Beauregard 1912:24–25). Trudeau noted, however, that two years previously (1792) a party of French traders had found the Arikaras to be wicked. As a result of this visit, the Arikaras had reduced their opinion of whites (Beauregard 1912:25, 26). Apparently, the Arikaras found the French to be wicked as well.

Through time, traders in particular developed a less favorable view of the Arikaras. To a large extent the negative views held by the traders were due to the increasingly hostile actions of the Arikaras against Euro-Americans, especially between the years of about 1805 and 1835. During this period fur resources in the Arikara area had declined drastically and the traders were less interested in trading with the Arikaras and more interested in proceeding up river. The Arikaras attempted to keep the traders from bypassing them (e.g., Dale 1918; Thwaites 1904b:127). Several instances of hostile acts were recorded, including the "Pryor affair," an attack on United States soldiers and traders of the Missouri Fur Company in 1807 (Jackson 1962:432–436; Oglesby 1963:50–51); threatened attacks (and theft of the fort cat) at Fort Manuel in 1812 (Luttig 1920:92, 110); the attack on the Ashley party in 1823 (Morgan 1964:27); and the reprisal shelling of an Arikara village (now known as the Leavenworth site) by the United States Army under the command of Leavenworth in 1823, with the support of several hundred Sioux (Morgan 1953:69; Robinson 1902:200). Leavenworth's attack did not end Arikara hostilities, and in 1830 the Arikaras attacked the Mackenzie trading party (De Land 1918:129). There were several other incidents of less dramatic scope. In general, attacks were directed against traders who were not interested in trading with the Arikaras.

In 1832 George Catlin passed the Arikara villages and noted (1842:204):

> When Lewis and Clarke [sic] first visited these people thirty years since, it will be found by a reference to their history, that the

> Riccarees received and treated them with great kindness and hospitality; but owing to the system of trade, and the manner in which it has been conducted in this country, they have been inflicted with real or imaginary abuses, of which they are themselves, and the Fur Traders, the best judges; and for which they are now harbouring [sic] the most inveterate feelings towards the whole civilized race.

Much the same sentiments are expressed by Maximilian (in Thwaites 1906a, vol. 23:386).

By the late 1830s the Arikaras had resumed trading with the Euro-Americans on a regular basis, but the traders continued to express their contempt for the Arikaras. In 1837 Chardon traded with the Arikaras, but described them as the "Horrid tribe" (in Abel 1932:110). Denig (1961:52) observed that "The domestic character and habits of the Arickaras are decidedly more filthy than any other nation on the Upper Missouri." The Indian sub-agent for the Upper Missouri (United States 1837a:500, 555) reported:

> The Ricaras have long been notorious for their treachery and barbarity, and, within my own recollection, have murdered and pillaged more of our citizens than all the other tribes between the western borders of Missouri and the heads of the Columbia river. . . . They make very fair promises and professions, as to their friendly feelings towards the whites, and their dispositions to maintain peaceable relations with the neighboring tribes, but no reliance can be placed in them.

Such relations of antagonistic trade continued through the mid-nineteenth century. Traders exchanged goods with the Arikaras, but were in constant fear of Arikara attack (e.g., Larpenteur 1933:213). In 1858, Boller (1959:29) described the Arikaras as "savage-looking Indians and more sullen and insolent than any we had yet met." Unfortunately, there are no documents for this period describing what the personal views of Arikaras might have been towards Euro-American traders, although an equally negative outlook is not difficult to predict.

In contrast to the disdainful views of the traders, the explorers, painters, and naturalists saw the Arikaras in a somewhat different light. Members of the Lewis and Clark expedition presented positive views of the Arikaras. Coues (1893:163) observed that

> The Ricaras are tall and well proportioned, the women handsome and lively, ... Both sexes are poor, but kind and generous, and although they receive with thankfulness what is given to them, do not beg as the Sioux did.

Gass (1958:52) noted that "They are the most cleanly Indians I have every [sic] seen on the voyage; as well as the most friendly and industrious." What a different view, compared to that of Tabeau (cited earlier), who was among the Arikaras at the same time as Lewis and Clark! Some of the different perspectives held by Lewis and Clark and the different ways they were treated, compared to the fur traders, were due to the fact that they presented themselves as representatives of the "Great Father" (Coues 1893:162). Apparently the Arikaras accepted as legitimate the high status of Lewis and Clark. By contrast, a Mandan chief observed that the iron worker and gunsmith were the only worthwhile men in the Lewis and Clark expedition (Mackenzie 1960, vol. 1:330).

The naturalist Bradbury visited the Arikaras in 1811. In speaking of the Indians of the Upper Missouri in general, he said (Thwaites 1904a:176, 178):

> I never heard of a single instance of a white man being robbed, or having anything stolen from him in an Indian village. . . . No people on earth discharge the duties of hospitality with more cordial good-will than the Indians.

Bradbury was under a false impression about theft, yet the passage reflects something of the way he was apparently treated in the Indian villages. Brackenridge, another interested observer of Indians, also visited the Arikaras in 1811, and was well treated (Abel 1932:205). In the early 1830s, however, known hostilities kept Maximilian (Thwaites 1906a, vol. 22:334) and Catlin (1842:204) from spending much time in the vicinity of the Arikara villages. Their views, however, suggest a more culturally equitable consideration of the Arikaras.

The contrast between Euro-American and Arikara motivations in the trade process are even more clearly highlighted when the differences between the fur traders and the explorers are considered. The strict economic motivations of the traders set a negative tone for the entire interaction process. In comparison, the explorers were less overtly economic in their goals and more willing to participate in the social obligations of interaction, as defined by the Arikaras. The different ways the two contrasting groups of Euro-Americans interacted with, and were treated by the Arikaras, highlight the importance of the social basis of exchange as it was practiced in the Arikara villages on the Upper Missouri.

PLACES OF INTERACTION

The social and economic aspects of exchange were also affected by the physical settings in which the interactions took place. For the first 100 years of direct contact with Euro-Americans, trade not only operated under Arikara control, it also took place within Arikara settings. The traders that visited the Arikaras came in small groups and took up residence with Arikara households within the earthlodge. Usually it was the lodge of the village chief or another chief who served as protector for the trader and his goods. For the next 100 years of trade with the Arikaras, most traders lived in forts—social and physical settings defined by the traders themselves.

The best example and account of a trader living in an Arikara village is that of Tabeau (Abel 1939). As already noted, Tabeau resided in the lodge of the chief Kakawita. From this location, and with the help of Kakawita, Tabeau conducted his trade. Within the earthlodge setting, Tabeau found himself immersed in a complex set of social relations and obligations. Tabeau, as the wealthiest resident of the lodge, was constantly expected to present gifts to the other occupants of the lodge, in reciprocal exchange for the food he was given (Abel 1939:136, 145). He, however, restricted his gift giving and made efforts to separate himself from contact with other people in the lodge.

Not long after Tabeau's residence with the Arikaras, Euro-

Americans established forts from which to conduct the trade. By the mid-1790s, British companies had established trading establishments in the vicinity of the Mandans, from which they conducted trade with nomadic groups (Nasatir 1952:92; Abel 1939:87). In 1812, Fort Manuel was established near the Arikaras (Luttig 1920; Smith and Ludwickson 1981). Although this fort only lasted about a year, it marked the beginning of a new type of setting for the conduct of trade. Traders were no longer even making the attempt to operate within the Arikara sociomaterial milieu. The forts allowed the traders to establish their own contexts for trade and to increase the number of traders in the region. Fort Manuel employed approximately 75 *engages* at various hunting and trading tasks (Smith and Ludwickson 1981:81). The traders no longer relied as heavily on the Arikaras for food or protection; in fact, relations deteriorated to the point that traders were often not safe in the Arikara villages. With the considerable manpower available to the forts, they were able to establish their own gardens and conduct their own bison hunts (Chardon in Abel 1932; Wishart 1975:53). By 1830, traders were planting potatoes at Ft. Tecumseh and corn at Ft. Clark, among other crops (De Land 1918:118, 203).

With the establishment of forts further up the Missouri, the role of the village groups as middlemen became less important (Meyer 1977:84). In 1829, Ft. Union was founded at the mouth of the Yellowstone River, and in 1832 Ft. McKenzie was built in the heart of the Blackfoot country (Meyer 1977:85).

Traders did continue to trade in the Arikara villages to some extent, but with the establishment of the forts, the Arikaras were more likely to come to the traders, rather than the reverse. The forts, in essence, continued the process of social separation of the Arikaras and Euro-Americans. The forts served the Euro-American goal of restricting contact with natives and restructuring trade as a more strictly economic activity. Yet, this did not mean that the Arikaras stopped viewing trade with Euro-Americans as a social process. The Arikaras continued to visit the forts to give and receive gifts, to trade, and to perform dances (Chardon in Abel 1932:143). Dances performed for gifts, in conjunction with trade, may have been a widespread practice long before Euro-American contact and may have fostered the spread of certain dances across the Plains (Blakeslee 1975:174). Even so, the forts and the increasing military strength of the traders did much to structure interaction and trade within a Euro-American context.

GOODS IN THE TRADE NETWORK

The Arikara villages and the forts of the traders were nodes in a vast trading network that spanned centuries and continents. In the preceding sections the discussion centered on attitudes in the interaction process and the social and physical settings for trade. In this section, a brief outline will be presented of the continuities and connections in the exchange process that extended beyond the bounds of the Upper Missouri. Further, those goods that were part of the trade, in prehistoric as well as historic times, will also be mentioned, as a way of providing some insight into the strategies both sides used in conducting trade.

The role of the Arikaras and other village groups as middlemen in trade on the Plains has been extensively documented by a number of researchers (Berry 1978; Blakeslee 1975; Ewers 1954:430; Jablow 1951:33; Wood 1972:158, 1974). Blakeslee's study (1975), in particular, provides an extensive view of an intergroup trade network that existed across the Plains, and with surrounding regions, from prehistory into the historic period (Fig. 4). Blakeslee argues that one of the primary roles of this exchange network was to maintain ties between groups which might be relied upon for support in times of localized regional subsistence stress (for example, drought). To support this contention he notes that much of the aboriginal trade was for foodstuffs and that the trade was highly redundant (see also Ewers 1954:433). "The generally uniform distribution of resources on the plains meant that the necessities of life could be obtained without recourse to trade" (Blakeslee 1975:200). Yet, trade did take place, and many of the kinds of goods traded were already mutually available to the respective groups involved in the exchange. Blakeslee (1975:82–149) notes that the calumet ceremony was one of the most important mechanisms for maintaining trade relations. The smoking of the calumet pipe and

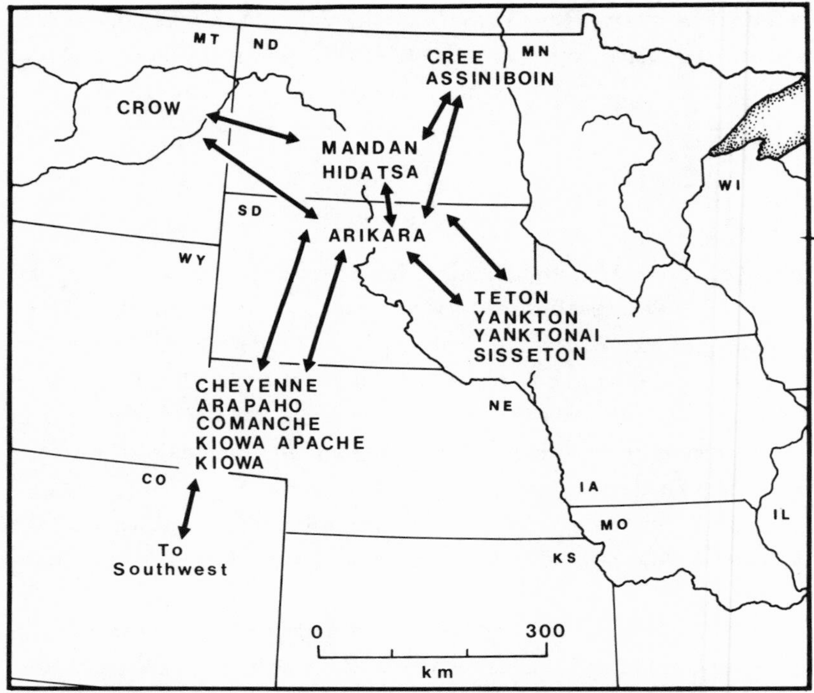

Fig. 4. Location of major links with the Arikaras, Mandans, and Hidatsas in the Plains aboriginal trading network. Adapted from Blakeslee (1975:xii) and Ewers (1954:441).

other aspects of the ceremony allowed the establishment of fictive kin relations between individuals from unrelated groups.

Archaeologically, the evidence for the existence of a long-standing trade network is restricted largely to nonperishable items, consequently it is difficult to substantiate trade in foodstuffs prehistorically. The evidence, from archaeological sources, extending into the historic period, does, however, point to the expansive nature of trade on the Plains. Wood (1974:12) reviews the archaeological evidence for long-distance trade at sites in North and South Dakota (Table 1). The evidence in the Post-Contact Coalescent (A.D. 1675–1780) and the Disorganized Coalescent (A.D. 1780–1862), the periods of primary concern for this study, indicates the continued exchange of goods that

TABLE 1. *Nonlocal Materials of Aboriginal Trade in Middle Missouri Sites (by trade items)*

Cultural Variant	*Dentalium*	*Olivella*	Obsidian	Steatite	Abalone	Copper	Conch	*Marginella*	*Anculosa*	Catlinite
Disorganized Coalescent A.D. 1780–1862	X	X	X	X	X		X			X
Post-Contact Coalescent A.D. 1675–1780		X					X			X
Terminal Middle Missouri A.D. 1550–1675	X	X	X				X			X
Extended Coalescent A.D. 1550–1675	X	X	X			X	X			X
Initial Coalescent A.D. 1400–1550		X								X
Extended Middle Missouri A.D. 1100–1550	X					X	X		X	
Initial Middle Missouri A.D. 900–1400	X			X		X	X	X	X	X

Source: Wood (1974:12).

had been a part of the trade inventory since A.D. 900, or perhaps earlier. Items such as *Dentalium, Olivella,* abalone, and conch shell, and lithic material, such as obsidian, steatite, and catlinite, were important exchange goods.

One of the primary factors that made the village groups important as middlemen was the permanence of their settlements. Because the locations of the Arikaras and other village groups were known from year to year, unlike those of the nomadic groups, the villagers represented effective points to which trading parties could easily travel. The flow of goods to the Arikaras, the Mandans, and Hidatsas took a number of routes. Wood (1972:158–159) describes three major routes:

> (1) The Crow came to the Mandan, Hidatsa, and Arikara villages from the upper Yellowstone River area with goods obtained at the secondary Shoshone rendezvous. There is archaeological evidence that this route is a very ancient one.
>
> (2) Another route was between the American Southwest and the Northern Plains via the Cheyenne, Arapaho, Comanche and other nomadic groups. Whereas this route may be an old one, as Ewers [1954:441] contends, the groups which participated in it are newcomers to the Plains, and may well have displaced earlier participants in the system.
>
> (3) The Mandan-Hidatsa and Arikara also exchanged goods with the nomadic Assiniboin and Cree in the northeastern Plains, as well as with the Teton and Yankton Dakota, the latter obtaining many of their goods at the secondary Dakota rendezvous.

Blakeslee (1975:68) provides some refinements to the trade routes listed above. He suggests that the third route actually includes two separate routes; one from the Cree and Assiniboin to the north and a second, originating with the Dakota groups to the east. An additional trade route from the south can also be included. These various trade links to the Arikara villages meant contact with a number of different groups from many parts of the Plains. In addition to the neighboring Sioux groups and the Mandans and Hidatsas, the Cheyennes, Arapahos, Kiowas, Kiowa-Apaches, and Comanches were some of the other groups trading with the Arikaras (Ewers 1954:430; Gilmore 1926c:15–16).

In historic times the major items that were traded between the Arikaras and other groups were various foodstuffs. The nomadic groups brought products of the bison and processed roots (e.g., prairie turnip) and berries they had collected (Abel 1939:98). These items were exchanged for agricultural produce—especially corn (Blakeslee 1975: 177–181; Gilmore 1926c). The tobacco grown by the Arikaras also had a high value in the aboriginal trade (Abel 1939:158). As mentioned above, a variety of shells and lithic materials were also exchanged. Other raw materials such as Osage orange wood for making bows, or finished products such as bows made with mountain-sheep horn were also important trade items (Ewers 1954:440). Before direct contact, the increasing availability of Euro-American goods also made these items major commodities in the intergroup trade network (Ewers 1954:436). The trader Larocque was much impressed to see the great quantities of Euro-American goods that had been acquired through native channels by the Upper Missouri groups (Larocque 1910:20).

The number of Euro-Americans trading on the Upper Missouri in the eighteenth and early nineteenth centuries increased, from less than 50 in 1807 to over 1,000 by the 1820s (Wishart 1975:45). This influx of traders caused some major shifts in the aboriginal trade routes. An overland route from the northeast established new links; however, the major change was the increasing flow of goods up the Missouri from St. Louis. In the 1700s most Euro-American trade was coming from Hudson's Bay Company trading establishments, or other traders (which later became the North West Company) on the lower St. Lawrence River (Lehmer 1971:170). The expedition of Lewis and Clark, however, fostered a shift away from the overland route, and towards the river route from St. Louis.

Soon the village groups along the entire Missouri were fighting to maintain their middleman status by discouraging direct Euro-American contact with groups further up river. Attempts by Indians to restrict access to more remote groups was not new to the Missouri region. In fact, such efforts to control trade were a common aspect of the expanding trade and settlement frontier. As early as Jacques Cartier's travels up the St. Lawrence in 1534–1535, native peoples were advising that it was too dangerous to go further or that groups up river were untrustworthy (Hoffman 1961:140–141). Much to the general dismay, Cartier continued on. So too, on the Missouri, Euro-Americans insisted on continuing past the middlemen to reach the ever-receding sources of furs.

The objects that Euro-Americans brought, or that were transferred through Indian intermediaries, constitute a very diverse inventory of goods. Many of the goods traded were specifically tailored for the Indian trade (Quimby 1966:11). Euro-American traders also included items in their inventories that had long been a part of the aboriginal trade. Such things as walnut wood for bows, turkey feathers, and tobacco were part of the traders' wares. It was also apparent to the traders that their goods must conform to Indian tastes, if their bartering was to succeed. Tabeau (Abel 1939:171) noted:

> Ammunition, knives, spears, blue beads, tomahawks, and framed mirrors are the only articles for which they are willing to exchange their robes. Hardware of every kind can procure skins of the common fox.

Later Boller (1959:302) remarked on the changing demands for blankets.

> White blankets (to make capotes) were in the greatest demand and so unusual was the rush for them that we began to fear we would not have enough left for the Sioux trade, their fancy also running on white, which is the favorite color for war-parties. Hitherto scarlet and blue blankets had been the rage, but they were now not even looked at.

The interest in white blankets, mentioned above, may well be linked to the demand for the highly valued robes made from the skin of albino bison (Dorsey 1904b:62, 67; Thwaites 1906a, vol. 23:390). Arikara interests in Euro-goods almost always included blue beads and vermilion. Bradbury, in 1811, remarked that these items were frequently exchanged for sexual favors (Thwaites 1904a:140). Coues, in 1804, noted that red paint (i.e., vermilion) was greatly in demand (1893:165). The same was commented on by Tabeau (Abel 1939:171), although he considered the red paint only as an accompaniment to other articles being traded. At the American Fur Company fort, Arikara women were trading corn and squash for "knives, hoes, combs, beads, paints, etc., also purchasing ammunition, tobacco, and other useful articles for their husbands" (Denig 1961:46).

As noted above, a major trade good preference of the Arikaras, and other groups on the Upper Missouri, were blue glass beads. Many of these beads were remanufactured, through a melting and molding process, into pendants of native design. The remanufacture of beads is another way in which Euro-American trade goods were incorporated within an Arikara frame of reference. The topic of Arikara glass pendants was mentioned in a number of early sources. Tabeau (Abel 1939:149) noted:

> A Spanish prisoner taught them how to melt our glass beads and to mold them into a shape that pleases them. This art which is as yet unknown to them is practiced only secretly and still passes for a supernatural and magical talent.

Whether the Spanish prisoner was actually the source of this innovation or not, is open to debate, considering that glass pendants were also manufactured by Indians in the Illinois country and other parts of the Mississippi Valley.

The making of pendants among the Arikaras continued through the middle and late nineteenth century (Denig 1961:51; Matthews 1877:22). Matthews (1877:22) expressed the essential fact of the glass pendants that has kept them a topic of interest to early observers and later scholars:

> It is strange that within a few years after glass beads of European manufacture were first introduced among them, and when such beads must have commanded a high price, they should pulverize them and use the powder in making ruder and more unsightly articles after their own design.

Matthews probably overestimated the value of beads, but even so Euro-Americans considered it odd that the crudely made pendants should hold a worth beyond the beads themselves. Several studies have reviewed the early sources and the techniques involved in making the pendants (Gilmore 1924a; Howard 1972; Stirling 1924; Ubelaker 1966; Ubelaker and Bass 1970). Howard's study, in particular, places the manufacture of pendants within a social context. He argues that the pendants were used in a status validation ceremony by the Arikaras, as well as by the Mandans, Hidatsas, Cheyennes, and Yanktonai and Teton Dakotas (1972:93). The presence of pendants in some burials from the Leavenworth and Sully sites suggests to Howard the importance of these objects in defining "individuals with special status in the community" (1972:96).

It is possible to go beyond the social and technical aspects of pendant manufacture and consider the implications from a more structural point of view. Although specific connotations for the evocative aspects of blue beads are lacking in the ethnohistorical record (without seriously overreaching the limits of credibility), it may be observed that the Dakota word for beads and pendants translates as "blue sky" (Howard 1972:94). Another reference to the symbolic meaning of the color blue is in the use of a blue cloth by Trudeau to obtain safe passage past hostile Indians. He states (Nasatir 1952:272): "I placed on the sand the blue cloth, symbolic of the clear road which I demanded of them." While interesting, these allusions to the symbolism of the color blue shed little light on the reasons for making blue beads into blue pendants. Yet there does seem to be an inescapable redefinition of meaning inherent in the transformation of Euro-American beads into Arikara pendants. Such a transformation implies the desire to incorporate at least some aspects of the Euro-American "otherness" into an Arikara encompassing ideal. To bring the power (defined loosely) of Euro-Americans within the Arikara cultural frame of reference was a consistent theme of the interaction process, from the Arikara point of view. The manufacture of glass pendants may have been part of this process.

The ever-changing nature of Indian interests and needs for trade goods required that the traders stock a diverse inventory of merchandise. A glimpse of what the trader "outfits" contained is available from several sources, including the records of the American Fur Company, now housed at the Missouri Historical Society in St. Louis (Missouri Historical Society 1822, 1829, 1831a, 1849; Thwaites 1904–05). Available inventory lists for "outfits" traded to the Arikaras, or at trading establishments in the general area cover the period of 1803–1849, and include quantities and prices for each item. The names of many of the items on these lists clearly indicate that goods were manufactured or at least intended for the Indian trade. Although the available inventories span a relatively short period of time, there are changes in the composition of the lists. It appears that there was a shift away from exotic or expensive items, including items of personal adornment, towards clothing and food.

5

EVENTS AND THE OUTLINES OF CHANGE

> A new nation is always disposed in favor of the whites; it worships them, sometimes up to the point of superstition and especially fears to displease them. A little familiarity destroys the illusion; the first ray of light convinces them that they are enlightened and that period is the most critical for the trader.
>
> TABEAU 1805

Much of the discussion in previous chapters has been oriented towards presenting a largely synchronic view of some of the social and cultural aspects of the interaction between the Arikaras and Euro-Americans. In this chapter the focus will shift towards a diachronic evaluation of factors that played an important role in the interaction process. Previously discussed factors will be placed within a chronological framework that will serve as a historical model of change, against which changes in the archaeological record can be evaluated. The historical outline will also include those major considerations, such as epidemics, that played a prime role in orienting the trajectory of Arikara change and interaction with Euro-Americans. The historical outline provides a

---

The epigraph that appears above is from Abel 1939:153–154.

means of ordering changes in attitudes and other factors that are presented largely synchronically in Chapter 4. In Chapter 8, a series of propositions about change in Arikara material culture will be evaluated against the historical background presented here.

In the second part of this chapter a general theory is described as a link between the historical trends and Arikara strategies for maintaining a viable social system. While the theory is specifically oriented towards the Arikara case, it incorporates broader implications concerning the differential success of various societies faced with acculturative pressures (see Champagne 1985).

HISTORICAL DYNAMICS

Some 180 years ago, the trader Tabeau (Abel 1939:153–154), continuing the theme expressed in the introductory quote to this chapter, remarked on the different "ages" of interaction with Indians.

> Intercourse with the Savages has three ages:—the age of gold, that of the first meeting; the age of iron, that of the beginning of their insight; and that of brass, when a very long intercourse has mitigated their ferocity a little and our trade has become indispensable to them.

In spite of Tabeau's pejorative terminology, his observations carry some general validity, especially from the trader's perspective, and reflect something of the history of interaction as viewed by Euro-American observers in the early nineteenth century.

Inherent in any consideration of change over the long run, whether it be the observations of individuals (like Tabeau) directly involved in the events under consideration, or those who observe history from the documents, is the construction of a *particular* history, one that is composed of only a limited set of points or concerns. All things considered, there is no one single history that is the "correct" history; as such, history is a hypothesis. The factors considered most relevant for this history of interaction include an orientation towards the significance of trade and the trade goods themselves, and the relevance of attitudes and perspectives held by both parties in the contact environment. Yet, these factors do not stand in isolation, and any consideration of the interaction process *must* take into account a variety of other variables. The chronological outline of interaction to be constructed here includes:

1. Growth and fluctuations in the economics of the fur trade, including changes in the availability of trade goods.
2. Changes in attitudes towards trade and the interaction process held by Arikaras and Euro-Americans.
3. The occurrence of epidemics and general population decline.
4. The changing nature and intensity of warfare with the Sioux and others.
5. The differential ability of Arikara society to function within culturally prescribed limits, given the variety of pressures interaction with Euro-Americans instigated (e.g., factionalism due to amalgamation of several villages into one).

There are certainly other factors that could be dealt with, however those listed above are considered the most important for the following discussion.

The history of interaction can be characterized for the Arikaras by six periods, including one period before contact and five periods after the presumed time of direct interaction with Euro-Americans. Each period will be considered in chronological sequence. Because much of the documentation and argument for this particular construction of the interaction process has already been given, the following characterizations will present, in summary form, the most important points about each period.

Period I is a pre-contact period dating from approximately the late 1500s until 1680. This period is included in the historical sequence primarily for archaeological purposes. The beginning date is intentionally left vague, but is designed to coincide roughly with the first archaeological data that may reasonably be identified as Arikara. The closing date is a rough estimate of the time of first direct European contact with the village groups on the Upper Missouri. The archaeological assemblages associated with this period will be used as a beginning point against which to consider post-contact changes in the artifact composition of various Arikara physical contexts (i.e., earthlodges, ceremonial earthlodges, and burials). Although this period serves as the beginning of the chronological sequence it is, nevertheless, recognized that the influences of Europeans on Arikara lifeways and material assemblages was taking place long before even the earliest direct contacts. Diseases introduced by Europeans may have had a significant impact on Arikara population levels well before the eighteenth century (Ramenofsky [1987:133] defines the seventeenth century as the period of greatest disease impact on the Upper Missouri). Early fur trader accounts point to the former existence of as many as 32 villages capable of fielding 4,000 warriors (Beauregard 1912:28, 29). Even without European influences it is apparent that prehistoric cultural interactions in the Middle Missouri region (used in the archaeological sense of the term) between A.D. 1400 and 1675, and especially within the Coalescent Variant (discussed in Chapter 7), were resulting in a number of changes in the material remains found in the archaeological record (Lehmer 1971:107–128).

Using Period I as a starting point against which to consider subsequent changes after the incorporation of Euro-American trade goods does at least present a general way to evaluate the composition of "traditional" Arikara material assemblages. A major theme of this study is the relationship between Arikara social change and their use of Euro-American trade goods. From this perspective, the use of archaeological assemblages associated with Period I, which contain virtually no objects of Euro-American origin, is a good way to gauge subsequent changes in the material record.

The first post-contact time frame is *Period II,* dating from 1681 to 1725. This is the first period of probable direct contact between the Arikaras and Europeans. It is characterized by continued indirect trade with other Indian intermediaries and sporadic direct trade with a small number of French visitors (Hyde 1952:39; Margry 1876–1886, vol. 6:455). As discussed earlier, the Arikaras would almost certainly have viewed Europeans as powerful beings with spiritlike qualities. The interaction process must have proceeded on hospitable and amiable terms.

The next period is *Period III,* dating from 1726 to 1775. Like Periods I and II, little direct historical information is available to describe this period; however, it is certain that contact with Europeans became more frequent. Due to disease and warfare with the Dakota, Deetz viewed the period of 1720–1750 as the time of greatest stress for the Arikaras. From his point of view, Arikara social stress was reflected in the "extreme variation seen in the [ceramic] design vocabulary of this period" (1965:101). Even if it was a period of great social stress, trading relations with Europeans continued to be good. Every indication points to Europeans maintaining their favored status as manipulators of supernatural powers. The Arikaras also managed to maintain their status as middlemen in the fur trade, considering that Europeans had as yet maneuvered beyond the Arikaras in only very limited numbers. The indirect trade in Euro-goods meant that the Arikaras had horses by at least 1738 (Burpee 1927:335–337). Arikara access to guns may have been delayed until about 1750 (Ewers 1954:437).

The next phase is *Period IV,* dating from 1776 to 1805. During this period direct trade with the Arikaras is noticeably intensified. Beginning in the 1790s, a series of expeditions made their way up the Missouri from St. Louis. The most noteworthy of these was the Lewis and Clark expedition in 1804–1805. During this period the first significant accounts of Arikara life appear in the historical record. Hyde (1952:48) defines the period of 1770–1800 as a time of crisis for the Arikaras, largely due to depopulation and warfare with the Dakota, the same reasons for which Deetz defined the earlier period of 1720–1750 as the time of greatest social disruption. Whatever the period of greatest crisis might have been, there was in fact no time of reprieve from the calamities connected with Euro-American contact.

By the beginning of Period IV the Arikaras were firmly established as participants in the economics of the fur trade. As the Euro-

American traders had planned, trade goods were becoming less of a luxury and more of a necessity (Abel 1939:153–154). Euro-goods were also available in ever-increasing quantities. Guns, which had previously been of limited utility due to the difficulty of maintenance and resupply, could now be used on a routine basis (Holder 1970:115). Although the bow and arrow were still preferred for hunting, the gun had become essential to warfare.

Disease was continuing to take its toll on the Arikara population in Period IV. Hyde (1952:33) suggests the occurrence of three epidemics between 1772 and the 1780s (Table 2). Stearn and Stearn (1945:46–48, 75–77, 130–131) suggest that there was an epidemic, probably smallpox, on the Upper Missouri in 1780–1781 (or 1781–1782) and another in 1801–1802. In a letter from Rengel to Miro (Nasatir 1952:109), dated 1785, seven Arikara villages were noted, with an estimated 900 warriors (Table 3). In 1794, Trudeau (Beauregard 1912:28) reported the existence of only two villages. Certainly

TABLE 2. *A Partial List of Epidemics Affecting the Arikara and Other Groups on the Upper Missouri*

Date	Epidemic	Reference
1772–1780s	Three possible	Hyde 1952: 33
1780–1782	Possible smallpox	Stearn and Stearn 1945: 46–48, 75–77, 130–131
1801–1802	Possible smallpox	Stearn and Stearn 1945: 46–48, 75–77, 130–131
1818–1819	Possible smallpox	Stearn and Stearn 1945: 78
1837	Smallpox	Abel 1932: 124, 127
1846	Measles	United States 1847: 290
1851	Cholera	Hewitt 1937: 69, 72–73, 76–77
1856–1857	Smallpox	United States 1857: 127

Note: There were certainly other epidemics before 1772; however, they went unreported. In general, the specific identification of the disease vectors responsible for an epidemic are tentative.

the information on the number of epidemics in this period is incomplete (Trimble 1986). By the end of Period IV (1805), the two villages reported about ten years earlier, had split into three villages with an estimated total population of 2,600 (Coues 1893:144). Tabeau estimated, for roughly the same date, that the Arikaras could field 500 warriors (Abel 1939:124–126) and also noted that there had formerly been 18 villages. In 1811, Brackenridge (Thwaites 1904b:122) reported that the Arikara villages were the remnants of "17 distinct tribes (i.e., villages)." Beyond the memory of Tabeau's or Bracken-

TABLE 3. *Selected Arikara Population Estimates*

Date	Observation	Reference
1904	380	Fletcher 1906: 84
1874	618–700	United States 1874: 242
1866	1500	Trobriand 1941: 281
1855 (approx.)	600	Denig 1961: 59–60
1850	1500	Culbertson 1851: 137
1833–1856	800 warriors	Denig 1961: 43
1841	2750	United States 1842: 268–269
1837	2750	United States 1838: 593–594
1836	3000	United States 1837b: 420
1835	3000	United States 1836: 295
1830	550 warriors	De Land 1918: 107
1829	2500	United States 1829: 102–103
1804–1805	500 warriors	Abel 1939: 124–126
1804	2600 (650 warriors)	Coues 1893: 144
1802	500 warriors	Le Raye 1908: 161
1794	500 warriors	Beauregard 1912: 28
1785	900 warriors	Nasatir 1952: 109
Prehistoric	9000	Meyer 1977: 14

Note: This table represents a listing of many of the available population estimates for the Arikaras. In general, the Arikaras were unwilling to allow the collection of accurate census data until the late nineteenth century; consequently many of the above estimates are probably very inaccurate. Typically, the figures almost certainly overestimate the population.

ridge's informants, the evidence for a larger number of villages is convincing.

A major effect of depopulation, leading to social disruption, was the incorporation of the remnants of a number of different villages into a much smaller number of villages. Several early observers commented on the nature and results of depopulation. Trudeau observed that there was much factionalism in the Arikara villages, due to the presence of many chiefs, who had formerly been village leaders (Nasatir 1952: 296–298). Dialectical differences, once associated with different villages, were now incorporated into the same village (Abel 1939:125–126; Osgood 1964:159). From Period I on, factionalism resulting from village agglomeration must have been an increasingly important problem. The traditional hierarchical organization of the Arikara authority structure was undoubtedly severely threatened by the presence of competing sources of authority within the same village. The ideal leadership structure called for a single overall hereditary chief assisted by four chiefs, each representing the villages associated with the four semicardinal directions (see Chapter 3 for details). To challenge or modify this organization was also to come into opposition with the very structure of the cosmos itself. As described in Chapter 3, the authority structure of the Arikaras paralleled the authority structure of the gods. Nesanu, the supreme god, had as his assistants the four semicardinal directions. The hereditary chiefs of the Arikaras were also called Nesanu, thus providing a clue to the cosmic link between the power of the gods and that of the hereditary chiefs. Factionalism in the Arikara villages was symptomatic of challenges to authority, and by extension, to the very nature of man's relationship to the gods. In an archaeological study of social status as exemplified by burial practices, O'Shea (1978:136) concluded, in part, that there was evidence for a decline in centralized authority at the Leavenworth site. This seems to be substantiated in the ethnohistorical record. In the epigraph to Chapter 2, Nesanu told the Arikaras they must always maintain the office of chief (Curtis 1970:85), yet the very attempts of each chief to keep his authority were working as a device of self-destruction.

Available accounts for Period IV indicate that trading relations between the Arikaras and Euro-Americans were good, although it was also a time in which the Arikaras were recognizing that the Euro-Americans did not fit the cosmological ideal of supernatural beings. In fact, if anything, Euro-Americans were like medicine men—controllers of powers derived from the earth rather than the heavens. This shift in perspective was important, given Arikara expectations about the social nature of exchange practices, and the apparent rejection (or at least minimalization) of social participation by Euro-American traders.

Another aspect of the fur trade that was becoming more of an issue, was the increasing efforts of the Euro-Americans to bypass the Arikaras and trade with groups having greater direct access to the best hunting territories. In 1793, D'Eglise and Garreau attempted to make their way up the Missouri to the Mandans, however, they were forced to abandon the effort due to the hostilities of the Sioux and Arikaras (Nasatir 1952:83). Truteau, also attempting to reach the Mandans, was in constant fear of being detained and having his goods pillaged (Nasatir 1952:262–263).

Period V dates from 1806 to 1835. This period represents a distinct departure in the nature of the relationship between the Arikaras and Euro-Americans. The Arikara view of Euro-Americans became decidedly more hostile and there were a number of armed encounters between the two groups. Some of these encounters have been mentioned in the previous section. The increasing hostilities correlate with the lessening ability of the Arikaras to participate in the fur trade and maintain their position as middlemen. By the beginning of this period the beaver resources in the Arikara area were severely depleted (Ewers 1959:vii) and there was, as yet, only a small demand for buffalo robes (Wishart 1975:46). As a result, the Arikaras had little to exchange for the desired trade goods. Brackenridge (Thwaites 1904b:29) observed, in 1811, that there was no profit to be made at the Mandan and Arikara trading posts. Not only was there no profit to be made, but there was also a sharp decline in the international market for American furs. Orser (1980a:161–164) has effectively argued that the most hostile Arikara actions occurred at a time of extremely low international demand for furs. Figure 5 presents a graph showing the quantity of American furs exported between 1765 and 1835. By 1805, the export

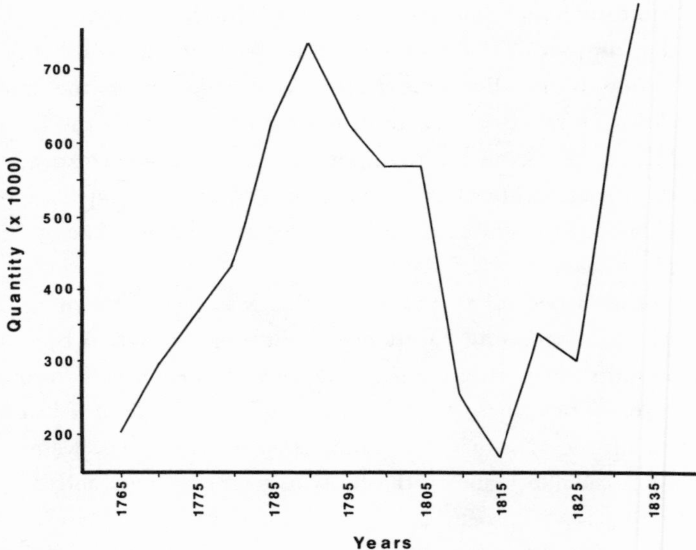

Fig. 5. American fur sales. Adapted from Orser (1980a:163).

of American furs had dropped drastically and did not rebound significantly until the 1830s, when bison hides became an important commodity. The drop in export of furs was also due to the war with England, which normally purchased most American furs. A trader named Biddle observed that between 1812 and 1819 the fur trade was "of little importance from a pecuniary point of view" (Missouri Historical Society 1819).

During Period V, the attempts of the Arikaras to participate in the fur trade were further hampered by new strategies of the traders. In 1822, William Ashley began sending whites to do the trapping, thus bypassing the Indians altogether (Meyer 1977:53). It was estimated that in the 1820s as many as 1,000 men were involved in the fur trade on the Upper Missouri (*Missouri Intelligencer* 1822). By 1831, there were an estimated 500 to 600 whites hunting beaver in the Rocky Mountains (Abel 1932:344; Missouri Historical Society 1831b; Russell 1965:3). Only a year later, the Arikaras had a major battle with

Ashley and his party of traders (Morgan 1953:56). For much of Period V, traders were making every effort to bypass the Arikaras (Orser 1980a:162). In 1832, the Arikaras left the Missouri Valley and took up temporary residence with the Pawnee on the Loup River (Meyer 1977:281), thus essentially abandoning their trade links and their position as middlemen.

By the beginning of *Period VI,* 1836–1862, trade and interaction with the Arikaras was again normalized to some extent, although the Arikaras no longer held the lucrative position of middlemen. The Arikaras had returned to the Upper Missouri, to the general dismay of the traders. The Arikaras participated in the trade, yet with an often unfavorable view of the traders, a view which the traders returned in kind (Boller 1959:28–30 and earlier discussion). Boller (1959:348), speaking somewhat facetiously, describes the character of the trade with the Arikaras:

> The agreeable prospect . . . presented itself of daily arrivals from the [Arikara] camp ostensibly to trade, but in reality to beg and steal. Like the Gros Ventres [Hidatsas], they, too, determined to extract the highest rates for their robes and were likely to leave no means untried to compass their ends.

In the 1830s the demand for bison hides had increased sharply and had replaced the dwindling supplies of beaver and other furs as the most profitable fur trade item. Indian subagent Hatton estimated that the total value of bison robes traded in 1849 would reach $330,000, whereas other furs would total only $60,000 (United States 1849:1073). The Arikaras were able to supply bison robes to the traders (Abel 1932:109, 173). De Land (1918:110–111) reports that a large number of bison robes were traded in the winter of 1829–1830. The ability of the Arikaras, and the other village groups, to participate in this trade was, however, continually hampered by the threat of Sioux raids. The epidemics (Table 2) that had so devastated the village groups (and were continuing to do so) had left the numerous Sioux groups relatively untouched. The dwindling Arikara military power placed them even more at the mercy of the Sioux than in Period V. Speaking of the time around 1805, Tabeau (Abel 1939:131) observed that the Sioux "steal the [Arikara] horses and they beat the women and offer with impunity all kinds of insults." The Sioux also kept the bison from coming near the Arikara villages (Abel 1939:131). The Sioux continued their domination of the Arikaras through Period VI (Denig 1961:47). As a result the Arikaras were often afraid to venture from their stockaded villages to hunt, or even to tend their fields (De Land 1918:107).

Depredations by the Sioux, social disruption, and natural disasters (i.e., flood and drought) contributed to the decreasing ability of the Arikaras to supply their own food needs. Towards the end of Period VI, United States Government Indian Agents began distributing annuities to the Arikaras and other Upper Missouri village groups. In some respects the annuities, as gifts of food and other supplies, could be viewed as traditional gift giving. Yet, this gift giving did not require a reciprocal repayment, but was instead clearly structured as the largess of the powerful, giving to those with little power. In typical fashion, however, the Arikaras saw their right to the annuities, as they had with Euro-American trade goods from the first, and made every effort to obtain their fair share, in spite of the clearly corrupt practices of the Indian agents (Boller 1959:30).

As Holder (1967:138) has noted, the first half of the nineteenth century (roughly Periods V and VI) witnessed a reversal of Arikara attitudes towards Euro-American traders. Realignments in the economics of the fur trade and increasing Arikara hostilities were interrelated factors, correlated with the perceived diminishing sanctity and power of the Euro-Americans.

HISTORICAL VULNERABILITY OF ARIKARA SOCIAL CATEGORIES

The historical record provides a variety of clues to the differential resiliency and vulnerability of Arikara society against the backdrop of interaction with Euro-Americans. In one sense, it is clear that Arikara society became increasingly less stable and susceptible to an erosion of cultural coherency; but in another sense it is equally evident that the

Arikaras managed to maintain a set of social and cultural ideals that have remained to the present. The hundreds of examples of volatile culture contact from around the world point to the great diversity in the ability of cultures to maintain a viable social system in the face of great pressure from external sources. The ability of a culture to maintain a viable system does not, however, necessarily imply a rejection of Euro-American influences, considering that change, and the ability to change, may be an inherent characteristic of some cultures.

The attitudes between the Arikaras and Euro-Americans and the history of interaction may be presented in a more general way, to encompass a broader understanding of how the Arikaras dealt with the realities of contact. The following discussion will center on a review of some of the changes in social roles that can be documented, and that had an effect on the interaction process. This discussion will be framed within an overall consideration of the material and documentary evidence for how social categories may or may not be susceptible to exogenous agents of change. Earlier, in Chapter 2, a part of the discussion was devoted to a consideration of the symbolic expression of cultural meaning in objects. The relationship of meaning to object (or more generally, material things such as earthlodges) is an underlying theme of this entire study, and as such, is included as part of the examination of the vulnerability of different social categories.

As the philosopher Peirce (1931–1935, vol. 4:447) pointed out in his authoritative presentation on semiotics, there are three types of "signs" that are aspects of what has been referred to as symbolism in Chapter 2. Parmentier (1985:840) has recently summarized the definition of these signs and pointed out the importance of the temporal link associated with each one:

> Signs that he [Peirce] classifies as 'icons,' in which the relationship between expressive sign vehicle and represented object is grounded in some formal resemblance, are inherently oriented toward the *past,* since these signs function meaningfully without the actual spatiotemporal existence of the represented object. In contrast, signs labeled 'indexes' require some relationship of contiguity between expression and object and are thus necessarily anchored to

> *present* experience, discourse, or action. Finally, signs that Peirce calls 'symbols' bring some formal representation into relation with an object represented only on the basis of further representation's action of imputing or endowing that relation with a conventional linkage. As such, symbols always point to the *future,* in that this semiotic relation is essentially a processual regularity.

The most important of these signs, for the present discussion, are icons, and especially a particular group of icons referred to as "diagrams" (Parmentier 1985:840). Diagrams illustrate a series of culturally defined connections between ideological or cosmological concepts and a physical context. In many societies, domestic houses, for instance, contain within their construction a set of cosmologically defined connotations (Cunningham 1973; Kuper 1980). Such cosmological connotations are not unique to houses, but may also be represented in ceremonial buildings, or at the level of the village or city. In Chapter 3, it was pointed out that the Arikaras defined a hierarchical set of relations that tied domestic earthlodges, ceremonial earthlodges, village organization, group organization, and the social hierarchy into a single unified system that constantly reminded the individual of his or her relationship to the powers that created the Arikaras and placed them in their villages on the Missouri River. Together, these hierarchies of social and cosmological dimension can be viewed as a diagrammatic icon in the Peircian sense. Although an iconic sign is often thought of as a material thing, the social hierarchy also served as an icon of cosmological relations. The degree to which the Arikaras were able to maintain coherency in the social and material hierarchical diagram was closely tied to the successful continuance of the indigenous cultural system (i.e., a reflection of their level of cultural vulnerability). An important element of this argument is the orientation of the icon towards past experience and, as such, themes of social concern and practice that were part of a pre-contact, or at least, non-Euro-American way of life.

The basic Arikara hierarchical structures have been presented in Chapter 3, however, it is worthwhile to briefly reconsider the fundamental aspects of these social and material hierarchies. The foremost of these hierarchies is the cosmological pattern itself. This pattern consists of Nesanu, the supreme deity, who is supported and assisted by four lesser gods, one associated with each of the four semicardinal directions. Nesanu and his assistants form a simple two-level hierarchy of the highest order. On a more earthly scale, the Arikara social hierarchy paralleled the cosmological organization, with the presence of a single overall hereditary chief who was aided by four assistant chiefs representative of the villages associated with each of the semicardinal directions (Curtis 1970:149). In Gilmore's (1927:332–345) perhaps somewhat idealized representation of Arikara social organization, there were also subchiefs, representative of each village. The numerical relation of one chief (or one god) with four assistants was reiterated at the overall group, regional, and village levels.

In the material realm, the domestic earthlodges and ceremonial earthlodges were Arikara-made representations of the cosmos (Reid 1930). The earthlodge's central hearth was representative of Nesanu, and the four interior support posts represented his four assistants. Stringer posts, forming the outside wall of the earthlodges were exemplary of the individual villages, at least in an ideal sense. The domed outline of the earthlodge was symbolic of the sky vault itself. During rituals held in the ceremonial earthlodge, seating of participants was arranged according to their regional affiliations and the other connotations associated with the semicardinal directions.

The Arikara sacred bundles were another important material element in the diagrammatic icon. Each village bundle contained objects recounting the Arikara origin myth, along with important events associated with particular villages.

The social hierarchy also had a spatial dimension. Early sources indicate that within the roughly circular palisaded villages, the earthlodges of high-ranking households were larger and tended to be located near the center of the village (Abel 1939:146–149; Beauregard 1912:36; Holder 1970:60; Thwaites 1904a:129–130). The centrally located earthlodges of the elite also meant that they were near the ceremonial earthlodges (Lehmer 1971:141).

Through time, gaps appeared in the hierarchical diagrammatic icon as a result of pressures resulting from Euro-American contact.

Three of the major disparities that developed in the diagram were tied to epidemic-induced depopulation. With the drastic decline in population, the Arikaras occupied an ever-smaller number of villages until 1862, when they were forced to join the Mandans and Hidatsas as part of a single village. The constant decline in the number of villages meant the destruction of the regional and village levels in the group organization aspect of the cosmologically based hierarchy. The gaps thus produced in the diagram almost certainly had a major effect on the decline of the authority structure and the general conception of the stability of future and past social action within the contact environment.

The amalgamation of villages also meant the incorporation of a number of chiefs and village population remnants within one or two villages (Abel 1939:124–126). The result of putting a number of hereditary chiefs in only a few villages, was rampant factionalism, also associated with the increasing inability of the group chief to execute an organized policy. The infusion of numerous chiefs within a village may also have worked to "devalue" the chiefly status category. The bringing together of chiefs produced gaps in the social aspect of the hierarchical diagram, the effects of which the Arikaras were unable to mitigate.

With population decline there was also a disruption of the priestly organization, which was a further aspect of the amalgamation of villages. With this type of disruption some of the all-important sacred bundles must have fallen into disuse with the death of priests and the subsequent loss of the intricate bundle rituals. Many bundles did fall into disuse, and perhaps were buried with the last priest who knew the rituals, or the bundles may have been taken to a hilltop and abandoned, but, even so, some did survive and were in use in the early twentieth century.

Beyond the material variables and disease-induced considerations, the presence of Euro-Americans also created other problems within the social authority hierarchy. Not at first, but eventually the power of the Euro-Americans had the effect of imposing two levels in the authority hierarchy above that of the hereditary chiefs. Immediately above the chiefs were the local traders at the forts, and above them was the "Great

Father" who lived in a place called Washington. The lower of these two levels was more physically real, yet Lewis and Clark had explained the power of the "Great Father," which the Arikaras were willing to accept. By the time the Arikaras had joined the Mandans and Hidatsas at Like-A-Fishhook village (Smith 1972), the Indian agents held enough power to depose traditional chiefs and replace them at will (Trobriand 1941: 172). The reliance on the authority or power of the Euro-Americans was such that the sacred bundles were left at Fort Berthold for safekeeping when the Arikaras moved to their winter camp (Mattison 1966:211).

Other dimensions of the social system that were apparently undergoing change are supplemental logical structures of the hierarchical diagram, but are included here because of their impact on the overall operation of the social system. In particular, some social groups may have been increasing in wealth, while other groups were finding expanded avenues to power. Throughout the contact period, hereditary chiefs maintained some level of control and normally served as the interaction point with the Euro-American traders. Chiefs received gifts from the traders, set prices, and had first access to the trade goods. The trader Tabeau (Abel 1939:143–144), irked by the low profit margin to be had from trade with the Arikaras and the demands of the chiefs, blamed the latter for the scarcity of goods available for sale to commoner Arikaras.

> I content myself with the slight satisfaction of boldly making them understand that, if the young men are in want of merchandise, they should put the blame on their chiefs, all of whom have demanded it gratuitously; that, from the time of my arrival, finding themselves the only ones provided with peltries, they had fixed munitions at a low price, only to take them all, despite my remonstrances; that, all the winter, they had not given over exhorting that meat should not be furnished except for balls, knowing well that there would remain none in the springtime for the robes of the young men; that today they wished to do likewise in the case of powder, of which I had very little left and of which a chief, in trading a robe, carried away the portion of a young man with his own.

Tabeau's experiences support the contention that chiefs were able to control access to important trade goods, like munitions. Chiefly control of Euro-American trade may have increased the access to wealth of high-status households (Holder 1967:132, 1970:62–63). Although chiefs gained in wealth, the general disruption of the status hierarchy may have allowed those individuals without hereditary claims to authority an increased opportunity to achieve status through the auxiliary route of the "war ladder." While achieved status had always been an option for those born to commoner families, there was no possibility of surpassing the authority held by hereditary chiefs. However, with the disruption of the established status hierarchy, the opportunity for newfound power may have presented itself. The result would have been a further undermining of the hierarchical diagram linking the many aspects of Arikara society into a unified whole. As an adjunct to this theme, it is instructive to note that the myths recorded by Dorsey (1904a) around the turn of the twentieth century make many references to the attainment of chiefly status through war deeds or other achievements, but almost no mention of the hereditary chiefly ranks.

Like the men, women, too, found new opportunities in trading with Euro-Americans. Although the effects are hard to substantiate, women were trading agricultural produce directly and receiving a variety of goods in exchange (Denig 1961:47). This may have increased the personal wealth of women and enhanced their status. The effect, ultimately, was a further subversion of the coherence of the social system.

In terms of changes in the residence and descent system associated with Euro-American contact, Deetz (1965:31–32) has argued that there was a shift away from a matrilineal, matrilocal system towards a generational, nonmatrilocal system. His support for these ideas is primarily the increasingly less settled nature of Arikara villages, the sharp decline in population, and archaeological evidence for a decline in earthlodge size through time. The latter factor may indicate fewer people living in the earthlodges, and thus implying a shift in residence patterns. A change from a matrilineal to a generational system would almost certainly put stress on the ideal relationships, as defined in the creation myth and continually reiterated in ritual. The importance of

Mother Corn in myth and ritual need not of necessity be tied to a matrilineal system, yet in the ancestral pattern the connection was strong.

The hierarchical, diagrammatic icon, as defined here, could easily be viewed as a complex set of overlapping subdiagrams. However, the overall hierarchical construct does have relevance for a broad consideration of social stability, and was an important complex of structures that the Arikaras used and continually redefined in the context of a changing set of social actions. In the period of interest for this study (late 1600s to 1862), it is clear that the Arikaras *did* manage to maintain a certain level of cultural stability. Even with drastic population decline, threats to the authority structure, and changes in the social system, the Arikaras continued to function as a viable social unit. The idea of cultural destruction of local systems may be overstated. At least in the first 160 years of contact, the Euro-Americans had to adjust, while the local systems devised ways of incorporating the strangers and their goods.

The moderate Arikara success in maintaining a viable social system, was, in part, due to the continuance of critical aspects of the hierarchical diagram. Nesanu told the Arikaras that they must always preserve three things: corn agriculture, the chiefly office, and the traditional teachings (Curtis 1970:85). The Arikaras did manage to maintain these three things, in spite of major disjunctures in social practice. Meaning in the cultural order is always at risk in social action (Sahlins 1985:ix). Those aspects of the iconic hierarchical diagram that continued to support a link with the past and were thus important elemental components of themes of social stability are:

1. Persistence of the sacred bundle system. Although fewer and fewer bundles were in use, their sacred contents provided a strong past-oriented connection.

2. The seeming permanence of the mythological system. The many myths recorded by Dorsey around the turn of the twentieth century reflect very few Euro-American influences

(1904a). Although Dorsey may have intentionally excluded those myths that were not "traditional" in character, still the sheer number and the cultural coherence of the ideological and value systems expressed in the myths is undeniable.

3. Continued use of prescribed techniques of earthlodge construction. At least some domestic and ceremonial earthlodges were built and used until the first decade of the twentieth century. By continuing to use earthlodges, the cosmological connotations of the building endured.

The three factors listed above are at least a few of the elements that maintained and integrated the past-present linkage in the hierarchical diagram. The authority structure continued to have a cosmological basis. Although beyond the scope of this study, the period after 1862 represented another crisis time in the maintenance of the social system. In the 1860s, missionaries appeared on the scene for the first time and made every effort to draw the Arikaras away from their ancestral belief system. The missionaries had their successes and it was a time of much change for the Arikaras. As Bruner (1973:233) points out, change does not, however, necessarily threaten the social identity of individuals or of the social system. For example, the Batak of Indonesia were able to construct a Batak image of social and personal modernity. On the other hand, Bruner (1973:228) argues that

> American Indians, until quite recently (Witt 1968), have had to renounce their Indian identity in order to change their culture, but the Batak do not have to change themselves in the process of becoming more modern. . . . The American Indian model [of a modern person] is a white man.

Although Bruner speaks in terms of the developing ethnic interpretations of modernity, it is also part of finding ways of dealing with exogenous stresses.

The ability of the Arikaras to successfully maintain at least some level of cultural integration, despite the pressures that produced gaps in the hierarchical diagram, was not a unique occurrence. Many other groups on the Plains were as successful as the Arikaras, or more so. Others, such as the Mandans, were much less successful (Bruner 1961:187). There is, of course, a broad cultural differential in the capacity for adapting to change. In some cultures, like the Batak, external pressures can be mitigated within the current cultural logic, without producing a destructive disjuncture between practice and ideal. By contrast, many Australian Aborigine groups were unable to cope with the exigencies of change, resulting in a near complete social demoralization. It would seem that to a large extent, the ability of the society to maintain the internal consistency of its own diagrammatic icons, whether through a rejection of external influences or the application of a culturally adaptive logic that accepts change, depends on the effectiveness of the linkages that tie together social units at different levels. The hierarchical diagram of the Arikaras had a number of linking elements, both material and social, that maintained strong social cohesiveness, until the 1860s and in modified form, to the present.

6

STRATEGIES FOR ANALYSIS

> Throughout nature, wherever man strives to acquire knowledge he finds himself under the necessity of using special methods, 1st, to bring order among the infinitely numerous and varied objects which he has before him; 2nd, to distinguish, without danger of confusion, among this immense multitude of objects, either groups of those in which he is interested, or particular individuals among them; 3rd, to pass on to his fellows all that he has learnt, seen and thought on the subject. Now the methods which he uses for this purpose are what I call the *artificial devices* in natural science,—devices which we must beware of confusing with the laws and acts of nature herself.
>
> BAPTISTE PIERRE ANTOINE DE MONET DE LAMARCK

CONTEXTUAL AND CHRONOLOGICAL CHANGE

In the above quote, Lamarck noted the tenuous and, perhaps, sometimes strained relationship that exists between the objects of inquiry and the analytical methods used to recognize order within those objects. Although Lamarck is speaking principally about classification schemes, from a larger point of view, any study, whether physical, biological, sociological, or historical, faces the problem of distinguish-

---

The epigraph that appears above is from Lamarck 1963:19.

ing between results or conclusions that are "real," and those which are a construct of the "artificial devices" used to measure the objects of inquiry. There is no simple way to insure a close fit between "reality" and the results of analysis, since the disjuncture is often a byproduct of our simplistic understanding of human action and thought. One way, however, to minimize the huge potential for misrepresentation of the "facts" is by presenting, in some detail, the theoretical and methodological strategies being used. This does not in itself bring reality closer, but it does allow others to evaluate the analysis based on their own conceptions of valid relationships.

In Chapter 4 the particulars of the relationships between the Arikaras and Euro-American traders were presented in conjunction with the objective of constructing a history of interaction for the Arikaras, which could then be used as a framework for examining changes in the material record. In this chapter the focus will shift away from the ethnohistorical data, and towards the archaeological. Specifically, I will lay the groundwork, in terms of analytical assumptions, hypotheses, and strategies, for the examination of the relationships between the known historical periods and associated changes in the archaeological data.

One of the most important factors to be considered in the analysis of any archaeological assemblage is the role of context, and how changes in artifact distributions are related to social, cultural, behavioral, or historical processes. If meaning, in a general sense, is at least partially context specific, as illustrated in Chapter 2, then analytical procedures should include a very careful consideration of context when making general comparisons. The use of trait lists to characterize one site or group of sites for comparison with another group of sites, without considering the potential variation in how a site is organized, is a common approach that fails to take contextual relevance into adequate consideration. The simple realization that artifacts are not randomly distributed within sites should indicate that trait lists are inappropriate and should strongly underscore the role of context. In practice, most archaeologists recognize this fact and are increasingly making efforts to consider context more specifically. But to consider context in appropriate ways involves new methodological problems, plus greater investments in analysis time. One of the major methodological issues is concerned with defining the relevant scale at which context should be considered. That is, what type of material context should be identified as the valid unit of comparison? In some cases it may be appropriate to compare one site with another, while in other cases the relevant unit of comparison may be individual features or even parts of features within a site. The most appropriate units for comparison are those believed to have cultural relevance. Whatever units are selected, care must be taken to avoid mixing contexts. It is appropriate to compare the contents of a domestic house with the contents of another, however, under most circumstances it is not suitable to compare a domestic unit with a refuse midden or to compare artifacts associated with a burial to those coming from a refuse pit. Although such comparisons would seem intuitively inappropriate, they are in fact used on a large scale to assign components to particular chronological phases. Or at a more encompassing level, such as the site, the actual composition of the site must be considered in order to insure comparability between sites.

If social and cultural relevance is to be considered, the role of the material context must be made explicit and examined within a framework of comparability. In this way, context can be considered as more than just the material set of relations, but also may include a vast array of culturally determined responses. This has relevance for defining what levels of context may be compared and under what conditions. One way to develop a comparative grounding for a particular set of material contexts is to identify a historical and cultural frame of reference. To develop the historical and cultural conditions for the material context of the Arikaras has been, in part, an objective of earlier chapters of this study. In particular, the historical chronology defined previously, will be used as the primary basis for examining changes in the Arikara material context. The specific Arikara material assemblages to be used in the analysis of changing artifact patterns through time are derived from three major contexts: (1) the domestic earthlodge, (2) the ceremonial earthlodge, and (3) the cemetery. Although there are certainly other important contexts at this level of analysis, such as hunting camps (e.g., Smith and Johnson 1968) or other types of specialized activity sites, these three are by far the most widely represented and are least ambiguous in terms of their ethnohistorical and archaeological documentation. The material assemblages associated with these three contexts are not a simple listing of the quantity of different kinds of artifacts, but are instead represented by the consistent occurrence of a number of artifact *categories* in the same type of context. Of the three artifact contexts, domestic earthlodges and burials will be considered in greater detail due to the limited sample of ceremonial earthlodges.

In conducting the archaeological portion of this study the general strategy will be to compare relative changes in artifact assemblage composition for each material context within each time period. The comparison of materials from these separate contexts is a basis for proposing change in the roles of various artifacts. For instance, most earthlodges in Arikara villages are domestic contexts occupied by coresident social units. The artifactual debris found in domestic earthlodges is assumed to have functioned primarily as part of a personal or domestic assemblage, and will systematically differ from assemblages associated with ceremonial earthlodges or burials. It is therefore assumed that the social interactions that define each of the three contexts produced distinct artifact assemblages. This is not to say, however, that there will not be considerable overlap in the types of items coming from each context. It is entirely probable that material contexts defined as ceremonial earthlodges functioned as a location for social and ceremonial events but also as a habitation for important individuals, at least on occasion. The overlap of activities in different contexts will produce material assemblages that differ in subtle yet important ways.

IDENTIFYING CHANGE IN MATERIAL ASSEMBLAGES

Any set of archaeological remains compared over a lengthy period of time will show change in the composition of the assemblage, at least at some level. This constant variation, coupled with analogies and assumptions about culture change (often remaining implicit), form the basis for archaeological studies of culture change. In most studies of prehistoric change, assumptions and analogies must be employed at two levels. First, chronologies must be constructed that define "significant" shifts in the composition of the material record. Defining such shifts is usually a matter of partitioning a continuum of material change based on one or a few perceived disjunctures in various artifact or feature classes. In most cases the relationship between change in the material remains and sociocultural change is poorly understood. Secondly, when examining variation within a previously constructed chronology, further assumptions and analogies must be made about specific changes in artifact categories and hypothesized relationships must be developed for how artifact change relates to some form of sociocultural variation. The assumptions and analogies made at these two levels often overlap, but also introduce unseen biases in the construction of methods for analyzing change. Whether implicit or explicit, analogies are used at all levels of analysis and interpretation. On the largest scale, an analogy can be defined as one of three types: direct historical, restricted cross-cultural, or formal. The direct historical approach pioneered by Dawson (1880) and systematized on the Great Plains by Strong (1935) and Wedel (1938), emphasizes the use of analogy in circumstances with known connections between the historic and the prehistoric. The restricted cross-cultural or the "new analogy" emphasizes comparison of societies with similar levels of subsistence under similar ecological conditions (Ascher 1961:319; see also Anderson 1969; Child 1956; Clark 1953). The formal approach (Binford 1967; Hill 1970) regards all sources of analogy as having comparable validity and is, instead, concerned with the construction of hypotheses that can be tested with "independent" archaeological data. Each type of analogy is concerned largely with the interpretation of archaeological patterning based on ethnographic examples. With the ethnographic pattern as a model, particular expectations are suggested for the archaeological record.

Another type of analogy in common use, but not directly linked to an ethnographic model, can simply be referred to as the "common sense" approach. This approach is usually employed where specific models are not available. This approach is not necessarily fortuitous in that it is connected to the theoretical biases of the researcher and perhaps to an intuitively defined cross-cultural sample. The common sense approach is similar to the "buckshot" approach described by Yellen (1977:7): "It is a form of specific analogy, usually of limited applicability, difficult or impossible to substantiate, and very difficult to avoid." Analytical models based on the common sense approach rely on a belief in the rationality of the people who lived in the past, "it just seems reasonable that they would have done it this way." The investigator's own theoretical and cultural biases play a large role in determining what may logically have happened in the past. Although the investigator's biases are an inseparable part of any analysis, too much of archaeological investigation is based on common sense analogies, with their built-in, unexamined assumptions, that may unnecessarily limit the range of interpretive possibilities for analysis of the past.

Analyzing change in protohistoric and historic periods offers a partial solution to the vagaries of the analogical process. In the case of the Arikaras, ethnohistorical documentation has allowed the construction of a historical chronology based on known social, cultural, economic, and demographic changes. Even so, there are many histories or chronologies that can be constructed from the same body of information, each emphasizing different sets of relations. The historical changes identified for the Arikaras emphasize their interactions with the Euro-American traders while also taking into consideration other social, economic, and demographic changes. Although these variables can not always be substantiated as thoroughly as might be hoped, they do incorporate a level of historical meaning absent in prehistoric culture-historical chronologies. It is the fact that historical biases can be specified for the Arikaras that eliminates the need to incorporate unverifiable assumptions in the construction of a historical chronology. The previously specified historical chronology for the Arikaras represents a reasonably explicit background against which changes in the material record can be examined.

In Chapter 2 a considerable portion of the discussion was oriented towards specifying the complex interactive relationship between objects and culture. Subsequent discussions in Chapters 3, 4, and 5 have sought to define the historical context of Arikara culture and trade with Euro-Americans while not loosing sight of the material component of social and individual action. As Csikszentmihalyi and Rochberg-

Halton (1981:21) point out with regards to the individual (but certainly also applicable to the larger social context):

> it is extremely difficult to disentangle the use-related function from the symbolic meanings in even the most practical objects. Even purely functional things serve to socialize a person to a certain habit or way of life and are representative signs of that way of life.

The fact that logical patterns do exist between social action and the material realm is, of course, an essential basis for the archaeological endeavor.

The outlines of Arikara history as specified in Chapter 5, represent a starting point from which changes in the material record may be examined. However, material change and historical change are not directly linked, and expectations must be defined about how sociocultural change can be identified in the material record. For the purposes of this study, five hypothesized artifact processes have been identified by which the archaeological artifact assemblages may be characterized, and thus compared. The hypothesized processes reflect the range of variability likely to be of direct relevance for understanding the conjuncture of social and material change. The five processes are: Maintenance, Addition, Replacement, Rejection, and Transformation. The term process refers to a specific conjuncture of sociocultural, economic, and demographic factors, explained below, hypothesized to result in an archaeologically recognizable pattern. These specific processes were developed to incorporate a level of analytical resolution with relevance to both social and material factors while remaining within the bounds set by the available data. In a more strictly ethnoarchaeological case, for instance, it would be possible to be much more specific about the nature of the activity processes linking social factors with the material component (Gelburd 1978). However, in the early historic period such fine detail is not available, hence the five artifact processes must be defined in a relatively generalized way.

The first process is characterized by an artifact complex undergoing relatively little change and is marked by *Maintenance* of the functional and symbolic meanings of artifacts. Under this contingency the native program of artifact usage continues largely intact, although functionally equivalent Euro-American goods may be incorporated as part of the system of usage. For instance, metal knives may be used in conjunction with stone knives. In this way, functional characteristics remain largely unchanged although stylistically the artifact assemblage may appear very different. The change in the general stylistic composition of the artifact system is a secondary aspect of material change and is related to the periodic "revaluation" of artifacts. The extent to which the stylistic composition of the assemblage varies from one period to the next is an additional measure of the coherency of that system. It is suggested that an artifact assemblage that is maintained in continuity, is associated with a particular aspect of a social system (i.e., domestic or ceremonial interactions) that is under relatively little stress in the culture-contact environment or that has retained coherency in the face of whatever pressures are being applied. In particular, economic pressures, in the sense of redefining economic roles, are assumed to be minor in artifact systems that are maintaining continuity.

Related to maintenance is the process of *Replacement*. In this process the overall composition of the material assemblage remains unchanged (like Maintenance); however, native artifact categories are replaced by similar types of Euro-American categories, such as metal knives replacing stone knives. The process of replacement is similar to Spicer's incorporative integration (1961:530). Replacement is not meant to imply the abandonment of one artifact category, which is then supplanted by another category of dissimilar type. The process of replacement, like maintenance, implies the existence of an artifact assemblage undergoing relatively little change, but also an artifact system open to certain kinds of change. The associated social system is hypothesized as maintaining coherency but is also open to the free exchange of goods in the trade interaction process. In terms of Arikara history, the process of replacement would be associated with periods of amiable relations with Euro-American traders.

A third characteristic process is *Addition*. In this process Euro-American trade goods, native trade goods, or additional Arikara artifact categories are incorporated as additional elements to an already existing system associated with one of the three major contexts. The composition of the basic assemblage sets remains intact. The process of addition suggests that a variety of pressures or patterns of social usage are at work and are affecting the composition of the artifact system, but the core set of relations is still in operation.

There is a potential disjuncture between how a culture uses objects in sacred and secular contexts, on the one hand, and how newly introduced trade goods are accepted and used, on the other. Cultures adopt or reject objects based on their own perceived role of the object, but the potential for change and disruption of the social system is high given the conceptually and materially exotic nature of some Euro-American trade goods. Even though the new objects are functioning within already existing cultural contexts, their unusual characteristics set them apart, to some extent, from native objects that had previously occupied those roles. Considering that objects help reify cultural values and categories, Euro-American exotica, if adopted into social contexts, may presage change in a variety of social circumstances by destabilizing the material component of social action. While the culture may be operating according to accepted notions of trade, including the acquisition of knowledge and power, the accumulation of material wealth, the formation of alliances, and the control of economic and social relations, it may also be contributing to the process of social disruption as part of the complex interactions of the contact environment. It follows that a period in which new categories of artifacts are being adopted may also be a time of rapid social change. For the Arikaras, Euro-goods never became an important part of ceremonial paraphernalia. Symbolic items associated with basic themes such as buffalo, corn, and the cosmic forces, did not take on Euro-American influences or connotations. But Euro-goods were incorporated into the personal and social life of every individual and in some cases, into the ceremonies that formed the pathway connecting the individual to the cosmos—those ceremonies associated with death and burial. Through time, Euro-goods became an increasingly important part of burial offerings, and eventually (by the late nineteenth century) became the dominant component of all contexts except the ceremonial.

In any case of culture contact, the transfer and acceptance of items between the groups will not be total or complete. Instead, some objects will fit within social, economic, and ideological usages while others will not. In some cases, the cultural constraints are such that, initially, very few objects of foreign origin are accepted. For example, the instance of Erromango Island mentioned in Chapter 2 certainly suggests the differential perceptions of the acceptability of European trade goods. A process that reflects the cultural constraints placed on some or all newly introduced goods is *Rejection.* In this process newly introduced artifacts, which do not fit within the current cultural logic, are ignored or accepted in only limited quantities. This would have an immediate impact on the supply aspect of various goods and traders would undoubtedly quickly modify their inventories to match the interests of their clients. Yet, such market modifications may only have a significant impact in circumstances in which the contacted group is open to the acceptance of goods in general. Such openness is not impled by the process of rejection, which is meant instead to denote a culturally motivated intent to reject external influences. It is assumed that a culture that rejects some or all objects offered by the contacting group is maintaining a high level of cultural coherency and is undergoing relatively little exogenous stress or has adapted mechanisms for coping with various pressures. The process of rejection will be most apparent archaeologically in circumstances where previously accepted objects cease to be incorporated in material assemblages.

The fifth process concerns *Transformation* of the material cultural system. When an artifact assemblage is transformed there is a distinct change in the overall composition of the assemblage. There may be the reduction or virtual elimination of several artifact categories and the inclusion of one or more functionally nonequivalent categories (like the addition process). The overall diversity of the assemblage may be expanded or reduced and need not conform to earlier patterns of usage, although the general character of the material assemblage will be maintained regardless (i.e., represented as domestic earthlodges, ceremonial earthlodges, or cemeteries). A transformed artifact assemblage indicates that the culture has undergone a significant redefinition of economic, social, or symbolic relations as expressed in material remains in the different archaeological contexts.

Each of the processes of change in artifact assemblages functions within an ever-changing social and cultural framework. The five processes that artifact assemblages may fall into do not represent segments on a continuum of change. As already mentioned, maintenance and replacement are closely related processes. The main difference between the two is that replacement implies a greater potential for change. The processes of addition and rejection have approximately opposite impacts on an artifact assemblage. The fifth process, transformation, represents a fundamental and abrupt shift in the composition of the material assemblage, the kind of change that might easily be recognized in the archaeological record. Transformation is an incremental representation of the combined processes of addition and replacement.

Of the five aspects, or artifact processes, each is hypothesized as being related to different characteristics of the social interactions taking place in the pre-contact period (Period I), and between Arikara and Euro-American traders in each of the five post-contact periods (Periods II–VI). The post-contact periods are the primary focus for considering changes in the three major artifact assemblages (contexts).

The five artifact processes, in effect, represent linking arguments that define relationships between the historic periods and the archaeological data. Each process incorporates implications for changes in the interaction process between the Arikaras and Euro-Americans, and implications for the material record. By providing this link between the social and the material aspects, it is possible to characterize the Arikara archaeological data based on the five processes, and by presupposition, to specify the social, economic, and attitudinal correlations (used in defining each of the historic periods) that exist with the physical record. A series of expected relationships among the historical periods, the artifact processes, and the archaeological contexts (i.e., domestic earthlodges, ceremonial earthlodges, and burials) are presented in Table 4.

In order to emphasize the rationale behind the construction of Table 4, some of the elements discussed in Chapter 5 and earlier parts of this chapter will be briefly summarized here. Also note that each context in each period is not assigned a single process, but that multiple processes are often involved with each context in a particular period.

Beginning at the bottom of Table 4, Period I was defined in

TABLE 4. *Suggested Relationship of Artifact Processes to Historical Sequence*

Period	Maintain	Add	Replace	Reject	Transform
I	D, C, M				
II		D, C, M	D		
III	D, C, M	D, C, M	D		
IV	D, C, M			D	
V					D, C, M
VI	C, M		D		D

Note: D = Domestic earthlodges; C = Ceremonial earthlodges; M = Mortuary (burials).

Chapter 5 as a pre-contact phase dating from approximately the late 1500s to 1680. During this period the Arikaras are under less stress from Euro-American sources than in later times and all three of the material contexts are considered to be in a state of Maintenance, at least from the point of view of direct contact with Europeans. It is acknowledged, of course, that there were aboriginal interactions between the Arikaras and other more long-term residents of the Missouri River region prior to European contact (see Lehmer 1971:124–128).

In Period II (1681–1725) the Arikaras are a relatively stable, functioning society enjoying a middleman status in the burgeoning economics of the fur trade. Trade relations with Europeans are very favorable. During Period II, Arikara material assemblages are expected to have undergone processes of addition and replacement. Specifically, it is suggested that domestic earthlodges underwent both processes, while ceremonial earthlodges and burial contexts only experienced addition. The basis for suggesting that addition is the principal process of change operating in the latter two contexts is that these are both ritually oriented and the ethnohistorical record indicates a clear conservatism in their material aspects.

Period III dates from 1726 to 1775, and is a time of continued trade relations between Europeans and Arikaras. It is also a time of increasing social stress, due to disease and warfare with nomadic groups, among other things. In Period III, the process of maintenance again becomes a factor in all three of the contexts, however, at the same time it is expected that the processes of addition and replacement are continuing in domestic material assemblages. Addition is also taking place in ceremonial earthlodges and burials. By Period III, it is suggested that the newness of the encounter with Europeans had worn off and that an awareness of the scope of potential social problems was causing a certain amount of retrenchment, or at least leveling off in the processes of addition and replacement and hence, a return to maintenance. A leveling off of addition and replacement, and an increased degree of maintenance does not necessarily mean a return to a "traditional" artifact inventory. During this and the previous period, many items of European manufacture had been introduced and adopted by the Arikaras. Already, generations had been born exposed to the presence of Euro-goods. For these cohort groups a return to maintenance did not mean throwing away metal knives in favor of stone knives, but only that those things that had become part of everyday life were maintained as such to a greater degree than in earlier periods.

Period IV, dating from 1776 to 1805, was also a period of relatively good trade relations with Euro-Americans, although there were the beginnings of a shift in the role of the Arikaras in the fur trade. Arikara fur resources were becoming less reliable and traders from St. Louis were making greater efforts to bypass the Arikaras to reach more lucrative trade sources. Period IV was also a time in which the supernatural status of Euro-Americans among the Arikaras was becoming a thing of the past. Period IV is difficult to interpret, in terms of the types of processes that may be affecting the material contexts, yet it seems that maintenance may be operating in all three contexts, and rejection also characterizes domestic earthlodges. This suggestion is made based on the shift in relations between the Arikaras and Euro-Americans, and the presumed somewhat more changeable nature of domestic artifact usage in contrast to material assemblages associated with ceremonial contexts.

In Period V (1806–1835), drastic changes were taking place in the trade and interaction processes. By this time the Arikaras were finding it more and more difficult to maintain their middleman status, in fact, Euro-American traders were making every effort to bypass them. The lack of access, by the Arikaras, to beaver and other desirable furs was the principal problem—Arikara interactions with traders became hostile. This period is hypothesized as a time of major social and economic change, and therefore a time of transformation in the composition of the material assemblages associated with all three contexts.

Period VI, dating from 1836 to 1862, is the final period to be considered. During this period the Arikaras remained somewhat hostile towards Euro-Americans, however, trade began to operate again under relatively stable conditions. Bison robes had become a major trade item, which the Arikaras were able to obtain, albeit, less successfully than nomadic groups. Socially, the Arikaras had redefined their role in the fur trade and their relationship to Euro-Americans. In association with the realignment of social relationships with Euro-Americans, it is suggested that ceremonial earthlodge and mortuary contexts were less likely to be experiencing major changes in the composition of their artifact assemblages. The lack of change in the ceremonial earthlodge and mortuary contexts is hypothesized as relating to Arikara attempts (through the structure of the hierarchical diagram, discussed in Chapter 5) to maintain social coherence in the face of extreme exogenous pressures. One way to maintain social coherence was to reduce the amount of change introduced into important ceremonial contexts, thus preserving a link with past social action. In contrast to the ceremonially related contexts, the domestic context probably continued to change rapidly, by incorporating a greater variety of Euro-goods and allowing items of native manufacture to fall into disuse. Such change in Period VI can be described as the process of transformation in the material assemblage. The ethnohistorical record supports the idea that changes in interactions with Euro-Americans, such as the introduction of annuity payments to the Arikaras and other forms of increased reliance on Euro-Americans, fostered the trend towards acceptance of a Euro-American oriented domestic material assemblage.

The expected relationships defined above, and presented in Table

4, are a way of hypothesizing how the historical record may be connected to the material record. The next major step in the analysis is to examine the expected relationships in conjunction with the actual data. However, before conducting the heart of the analysis, it is necessary to specify the analytical techniques and the data to be used.

MEASURING CHANGE

In order to examine the kinds of relationships that have been discussed in previous sections, two factors, in particular, should be considered: the appropriate units of analysis; and the specific ways of measuring change in the units. In the first part of this chapter an effort was made to point out the importance of considering contexts when defining units of analysis. The primary contexts under consideration are domestic earthlodges, ceremonial earthlodges, and burials. Each of these contexts can be regarded as a unit of analysis, but there is also another, more specific, unit to be considered—the artifact category. The basic analysis strategy is to compare the composition of artifact assemblages from one time period to the next, within each of the three major contexts. To make the comparisons in artifact assemblages, individual artifact categories must be considered.

To be concerned with the concept of artifact category is at once to acknowledge a dual set of interests. The first of these interests, of course, has to do with the larger questions that form a basis for the study in general, while the second is often an implicit interest or concern with the inherent logic and validity of any scheme of categorization. To place something within a classification is to define a set of relationships that link it in some logical way with other things. Classification is part of the analytical process, and while archaeologists work at finding better and more appropriate ways of constructing typologies (Whallon and Brown 1982), it remains that classifications of some kind are invariably necessary (Ellen 1979:2).

The necessity of utilizing a classification scheme comes back to the issue of artifact categories as employed in the analysis at hand. As far as this study is concerned, an ideal classification of objects found in

Arikara sites would be based on the way the Arikaras themselves classify the items. If this could be done, it would, among other things, allow a better understanding of how the Arikaras integrated Eurogoods into existing material systems. There is a problem, however, in that the ethnohistorical record does not allow the fine level of resolution necessary to reconstruct this type of classification system. The objects that make up the archaeological record are only a subset of the many things the Arikaras made use of on a day-to-day basis. Most of the items mentioned in the ethnohistorical sources or in Arikara mythology are simply not preserved in the archaeological context. Those items that are mentioned and are part of the material record are usually things for which the function is not in question (i.e., hoes and projectile points).

The solution to the problem of assigning artifacts to particular categories is, of necessity, one that makes use of both ethnohistorical information and existing archaeological typological practice. For many years, archaeologists working on the Plains, especially those dealing with the later time periods, have used ethnohistorical sources to refine their functional interpretations of artifacts. Therefore, existing typological schemes have attempted to take into account at least some aspects of emically defined functionality. The specific artifact categories used in the study are presented in detail in the next chapter, where they will also be considered in relation to hierarchical cover sets and overlapping categorical membership.

The brief consideration of categorization presented here has regarded classification as part of the analytical techniques necessary to evaluate the themes under study. Other techniques that must be dealt with are those of a more numerical nature, used to evaluate the statistically based comparisons. Because the comparisons of artifact assemblages will be based on categorical or count data, complex multivariate statistics such as cluster or factor analysis will not be used (see Doran and Hodson 1975:136; Thomas 1978:241). Most of the numerical analysis of changes among artifact assemblages will be based on the relational comparison of artifact categories, as in the use of correlation techniques, simple comparison of graphs, and Q-Analysis. The use of each of these techniques will be considered in detail in Chapters 7 and 8.

7

SITES AND ARTIFACTS

> The ruins of the village are quite interesting. Here for the first time I have seen the dirt houses of the Upper Missouri, and they far surpass my expectations.
>
> LEWIS HENRY MORGAN [1862]

The archaeological data available on the Arikara are extensive and possess a reasonably accurate and well-defined chronology. There are, however, a number of potential pitfalls that must be considered prior to the selection and use of particular contexts in a chronologically based study of changing artifact patterns.

Before proceeding with a discussion of the archaeological chronology, a clarification should be made regarding terminology. Throughout the early historical sources, and the ethnohistorical studies based on these sources, the region of the Missouri River Valley from at least southern South Dakota, through North Dakota, and beyond is referred to as the Upper Missouri. In the archaeological literature, however, the portion of the Missouri Valley in North and South Dakota is known as the Middle Missouri. In the earlier chapters of this study, dealing with ethnohistorical data, the term Upper Missouri was used, but to be

---

The epigraph that appears above is from Morgan 1959:161.

consistent with established nomenclature, the term Middle Missouri will be used when discussing the archaeological data. As far as the study of the Arikaras is concerned, the terms are interchangeable.

MIDDLE MISSOURI CHRONOLOGY

Over the years the taxonomic units used to described the relationship of archaeological sites in the Middle Missouri region have undergone a number of revisions (Lehmer 1954a, 1954b:138–154; Lehmer and Caldwell 1966; Spaulding 1956:67–83; Stephenson 1954). Concerned primarily with the sedentary village horticulturalists, three broad cultural traditions were defined: the Central Plains, Middle Missouri, and Coalescent. The Coalescent tradition is considered to be later than the Central Plains or Middle Missouri traditions. The Coalescent is also considered to be the combining of the other two traditions resulting from the influx of peoples from the Central Plains area. Historic and protohistoric Arikara sites are part of the Coalescent tradition. In 1971, Lehmer published a synthesis of Middle Missouri archaeology that has become the standard work for description of the various chronological units since that time.

Within Lehmer's framework (1971:33) the Middle Missouri and Coalescent are the traditions associated with the region under study. The Middle Missouri tradition has been divided into three variants: Initial (A.D. 900–1400); Extended (A.D. 1400–1550); and Terminal (A.D. 1550–1675). The Coalescent tradition is divided into four variants: Initial (A.D. 1400–1550), Extended (A.D. 1550–1675), Post-Contact (A.D. 1675–1780), and Disorganized (A.D. 1780–1862). It may be noticed that within this taxonomic plan there is some overlap of dating between the several variants. This is because the traditions and variants are not viewed as regionwide time periods, but are instead meant to consist of related groupings of artifacts and features. This means that the Initial Coalescent, for instance, may begin in some areas earlier than in others. The Middle Missouri subarea of the Plains is divided into six regions (Fig. 6). These regions, from south to north, are Big Bend, Bad-Cheyenne, Grand-Moreau, Cannonball, Knife-

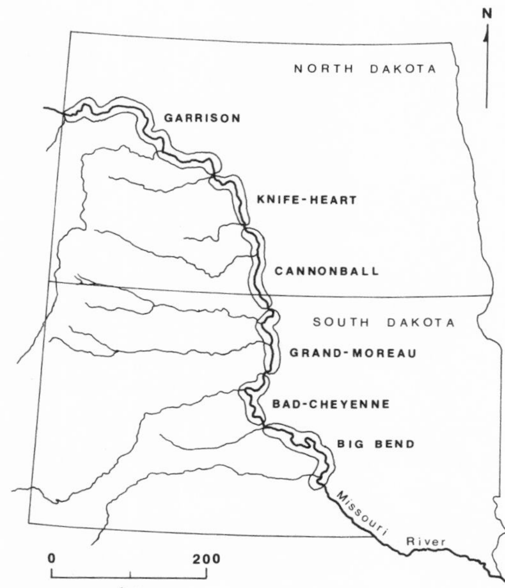

Fig. 6. Six archaeological regions in the Middle Missouri subarea. Adapted from Lehmer (1971:29).

Heart, and Garrison (Lehmer 1971:29). Each of these regions is associated with a different archaeological phase sequence.

The Middle Missouri and Coalescent traditions represent the archaeological ancestry of the Arikaras, Mandans, and Hidatsas. The Middle Missouri tradition relates to the Mandans and Hidatsas and the Coalescent tradition appears to incorporate the culture history of the Arikaras once they arrived in the Missouri Valley from the Central Plains. Initial, Extended, and Terminal Middle Missouri variants are characterized by the remains of horticultural villages, composed of rectangular houses with extended entrys (Fig. 7). Rectangular houses of the Middle Missouri tradition continue in use as late as A.D. 1675. Many villages were fortified but others were not. Almost nothing is known of the mortuary practices of the Middle Missouri tradition. Lehmer (1971:70) has suggested that either inhumations were placed at a distance from the village or that some form of above-ground disposal was practiced. The latter possibility seems more likely, especially considering the extensive use of scaffold burial by the Mandans

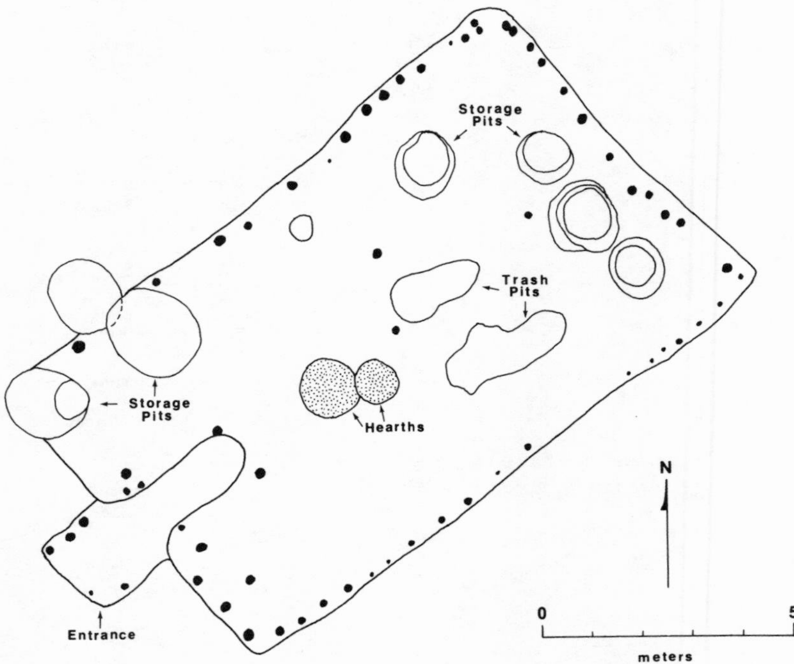

Fig. 7. Initial Middle Missouri variant house plan from the Breeden site, Excavation Unit 3 (House 2). Adapted from Brown (1974:6).

and Hidatsas in the historic period. By historic times the Middle Missouri tradition had been completely absorbed into the Post-Contact Coalescent variant. Lehmer (1971:136) points out that "On the basis of the archeological record alone, the uniformities of Post-Contact Coalescent culture are much more apparent than the tribal differences." By the time of contact with Europeans, the Mandans and Hidatsas, for instance, were living in round earthlodges characteristic of earlier variants of the Coalescent tradition.

As for the Coalescent tradition, the Initial variant presents a large number of similarities with the Central Plains tradition, related to Pawnee ancestry. The Initial Coalescent is the first stage of convergence with the Middle Missouri tradition. The Arzberger (Spaulding 1956)

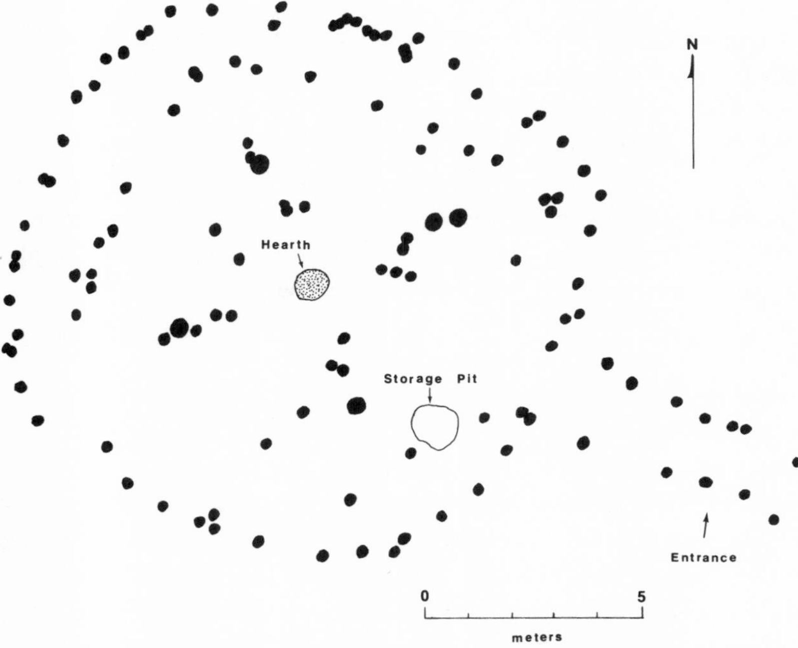

Fig. 8. Initial Coalescent earthlodge from the Arzberger site (House 3). Adapted from Spaulding (1956:24).

and the Black Partizan sites (Caldwell 1966) are important components of this first phase of what appears to be an excellent example of prehistoric culture contact. Although most houses of the Initial Coalescent horticulturalists are round with extended entrys, there are some that are square with heavily rounded corners (Fig. 8; Lehmer 1971:111). The villages are characteristically fortified. Nothing is known about Coalescent mortuary practices until the period of European contact (see Chapter 3 for mortuary practice details regarding the Arikaras).

In the Extended, Post-Contact, and Disorganized Coalescent variants, the material culture continues to become more closely integrated with that of the Middle Missouri tradition. By the Extended Coalescent, houses are almost always round with extended entrys and centrally located hearths. In the Extended Coalescent, villages are fortified at the northern and southern extremes of the zone of occupation on the Missouri River (Lehmer 1971:116). In later times most villages were fortified throughout the region. Evidence indicates that the Terminal Middle Missouri, located in the northern Middle Missouri area, coexisted with the Extended Coalescent, located in the southern part of the Middle Missouri area, between about A.D. 1550 and 1675 (Lehmer 1971:120–121). By the historic period the convergence of the Middle Missouri and Coalescent traditions was virtually complete.

EXCAVATING SITES ON THE MIDDLE MISSOURI

The archaeological data on which this analysis is based was brought together over a period of 75 years by a legion of archaeologists. In this section the methods and strategies used to excavate and analyze Arikara sites by the original fieldworkers will be considered as a way of evaluating and making explicit the strengths and weaknesses of the data. Most of the archaeological data used in this study was accumulated through a series of salvage projects related to reservoir construction. Today, the salvage programs conducted on the Middle Missouri between 1949 and 1969 would be called Cultural Resource Management, but the basic goal is the same—learn as much as possible before sites are bulldozed or washed away.

In 1944 Congress passed the Flood Control Act, which in part had the aim of constructing major reservoirs on many of the nation's rivers (Helgevold 1981:39). Plans being formulated for such major projects, involving the inundation of many river valleys, caused a considerable amount of concern among members of the archaeological community. To deal with the impending loss of important archaeological resources, a cooperative agreement was signed between the National Park Service, the Bureau of Reclamation, the Corps of Engineers, and the Smithsonian Institution (Jennings 1985:282). With the support of federal funding, the Smithsonian initiated a number of major projects in various portions of the country.

The region of the Missouri River Basin was given top priority and for years the Missouri River Basin Survey (MRBS) was the largest archaeological research program in the United States (Roberts 1952: 352). The sheer size of the program, the annual fluctuations in funding, the scarcity of trained archaeologists, and the rapid turnover in personnel contributed to a number of problems experienced by the MRBS (Lehmer 1965; Wedel 1967). One of the major criticisms was that a relatively small number of reports were written and published in comparison to the large number of excavated sites.

The Smithsonian River Basin Survey was not the only organization that became involved with research in the Middle Missouri region. Through the years historical societies and major museums and universities in Idaho, Montana, North Dakota, South Dakota, Minnesota, Wisconsin, Nebraska, Kansas, and Missouri were involved in the field research, sometimes using funds supplied by the National Park Service and at other times using funds from other sources. A notable project funded by the National Science Foundation and the National Geographic Society was the systematic excavation of several major Arikara cemeteries by William Bass of the University of Kansas.

Whatever its faults might be, the MRBS program was a systematic effort to preserve and study archaeological information, and it has left a valuable legacy. The systematic nature of the program is most evident in the use of standardized excavation and laboratory processing techniques. Although the quality of the excavations and subsequent cataloging naturally varied according to the skills of the individuals involved, the use of standard forms and procedures (Lehmer 1971:17–18) meant that at least a minimal criterion was likely to be met. In addition, most excavation collections were cataloged at a central laboratory in Lincoln, Nebraska. This procedure insured some level of comparability between collections, which is especially useful for the numerous sites having no published reports.

Like the laboratory procedures, most excavations were also conducted using a standardized set of techniques. Given the basic salvage orientation of most of the fieldwork, however, excavations were not always done in the most careful fashion. Systematic, time-consuming methods were often set aside for the sake of speed. The focus of most of the excavations in the villages was the delineation of a sample of the houses and testing of the surrounding palisade. In few cases were attempts made at excavating more than 10 or 15 percent of the houses in a village and rarely were areas between houses tested. A culture-historical perspective coupled with time and budgetary constraints seemed to necessitate the sampling of as many sites as possible, rather than the systematic excavation of a few sites. To excavate more than a small portion of a village seemed to have been viewed as wasting time to collect redundant data.

Most individual houses were excavated as a single unit, although occasionally arbitrary 5 or 10 ft squares were placed over the house area. Often, house depressions were visible from the surface, thus limiting the necessity for broad-scale testing. Generally the top soil or plow zone was cleared away by shovel, or occasionally by heavy machinery. The fill from houses was excavated by shovel and trowel and was generally not screened. Where encountered, stratigraphic units were used to segregate the collection of artifacts. Many houses contained refuse-filled storage pits. These pits were excavated and catalogued as separate features. The lack of screening limited the thorough recovery of artifacts, however, considering that this was the general practice, the same biases were introduced at most sites.

CONSTRUCTING THE DATA SET

Although many sites could potentially be used in the analysis, a specific set of criteria had to be employed for site selection in order to insure the validity of the sample. Considering that the analysis involves six different time periods, it was necessary to identify sites representative of each of these time frames. In general, for a site to be included in the analysis, the following criteria had to be met:

1. The site must be well defined chronologically, through radiocarbon dating, dendrochronology, ceramic seriation, direct historic observation, or a combination of these.

2. The site must contain one or more excavated domestic earthlodges, ceremonial earthlodges, or cemeteries.

3. Excavation techniques must at least reflect the standard of the day.

4. If the site is multicomponent, only structures or burials that are not superimposed with another component will be used.

5. Evidence of physical disturbance or the disruption of deposits through subsequent human actions, including the reuse of abandoned house locations as trash dumps by the Arikara, must be minimal.

Sites, or components of sites, that did not meet all five criteria were excluded from the analysis.

Of the above criteria, the chronological assignment of specific components to a particular time period is the most fundamental. The chronological assessments published for sites by the original investigators working in the Middle Missouri region in the 1950s and 1960s were often based on the relative frequency of Euro-American artifacts recovered from a site when other more reliable dating strategies were unavailable. While particular Euro-American objects (for example, coins) may be very useful for dating, the more common use of artifacts frequencies relies on the assumption of steady and predictable increase in the use of Euro-goods by Indians over a specified period of time. Ray's Middleman hypothesis (1978; see Chapter 8 for additional details) calls into serious question the assumption of uniform increase by pointing out variations in trading behavior. Similarly, this study rejects the notion of uniform increase because it does not address the significance of sociocultural factors in determining patterns of adoption or exclusion of Euro-American trade goods. It is, therefore, inappropriate to use change in Euro-American artifact frequencies as a chronological criteria. A more appropriate substitute is the detailed ceramic seriations conducted by Craig Johnson (personal communication, 1986) on numerous Middle Missouri site collections. Preliminary results from Johnson's ongoing research have helped to clarify particular chronological assessments. The chronology used here is further supported in research conducted by Ramenofsky (1987:221–249). A combination of

TABLE 5. *Sites for Inclusion in Analysis (by time period)*

Period	Site Name	Reference(s)
I (late 1500s–1680)		
	La Roche (39ST9A, B, & E)	Hoffman 1968
	La Roche (Bower's) (39ST232)	Hoffman 1968
	Molstad (39DW234)	Hoffman 1967
II (1681–1725)		
	Oacoma (39LM26)	Kivett 1958
	Swan Creek (39WW7)	Hurt 1957
	Black Partizan (39LM218)	Caldwell 1966
	Sully Cemetery (39SL4)	Bass 1965
	Hitchell (39CH45)	Johnson 1967
III (1726–1775)		
	Crazy Bull (39LM220)	Frantz 1962
	Indian Creek (39ST15)	Lehmer and Jones 1968
	Buffalo Pasture (39ST6)	Howson 1941; Lehmer and Jones 1968
	Mobridge Cemetery (39WW1)	None
	Phillips Ranch (39ST14)	Lehmer 1954a
	Peterson (39LM215)	Jensen 1966
	Fort George (39ST17)	Hoffman 1970
	Cheyenne River (39ST1)	None
IV (1776–1805)		
	Spotted Bear (39HU26)	Hurt 1954
	Red Horse Hawk (39CO34)	Hoffman 1970
V (1806–1835)		
	Leavenworth (39CO9)	Krause 1972
	Leavenworth Cemetery (39CO9)	Bass, Evans, and Jantz 1971
	39ST50	Cooper 1953
VI (1836–1862)		
	Star Village (32ME16)	Metcalf 1963

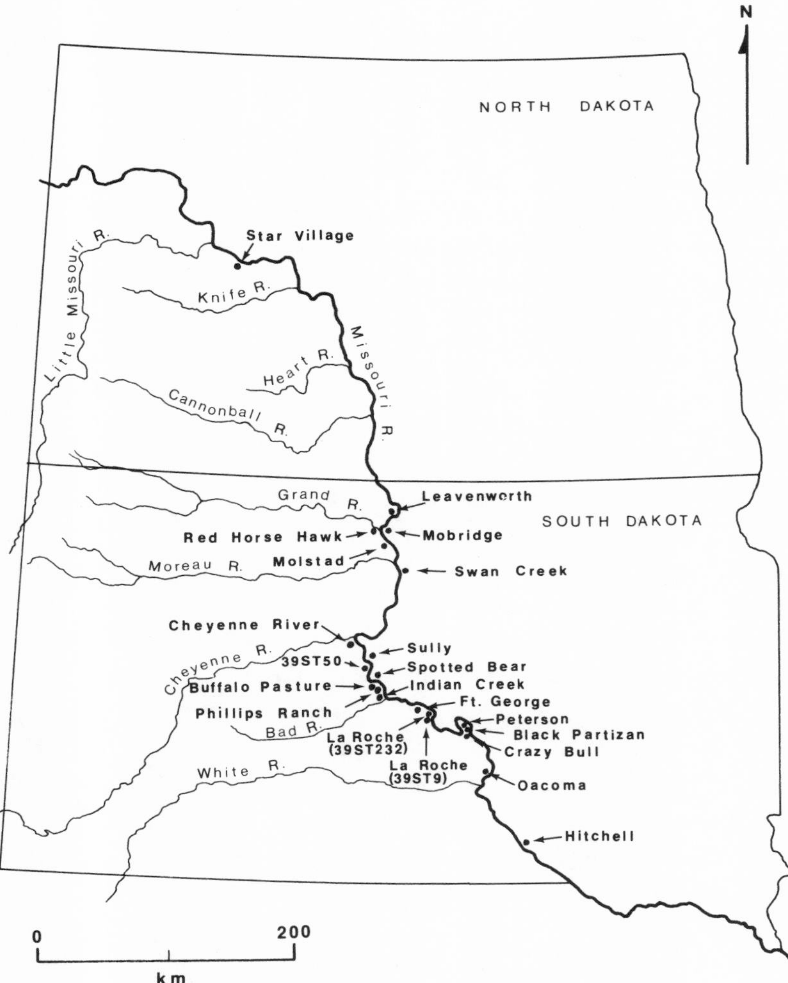

Fig. 9. Middle Missouri region showing location of sites used in the analysis.

chronological tools, especially ceramic seriation, were used by Ramenofsky to establish the dating sequence in her analysis of disease impact on the Middle Missouri village groups. Although relatively few of the total number of sites examined are used jointly by both studies, there is general chronological agreement where overlap does occur.

The sites used in this analysis are listed in Table 5 according to their chronological position. Information on a total of 21 village sites are included in the analysis. Table 5 clearly illustrates that sites meeting all of the necessary criteria are not equally numerous in each period. The total number of Arikara sites, in general, dropped sharply in the eighteenth and nineteenth centuries, so that by Period VI there was only one or two sites occupied at any one time. The Star Village is the only one of these few sites to have been excavated and therefore the only one available for inclusion in Period VI. Each site used is located on the map in Figure 9.

Domestic Earthlodges, Ceremonial Earthlodges, and Burials

Within the several sites designated for use in the study, three major contexts were identified to examine changes in the material record. The three contexts are domestic earthlodges, ceremonial earthlodges, and burials. In earlier sections it was noted that these contexts were most appropriate for inclusion in the analysis because they were discrete, unambiguous units that had been excavated using relatively standardized techniques. Before continuing on to an explanation of the data parameters that form the basis for inclusion of individual lodges or burials in the analysis, it is appropriate to provide some background to the archaeological characteristics of these three contexts. In Chapter 3, earthlodges and burials were described from an ethnohistorical point of view, but an archaeological viewpoint provides a different and supplementary set of information.

The archaeological remains of domestic and ceremonial earthlodges generally consist of a depression visible from the surface. Upon excavation, a circular arrangement of post holes is usually discovered, defining the margins of the lodge (Figs. 8 and 10). There is often an extended, post-lined entryway to the lodge. Inside the outer circle of posts, there is usually evidence for a series of four large interior support posts, set in a square arrangement. In the center of the lodge, evidence for a hearth is usually found. Also, usually located in the interior of the lodge, are one or more storage pits. Many of these pits have a relatively narrow opening with walls that expand outward to form a rough bell

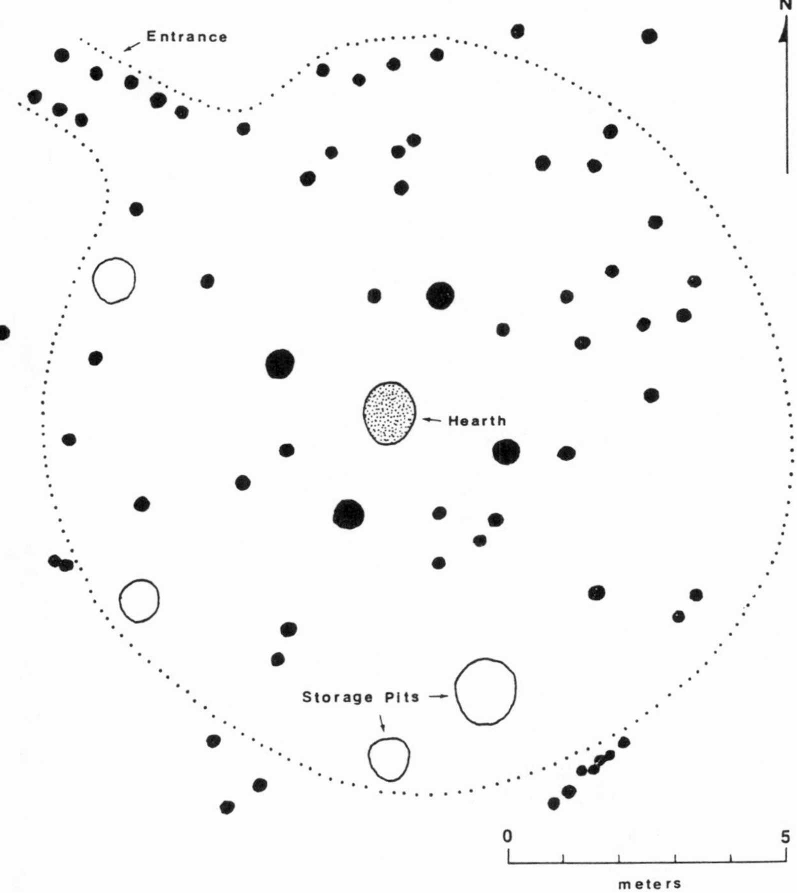

Fig. 10. A Post-Contact Coalescent domestic earthlodge from the Buffalo Pasture site (House 1). Adapted from Howson (1941:104).

shape. Some pits are two meters or more in depth. The floor of the earthlodge was often set a few centimeters to a meter or more below the ground surface. Most of these characteristics are verified in the ethnohistorical record.

Ceremonial earthlodges are basically the same as domestic earthlodges, but they can be distinguished by their size, location in the

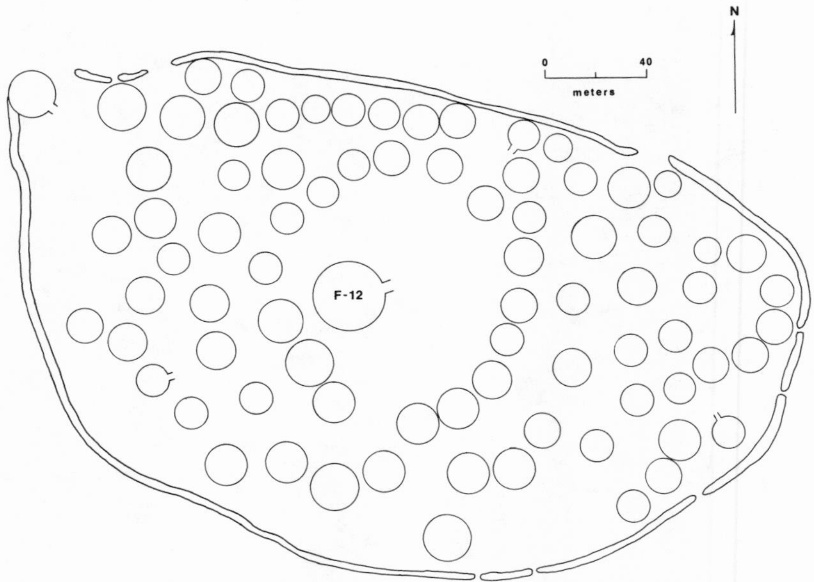

Fig. 11. The location of the ceremonial earthlodge (F-12) at the Star Village site. Adapted from Metcalf (1963:70).

village, and often the presence of an earth "altar." Ceremonial earthlodges are defined as considerably larger than domestic earthlodges and are usually located towards the center of the village (Lehmer 1971:141; Fig. 11). Most earthlodges defined as ceremonial contain few internal storage pits. The "altars" that are often associated with these buildings are low earth platforms positioned along the wall opposite the extended entryway (Fig. 12). Most of the characteristics attributed to ceremonial earthlodges are verified in the historical accounts.

The final context to be considered is that of the cemetery or burial. In Chapter 3, most of the historical information on Arikara burials was reviewed and it was determined that the archaeological data supported the ethnohistorical documentation. Most burials are clustered in cemeteries located near villages. At the Leavenworth site, for instance, there were four major cemetery areas located on the ridges above the site. Arikara burials consist of one or more individuals placed

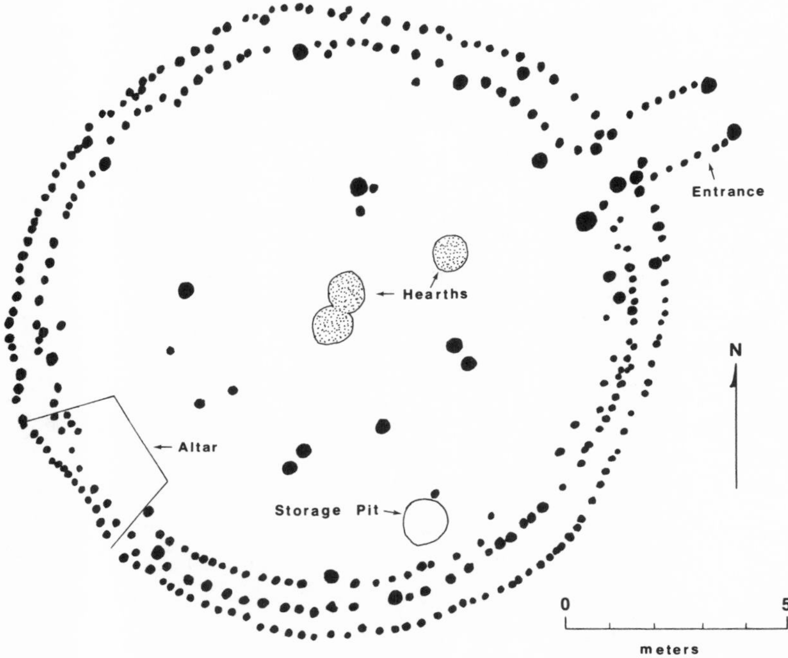

Fig. 12. A ceremonial earthlodge from the Phillips Ranch site. Adapted from Lehmer (1954a:84).

in a shallow grave. The opening to the grave was often covered with a series of sticks or small poles, placed at a slant to the ground surface. Frequently a grave might be reused, the former inhabitants were often dug through or pushed to the side. More than half of all burials contained no evidence of objects intentionally included as offerings.

DATA PARAMETERS

In the previous section a variety of factors affecting the validity and comparability of the archaeological data were presented. In this section, more specific criteria will be examined concerning the justification for inclusion of individual earthlodges or burials in the analysis. Also included in this section is a hierarchical cover set model describing the relationship between artifact categories, and how these categories will be used as analysis variables in Chapter 8.

Factors Influencing Comparison Validity

The composition of the archaeological record is influenced by both physical and cultural processes (Schiffer 1983). Some of the physical processes that may alter the deposits in a site include such things as erosion, fluvial and eolian deposition, and the translocation of artifacts due to freeze and thaw action or bioturbation. All of these factors, and more, can introduce error into an analysis that assumes a nonrandom cultural basis for the distribution of artifacts in a particular context. In the previous section, evidence for the physical disturbance of site deposits was considered one of the criteria for exclusion of a site from the sample. Given the nature of the data, the damaging effects of physical processes have been considered as much as possible in the selection of sites and in deciding at what level of analysis comparisons can be made.

Within the sample of sites reasonably free from major physical disturbance, there are other processes, of a cultural and data structural nature, that must be considered as affecting the formation of the archaeological record, especially with regard to domestic earthlodges. Although many aspects of human behavior affect the deposition of artifacts or the nature of features, some in particular may work to disguise the relationships being sought. Two of the most important factors that can be controlled for are the length of time an earthlodge was occupied and the effect of sample size on the comparability of earthlodges and burials from different periods.

The length of time an individual earthlodge was occupied will obviously have an effect on the amount of refuse accumulated in that structure when it was abandoned (a factor also influenced by such things as the level of household maintenance). For the Pawnees (Weltfish 1965:106), the average life-span of an earthlodge was about 12 years and for the Hidatsas, Wilson (1934:358, 372) estimated that an earthlodge lasted from 7 to 12 years. These estimates are interesting, but provide little insight in the archaeological context. Without a basis for judging the length of occupation for a building, comparison of the composition of artifact assemblages in earthlodges in one period with those in another might to some extent reflect the unequal mean length of occupation for earthlodges from each period. Although a difficult proposition, the solution is to standardize the sample size based on length of occupation of the earthlodge. While the precise length of use for any one earthlodge is not known (even at historic villages, like the Leavenworth site), there are two possible indicators that may reflect something about how long a structure was used: the number of internal storage pits and evidence for rebuilding and maintenance. With storage pits it is assumed that longer occupations will extend beyond the use-life of any one storage pit, requiring that some pits be abandoned (and subsequently filled with trash) and new pits be dug. With building maintenance, it is simply assumed that the longer a structure is used the more maintenance it will require, as evidenced by the addition of subsidiary central supports and wall posts.

Based on storage pit and maintenance criteria, earthlodges were identified as having been occupied for short periods of time (one) or long periods of time (two). If an earthlodge had three or fewer major internal pits (small basin-shaped pits were excluded) and no evidence of structural maintenance, it was assigned as a short-term occupation (one). If an earthlodge had more than three major pits and/or evidence of structural maintenance, it was assigned as a long-term occupation (two). Attempting to estimate a greater than two-part division of the occupation span is unrealistic given the nature of the available information. In the overall sample, earthlodges with short-term occupations were much more numerous than those with long-term occupations. In the final data set selected for analysis, comparable proportions of short- and long-term occupation earthlodges were chosen for each period. Long-term occupation earthlodges represented between 22 and 29 percent of the sample for each period.

Two additional factors, important for understanding how earthlodge material assemblages come into being, are the nature of lodge abandonment and activities carried out subsequent to abandonment, such as trash disposal. These factors are difficult to recognize archaeologically, especially when dealing with records from excavations conducted decades ago that employed "coarse-grained" recovery strategies. Even so, the implications were considered in constructing the data set and resulted in the exclusion of more than one earthlodge that was otherwise acceptable. Concerning the first of these elements, abandonment, the principal issue is whether the building was vacated under normal or unplanned circumstances (Brooks 1984). If normal, that is, planned, then fewer artifacts are likely to be left for the archaeologist to discover. For instance, when an earthlodge reached the end of its useful life span, it might be abandoned in favor of constructing a new dwelling nearby with useful gear being moved to the new location. Likewise, central support posts, other building elements, and marginally transportable equipment, such as large grinding stones, may be reused. If on the other hand the distance being moved is great, say several kilometers, then it is unlikely that heavy or cumbersome items are transported to the new location. It is, in fact, well known that the Arikara and other groups moved their villages periodically over fairly large distances, probably requiring heavy items to be left behind. For relatively small objects, whether the distance being moved was great or small, usable items (complete projectile points or ceramic vessels) were probably removed under normal abandonment. If by contrast abandonment was unplanned, say as a result of fire, then the entire domestic inventory might be present. Brooks (1984:4–5) suggests that the floor remains excavated from buildings that underwent unplanned abandonment are likely to include a wider range of serviceable items, and of the broken artifacts that are present, it may be possible to refit or reconstruct a higher proportion of them.

Whether abandonment was normal or unplanned there will, of course, be debris resulting from the gradual accumulation of normal day-to-day activity refuse. In addition to the materials associated with use, it is also possible that debris will become part of the post-abandonment building remains, through such activities as trash disposal by village inhabitants in the depression left by a collapsed earthlodge. Such an activity has the potential of greatly skewing the picture that would be derived from the artifacts associated with the actual use of the standing building. Archaeologically, there are clues to the nature of post-abandonment activities, such as stratigraphically separate layers of debris indicating a later episode of deposition on top of the collapsed lodge roof. Such was the case at the Oacoma site (Kivett 1958) in which the excavators noted one lodge (F40) that contained a large number of objects. Evidence indicated that much of the debris had been dumped there after the collapse of the building. This earthlodge was not used in this study because of the clear evidence for post-depositional disturbance and the lack of excavation precision that might have allowed separation of pre- and post-abandonment artifact assemblages.

In addition to the depositional consequences of various activities described above, another important data characteristic concerns the effect of differential sample sizes on comparison validity (Conkey 1980:618; Kintigh 1984:44; Thomas 1983:425). It is widely acknowledged that as the number of sample units (in this case earthlodges and burials) increases, so does the number of different artifact categories, unless the sampling units represent maximal diversity (i.e., every earthlodge or burial has exactly the same number of artifact categories), which is extremely unlikely. If sample size is not controlled for, the variation measured between periods may be unduly influenced by the number of sample units. The obvious solution, as with length of occupation, is to use identical sample sizes for each period, but like much archaeological data, it is nearly impossible to achieve this ideal. The archaeological data on the Arikaras are one of the largest and most internally consistent sets of information in North America for the contact period, and the extremely large number of burials (approximately 2,500) made it possible to select samples of identical size. Such was not the case for domestic earthlodges and certainly not for ceremonial earthlodges. Implementing the five criteria for selection of sites and controlling for length of lodge occupation greatly reduced the number of structures available for analysis. Also, the small number of sites available at either end of the time sequence further hampered achieving a numerically uniform sample.

As a way of further evaluating the sample size effect and estimating the number of earthlodges necessary to account for most of the variation, a regression analysis was run to evaluate the relationship between the number of domestic earthlodges and the number of artifact categories found in those lodges. The regression was based on a sample of 26 domestic earthlodges from Period II, 13 of which were identified as short-term occupations and 13 as long-term occupations. The sample used in the regression was selected from only one period to minimize the effects of chronological and other sources of variation. Because the order in which the sample is input into the equation can affect the results (Rogers 1979), the data were randomized prior to input.

The results of the regression analysis indicate a strong curvilinear relationship between the number of artifact categories and the number of houses (after a log transformation, correlation coefficient = .983, coefficient of determination = .968). This analysis is also useful in estimating the sample size necessary to account for most of the variation in the number of categories present. From the analysis, it is apparent that a reasonably small number of houses contain most of the artifact categories. That is, after a certain point the inclusion of additional earthlodges in the sample becomes redundant. This conclusion is similar to the results of a preliminary analysis of 47 Period II domestic earthlodges for which length of occupation was not controlled. It is estimated that a sample of between 9 and 11 domestic earthlodges for each period will account for most of the variation. In some periods it was possible to bring together a sample of more than 11 earthlodges, however, it was not possible to achieve the minimum sample size of 9 lodges for all periods. The final sample breakdown for each period is presented in Table 6.

TABLE 6. *Domestic Earthlodge Sample Sizes (by time period)*

Period	Domestic Earthlodges (quantity)
I (late 1500s–1680)	10
II (1681–1725)	14
III (1726–1775)	14
IV (1776–1805)	14
V (1806–1835)	9
VI (1836–1862)	4

The number of available domestic earthlodges for Period VI is well below the acceptable sample size limits. The small number of domestic earthlodges makes Period VI highly problematic as far as its validity in the analysis is concerned. The single site (Star Village) available for Period VI is also unusual in that it was occupied for only a few months. The quantities of debris recovered from the buildings at this site were much less than typical quantities recovered from earthlodges in other periods. It is also apparently the case that one of the excavated lodges was occupied by a Mandan family (Metcalf 1963:77). There is also no burial sample available for Period VI. Due to the various problems, Period VI will not be included in the major part of the analysis, but will be handled on an impressionistic basis for comparison with other periods.

Before proceeding with a discussion of the next major context to be used in the analysis, two additional characteristic of domestic earthlodges should be mentioned: earthlodge size variation and the possible effects of artifact and category frequency variation within a period sample. The first factor can play an important role in the comparison of artifact assemblages from different earthlodges, considering the amount of variation in building diameters in each village. This variation relates to the size and relative status of the family groups occupying each lodge. If there are more people living in the larger lodges, then it follows that more artifacts will be recovered from those earthlodges than from smaller earthlodges, assuming the length of occupation is comparable. It is, therefore, important that earthlodge samples have similar size ranges. The mean diameters for the domestic earthlodges used in this sample are listed by period in Table 7. Owing to the unavailability of some data, mean diameters from Periods III and V are based on samples smaller than those used in the overall analysis.

The mean diameters for each period range from 9 to 12.5 m. Although there is variation in the sample, it is not considered excessive. Furthermore, there is no consistent relationship between the mean diameter for a period and the overall artifact frequency. For instance, Period I has earthlodges with the largest mean diameter, yet it has a lower mean number of artifacts per earthlodge than any other period except Period II (the variation between mean number of artifacts in each period is discussed below). Likewise, Period IV has a sample with

TABLE 7. *Domestic Earthlodge Diameters for Each Period*

Period	Sample Size	Mean Diameter (m)
I	10	12.5
II	14	9.1
III	12	10.4
IV	14	9.0
V	7	11.0
VI	4	11.0

a relatively small mean diameter (9 m) but the mean number of artifacts in each Period IV earthlodge is only slightly smaller than the mean for Period V (57 versus 64). The difference between these two means is not considered significant. It would appear that earthlodge size is a factor closely interrelated with other characteristics of the sample, and is probably not a major source of potential error.

Another factor that should be considered for domestic earthlodges is the relative variation within the sample and how individual lodges with unusually large or small artifact inventories might be influencing the means used to characterize each period. In the next chapter, artifact mean frequencies and category means are used to describe changes between periods as they relate to the artifact processes described in Chapter 6. Although the specific artifact categories are not described until the next section of this chapter, it is useful to consider here the variation in the number of categories between lodges. The diversity present in the domestic earthlodge sample for each period is presented in Tables 8 and 9 as a series of basic descriptive statistics, including mean, standard deviation, and range. The sample size listed in these tables refers to the number of domestic earthlodges.

The standard deviations and ranges for artifact frequencies listed in Table 8 indicate considerable variation in the number of artifacts found in each earthlodge. Such variation is expected given the nature of earthlodges as a depositional context. Likewise, considering that earth-

TABLE 8. *Basic Statistics Describing Artifact Frequencies for Domestic Earthlodges (by period)*

Period	Sample Size	Mean	Standard Deviation	Range
	Arikara Artifacts			
I	10	93.5	79.0	51–274
II	14	72.2	87.4	15–355
III	14	120.5	100.0	19–344
IV	14	57.2	35.6	18–130
V	9	63.7	48.9	22–179
VI	4	5.5	2.9	2–9
	Euro-American Artifacts			
I	10	0.3	0.9	0–3
II	14	5.4	15.8	0–60
III	14	8.1	6.0	1–21
IV	14	2.2	2.4	0–8
V	9	46.4	67.8	3–210
VI	4	37.5	45.0	8–104

Note: Data in this table refer to the frequency of objects in domestic earthlodges, summed for each period. Because Arikara ceramics (sherds) are present in large numbers in all lodges, these artifacts were excluded from the tabulations.

lodges believed to be of different occupation spans are intentionally included in the sample for each period, the amount of variation is not unexpected. In Table 9, basic statistics for category frequencies are tabulated for each period. Category frequency refers to the total number of different categories of objects found in each earthlodge. Comparisons of the number of categories of objects in each period becomes an important part of the analysis in the next chapter, considering that category frequencies are less susceptible to variation than artifact frequencies, due to the essentially presence/absence character of the data. The standard deviations in Table 9 reflect the relatively consistent

TABLE 9. *Basic Statistics Describing Artifact Category Frequencies for Domestic Earthlodges (by period)*

Period	Sample Size	Mean	Standard Deviation	Range
		Arikara Artifacts		
I	10	17.1	5.3	12–28
II	14	14.7	5.7	9–31
III	14	21.7	6.8	10–36
IV	14	17.3	3.5	12–24
V	9	16.3	3.4	12–21
VI	4	4.3	2.3	1–7
		Euro-American Artifacts		
I	10	0.1	0.0	0–1
II	14	1.0	1.4	0–5
III	14	4.4	2.9	1–12
IV	14	1.9	1.8	0–5
V	9	10.0	5.7	4–19
VI	4	6.8	3.6	4–13

frequency of category occurrences compared to the artifact frequency standard deviations in Table 8. Considered overall, the variation in the number of objects or categories in each domestic earthlodge reflects the complex processes involved in the formation of the archaeological record. These processes have been taken into consideration in the constraints applied to the construction of the data sets.

The second major contextual class considered in the analysis is ceremonial earthlodges. Although ceremonial earthlodges represent an important source of comparative information to contrast with the domestic earthlodges, the very small number of usable ceremonial earthlodges precludes any sort of statistical analysis, and therefore will not be part of the primary analysis. However, ceremonial earthlodges will be included in examinations of possible trends or where general contrasts with domestic structures may be considered.

It was mentioned earlier that there was no problem concerning cemetery sample sizes. This is correct, however most of the excavated Arikara burials cluster within only three periods (II, III, and V). This means, again, that the full chronological sequence is not represented. Yet it will be possible to examine change through time based on the samples from Periods II, III, and V.

The criteria used to select burials for inclusion in the analysis was somewhat different than that used for earthlodges. Because only burials with associated artifacts were relevant to the analysis, those with no associations were excluded. This factor alone reduced the potential sample size by over 50 percent. Additionally, many burials were considered unusable because of disturbance, due to pothunters or the reuse of burial pits by the Arikaras. Some artifacts may have been removed or repositioned in disturbed burials, thus making it impossible to be sure of contextual validity.

The potential misleading effects of different sample sizes in each period were also considered. An appropriate solution was to select a comparable number of burials for each period. It was also necessary to take into account differences that might be consistently associated with age and sex criteria. A study of Arikara mortuary practices by O'Shea (1984) discusses in detail the changes through time related to the kinds of artifacts associated with different age and sex groups. O'Shea's work points to age and sex as important sources of variation within the burial population. Considering this observation, the sample composition was standardized according to age and sex as well. Age and sex are interrelated variables; consequently it was difficult to achieve exactly the same numerical breakdown within each period sample. Given the large number of available burials, it was possible to select identical sex category compositions for each of the three periods. The sample for each period consists of 19 males (1), 15 females (2), and 40 indeterminate (0). The latter category includes immature individuals and burials with fragmentary or poorly preserved skeletal material. The age variable was dependent on the sex variable, and is therefore not identical for each period. The age composition of the samples is presented in Table 10. Although not the same, the age groupings for each period are comparable. The final sample consists of 74 burials from each of three sites: Sully (Period II), Mobridge (Period III), and Leavenworth (Period V).

TABLE 10. *Number of Individuals in Burial Sample (by age and period)*

Period	Age (in years) 0–2	3–12	13–17	18–30	31–40	41–50+
II	20	13	5	19	6	11
III	17	15	4	24	12	5
V	24	12	5	15	12	6

In the previous discussion of factors relating to the selection and character of data used in the domestic earthlodge sample, two tables were used to present some basic statistics on variation within the sample for each period. Table 11 presents a similar set of information for the burial samples from Periods II, III, and V. This table shows the mean number of categories present in burials and the standard deviation and range for category occurrences. Burials typically have only one or two different kinds of associated objects. There are a few burials, however, that may have as many as 11 different categories present. The few burials with many objects figure prominently in O'Shea's (1984) analysis of status categories. The intentional inclusion of different age and sex categories in the samples for each period accounts for the variation evident from the standard deviations and ranges listed in Table 11.

Artifact Categories

Earlier it was mentioned that the artifact categories represent a combination of historically observed and inferred usage. The inferred usages are based on common classifications found in most archaeological studies of Arikara sites. The relationship between categories, however, is being viewed differently than is presented in most classification schemes. The objective here is to explicitly describe the relationship between categories within a framework that does not force categories

TABLE 11. *Basic Statistics Describing Artifact Category Frequencies for Burials (by period)*

Period	Sample Size	Mean	Standard Deviation	Range
	Arikara Artifacts			
II	74	0.8	0.6	0–2
III	74	1.4	1.8	0–11
V	74	1.6	2.0	0–10
	Euro-American Artifacts			
II	74	0.4	0.6	0–2
III	74	0.2	0.5	0–2
V	74	2.2	1.8	0–11

into a partitional hierarchy, which prevents an adequate recognition of interrelationships. The linking of data categories concerns what Aldenderfer (1987:105) defines as a "relational structure."

> Relational structure is concerned primarily with the definition of observations relevant to the study of the problem at hand, the definition of data (how we give meaning to data), the linkage between concept and data, and the linkage between concepts to form models.

The definition of observations and the linking of data are part of explicitly presenting the relationship between categories.

Initially, 189 artifact categories were defined. These categories are listed in Table 12, along with code designations. Of the 189 categories, 164 were identified in the sample selected for analysis. The other 25 categories have been retained in Table 12 to give a more complete picture of the overall material assemblage that may occur in Arikara domestic and ceremonial contexts. If contexts such as middens or other features were included in the analysis, there would certainly be addi-

TABLE 12. *Artifact Categories*

Code	Items
Arikara	
CER	ceramics (sherds)
POT	ceramic vessel
CEB	ceramic beads
CLP	clay pipes
CGP	clay gaming piece
CEE	ceramic effigy
ANE	carved animal effigy
SP	stone pendant
STP	stone pipe
SPP	stone projectile points
SC	scrapers
GR	gravers
SD	stone drills
WKF	worked or utilized flakes
STC	stone core
STK	stone knives
MA	mauls
CE	celts
SSA	sandstone abraders (including sharpening stones)
SCA	scoria abraders (including worked scoria)
SHA	shaft sanders
BOA	bone awls
BPI	bone pipe
BOF	bone fleshers (including elk, bison, and antler)
BSW	bone shaft wrenches
BHS	bison horn scoops
BFT	bison frontal-horn digging tools
SCH	scapula hoes
SCK	scapula knives (including cleavers)
WKS	worked scapula fragments (including hoes and knives)
BOP	bone or antler punches and perforators (usually scapula)
BOG	bone grainers
BOT	bone tubes
BOB	bone brushes
BOC	bone comb
BON	bone needles
BPA	bone paddle (and spatulas and digging tools)
BWE	bone wedge

TABLE 12—*continued*

Code	Items
BFH	bone fishhook
WKR	worked ribs (usually gliders, handles, or misc.)
QUF	quill flatteners (bone, also possible pottery tools)
BOW	bone whistles
BPE	bone or antler pendants
GPD	glass pendants (remanufactured trade beads, usually blue)
BBR	bone bracelet
BKH	bone knife handles
BPP	bone or antler projectile points
DRC	drilled claw or tooth pendants
ULB	ulna and other beamers
ULP	ulna picks
BSP	bone or wood stamp paddle
OWB	other worked bone
BIB	unworked bison bones (burial associations only)
TUS	turtle shell (burial associations only)
RAB	rabbit or other small mammal skeletal parts (burial associations only)
DUB	duck bills (burial associations only)
BIC	bird and mammal claws (burial associations only)
ANT	animal teeth (burial associations only)
BIS	bird skeleton or beak (burial associations only)
WKA	worked antler
WMS	worked mussel shell
SS	shell scrapers
SHP	shell pendants
SHB	shell beads
SMA	marine shell
SHD	shell disc
SCL	stone club head
HS	hammer stones (including "pecking stones")
AS	anvil stones
PM	paint mortar
SB	stone bead
ST	stone tablets (including paint palettes)
SR	stone ring
GS	grinding stones (including manos and metates)
GSD	ground stone disc
STB	stone ball
CH	choppers

Continued on next page

TABLE 12—*continued*

Code	Items
SMS	smoothing stones (including polished stones)
STW	stone wedge
NGF	native gun flint
OWS	other worked stones
WBW	wood bow
WBO	wood bowl
WHA	wood handle
WKW	worked wood
LEA	leather
MAT	matting
BP	brown pigment
RP	red pigment (hematite)
YP	yellow pigment (limonite)
WP	white pigment (chalky materials)
GP	green pigment
GA	galena
FO	fossils
CP	catlinite pipes
OWC	other worked catlinite
QC	quartz or gypsum crystals
BSK	bison skull
BES	bear skull
UOB	unusual objects (including concretions, petrified wood, and coal)
Euro-American	
EAC	Euro-American ceramics
EAP	Euro-American ceramic pipes
MTA	metal awl
IN	iron needle
BN	brass needle
MG	metal gun fragments
EAH	bone knife handles
IPP	iron projectile points
CPP	copper projectile points
BPP	brass projectile points
MPP	metal projectile points (unidentified metal)
IF	iron fragments (including small bands, coils, strips, wire, etc.)

TABLE 12—*continued*

Code	Items
CF	copper fragments (including small bands, coils, strips, etc.)
BF	brass fragments (including small bands, coils, strips, etc.)
ZF	zinc fragments (including small bands, coils, strips, etc.)
LF	lead fragments (including small bands, coils, strips, etc.)
OMF	metal fragments (including small bands, coils, strips, etc.)
GM	glass mirror
BGF	bottle glass fragments
OGF	other glass fragments
MAR	marbles
IT	iron tubes
CT	copper tubes
BT	brass tubes
OMT	other metal tubes
EAF	Euro-American gun flints
BU	bullets (lead balls, etc.)
MCC	metal cartridge casings
GTB	glass trade beads
OTB	other trade beads
INA	iron nails
IS	iron spikes
IB	iron bangles
CB	copper bangles
BB	brass bangles
OMB	other metal bangles
IK	iron knives
CK	copper knives
BK	brass knives
OMK	other metal knives
MKH	metal knife handle
IKH	iron knife handle
IBU	iron button
CBU	copper button
BBU	brass button
OBU	other metal button
GBU	glass button
MBP	metal breast plate
IBE	iron beads
CBE	copper beads
BBE	brass beads
OBE	other metal beads
MF	metal file
MHA	metal hand auger

Continued on next page

TABLE 12—*continued*

Code	Items
IC	iron collar
HOS	horse shoes
ICO	iron cones
CC	copper cones
MR	metal receptacles and fragments
TC	tin cups
IRB	iron bucket
BRB	brass bell
OIO	other iron objects (unidentified)
OCO	other copper objects (unidentified)
OBO	other brass objects (unidentified)
CRC	copper ring clasp
BD	brass disc
CD	copper disc
BRR	brass rods
IR	iron rods
IRR	iron rings
BR	brass rings
SR	silver ring
MER	metal rings
LR	lead rings
MBR	metal bracelet
MMO	miscellaneous metal ornaments
MM	metal mattocks and hoes
MAX	metal axe
MFH	metal fishhook
IRC	iron chain
ISC	iron scraper
IW	iron wedge
IRB	iron buckle
BRH	brass hinge
BRC	brass celt
BCL	brass clip
BRS	brass saw
SCI	scissors

tional artifact categories that could be added to the list in Table 12. In the primary analysis, categories will often be referred to by their code designations. Categories listed in Table 12 are subdivided based on whether they are of Arikara or Euro-American origin. Initial level categories include individual Arikara items, such as stone projectile points (SPP), drilled claw or tooth pendants (DRC), and shell beads (SHB); or Euro-American items, such as iron projectile points (IPP), metal fragments (OMF), and brass rings (BR). Each of the artifacts recovered from Arikara domestic earthlodges, ceremonial earthlodges, or burials have been assigned to one of the 189 artifact categories. While attempting to provide as much detail as possible, it should also be apparent that the 189 categories do not approach the level of detail often found in archaeological site reports on the Arikaras (e.g., Hurt 1954; Hoffman 1967). The difference in level of detail is especially apparent within ceramics and lithics. No attempt has been made to subdivide ceramics using specifically defined ceramic types. The value of defining individual ceramic types, for the present study, is dubious, and in any case would be nearly impossible given the available archival or published sources. Lithics, such as scrapers, are often divided into stylistic varieties that may or may not relate to differences in usage. Here too, such a refined categorization of lithics has questionable validity for this analysis.

Although most of the categories refer to patterned artifacts, like pottery or stone tools, there are also several for unpatterned artifacts, primarily various kinds of metal fragments and worked or utilized flakes. It is possible to argue that this type of object might have been collected less systematically by the archaeologists excavating the sites than pottery or other more recognizable items. If such were true, then it might be inappropriate to include unpatterned artifacts in the data set; however, an examination of the house data presented in the Appendix (Tables A-1 and A-2) shows, in general, that the quantity of unpatterned artifacts recovered from a building parallels the quantity of other types of artifacts. That is, if the number of patterned artifacts recovered was high, then the number of unpatterned artifacts removed from the excavations was also high. This strongly suggests that similar collecting strategies were followed for both patterned and unpatterned types of objects and that it is therefore reasonable to include items like metal fragments in the general data set.

The 164 categories defined for use in the analysis are viewed as the initial level in a hierarchical or intersecting cover set model. By constructing a cover set model, the relationship between categories at different analysis levels can be more clearly understood, and the "mixing" of categories that should logically exist at different levels can be avoided. An example of "mixing" is apparent in the definition of a set of activities that, for instance, includes digging, grinding, cutting, lodge construction, and hunting. Clearly, these five activities are not on the same analytical level; that is, at the very least, digging and cutting can be included under lodge construction, if not hunting as well. This is a "mixed" activity set because the components are not logically equivalent or separate.

The comparison of things at a single level that are better defined at different levels (i.e., "mixing") is a much too common problem in the social sciences (Russell 1956). The idea of using hierarchical cover set models to more clearly define the relationships being examined in a set of information was developed by Ronald Atkin as part of what is called Q-Analysis or Polyhedral Dynamics (1974, 1975, 1977, 1978). Q-Analysis is a mathematical language used to identify the structure of a set of relations (P. Gould 1980:169). The proponents of Q-Analysis argue that traditional statistics, and indeed, much of western analytical thinking are partitional in nature (P. Gould 1981). Such thinking is most overtly expressed in hierarchical dendrogram (tree diagram) or organizational chart classifications, in which items at one level in the hierarchy belong to only a single class at the next higher level. This is a basic characteristic of almost all hierarchical classifications commonly in use. Q-Analysis, by contrast, employs a different logic in defining hierarchical classifications. In the case of cover set hierarchies, one level is defined as different from another using the "nested base rule, in which one set is below another if it is a proper subset of the other" (Chapman 1984:214). One of the principal aspects of considering subsets of higher level sets, is that items in the lower set may end up belonging to *more than one* higher level set (Chapman 1984:214).

> Partitionalists do not like this approach, because (i) at some points some sets overlap each other, so that the isolation of some problem or quality for study is impossible; (ii) at any one level numbers, . . . of individuals in the classes . . . do not add up to a predetermined total; (iii) the problem of resolving levels is exceedingly tedious and gives rise to 'untidy' situations.

While each of these criticisms is valid from a partitional perspective, they also reflect unspoken advantages when emphasizing relationships between things. Naturally, if the objective is to analyze the structure of a set of relations then overlapping sets are not a problem but become a logical part of the analysis. From the same viewpoint, a potential criticism such as autocorrelation of higher order sets composed of overlapping categories from lower order sets, does not exist given the objective of examining the relation between things, and that the definition of cover sets does not require the number of things at one level to sum to the number of things at the next highest level. Again, the definition of hierarchical cover sets is dependent on relations between things and not discrete numerical partitioning. In this way the very notion that things can, and often do, belong to overlapping sets is almost certainly a truer reflection of reality.

The specific hierarchical cover set model used in this study is presented in Figure 13. This model is composed of six levels designed to represent the objects and activities associated with domestic earthlodge, ceremonial earthlodge, and burial contexts at different encompassing levels. The activities represented in the model are only those that may reasonably be inferred from the associated objects and are not necessarily part of all three of the above contexts. The model is not intended to represent all possible activities associated with the three contexts under study, only those activities associated with the artifacts recovered from the archaeological excavations. Reading from right to left, the lowest level in the model is that of the categories representing individual objects. By convention, this level is referred to as the $N-1$ level. At the next level, referred to as N, objects are identified as having a relationship to a particular activity by a connecting line. The

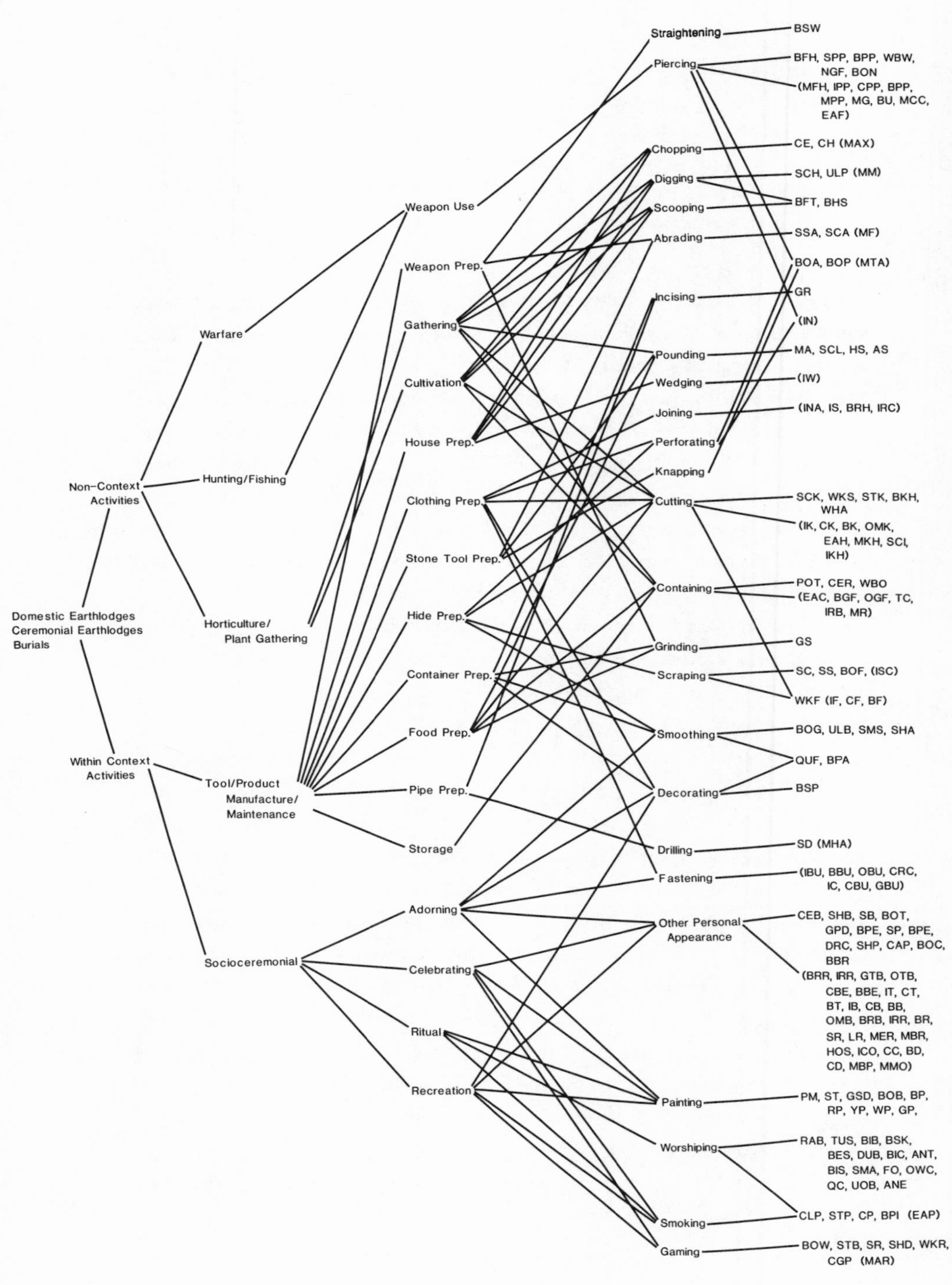
Straightening
BSW
Piercing
BFH, SPP, BPP, WBW, NGF, BON
(MFH, IPP, CPP, BPP, MPP, MG, BU, MCC, EAF)
Chopping
CE, CH (MAX)
Digging
SCH, ULP (MM)
Scooping
BFT, BHS
Abrading
SSA, SCA (MF)
BOA, BOP (MTA)
Incising
GR
(IN)
Pounding
MA, SCL, HS, AS
Wedging
(IW)
Joining
(INA, IS, BRH, IRC)
Perforating
Knapping
Cutting
SCK, WKS, STK, BKH, WHA
(IK, CK, BK, OMK, EAH, MKH, SCI, IKH)
Containing
POT, CER, WBO
(EAC, BGF, OGF, TC, IRB, MR)
Grinding
GS
Scraping
SC, SS, BOF, (ISC)
WKF (IF, CF, BF)
Smoothing
BOG, ULB, SMS, SHA
QUF, BPA
Decorating
BSP
Drilling
SD (MHA)
Fastening
(IBU, BBU, OBU, CRC, IC, CBU, GBU)
Other Personal Appearance
CEB, SHB, SB, BOT, GPD, BPE, SP, BPE, DRC, SHP, CAP, BOC, BBR
(BRR, IRR, GTB, OTB, CBE, BBE, IT, CT, BT, IB, CB, BB, OMB, BRB, IRR, BR, SR, LR, MER, MBR, HOS, ICO, CC, BD, CD, MBP, MMO)
Painting
PM, ST, GSD, BOB, BP, RP, YP, WP, GP,
Worshiping
RAB, TUS, BIB, BSK, BES, DUB, BIC, ANT, BIS, SMA, FO, OWC, QC, UOB, ANE
Smoking
CLP, STP, CP, BPI (EAP)
Gaming
BOW, STB, SR, SHD, WKR, CGP (MAR)
Weapon Use
Weapon Prep.
Gathering
Cultivation
House Prep.
Clothing Prep.
Stone Tool Prep.
Hide Prep.
Container Prep.
Food Prep.
Pipe Prep.
Storage
Adorning
Celebrating
Ritual
Recreation
Warfare
Hunting/Fishing
Horticulture/ Plant Gathering
Tool/Product Manufacture/ Maintenance
Sociceremonial
Non-Context Activities
Within Context Activities
Domestic Earthlodges
Ceremonial Earthlodges
Burials
N+4
N+3
N+2
N+1
N
N-1

connecting line merely indicates that artifact categories or activities at one level are associated with other artifact categories or activities at a different level. It will immediately become apparent that some objects are connected to more than one activity class at the N level. This is a characteristic of overlapping cover sets as defined previously. In the analysis to be conducted in Chapter 8, constant reference will be made to objects or activities at the N − 1 or N levels as part of the consideration of the artifact processes discussed in Chapter 6.

At the next more encompassing level (N + 1), the multiple connectivities and the overlapping set memberships become a barrage of linkages. As an example of the linkages that exist at the N + 1 level, the set food preparation consists of the N level sets, containing, cutting, grinding, pounding, and scooping. The set, cultivation, also at the N + 1 level is composed of the N level sets, containing, cutting, scooping, digging, and chopping. There are, therefore, three N level sets that have overlapping linkages at the N + 1 level: containing, cutting, and scooping. It must be reiterated that only activities reflected by the artifacts are included in the model. There are, of course, other activities associated with food preparation or cultivation, or any of the other activities, that are not included here.

At the N + 2 level the activity sets become more encompassing, and include such things as adorning, gathering, and hide preparation. At the next level (N + 3), the N + 2 level sets become part of five major activity sets: warfare, hunting/fishing, horticulture/plant gathering, tool or product manufacture/maintenance, and activities that can be identified as socioceremonial in nature. At the N + 4 level all activities are identified as belonging to either the within context or non-context activity sets. The set, within context, refers to those lower level activity sets that would probably have taken place within the domestic earthlodge, ceremonial earthlodge, or as part of burial processing. The non-context activity set includes those activities that would probably

Fig. 13. Hierarchical cover set model showing interconnected set memberships. Individual artifact category codes are listed at the right (N -1 level). See Table 12 for code identifications.

have taken place outside of the three major contexts, such as horticulture/plant gathering or warfare. The next level (N +5), consists of a single cover set encompassing all of the lower order sets. The N +5 level set includes all activities associated with domestic and ceremonial earthlodges and burials, as represented by the artifacts contained in those three contexts.

Figure 13 incorporates many activity and relational definitions that may or may not agree with other approaches. However, the objective has been to make the components of the analysis process explicit to allow a more thorough evaluation of the results. By constructing the cover set model, several definitional problems were solved in a way that helps prevent the mixing of categories (or sets) that are not actually of a comparable scale, and should instead be considered at different levels. The 164 categories of objects at the N −1 level represent a set of information too large to be effectively analyzed at this basic level. At the N level, however, the 164 categories are assigned to 25 cover sets associated with meaningfully defined activities. This is an important data reduction step in the analysis. Most of the analysis to be conducted in the next chapter will focus on activity sets at the N level. It should be remembered that, as part of the Q-Analysis approach, that things, in this case Arikara artifacts and Euro-American trade goods, at higher levels incorporate overlapping sets at lower levels. This means that at the N level a "count" of the objects will reflect a larger number of objects than at the N −1 level. Objects at any lower level may be counted more than once for inclusion in the next higher level. At the N −1 level, such things as bone awls (BOA) or bone punches (BOP) belong to more than one N level set, and are therefore counted as part of the knapping set as well as the piercing set.

8

ANALYSIS AND RESULTS

> The analysis is complicated because the situation to be analyzed is complex. There is no escape from this problem.
>
> ALBERT C. SPAULDING

The analysis presented here focuses on change in artifact assemblages through time. The major argument of this study is that major shifts in the political, economic, and social relationship between the Arikaras and Euro-Americans in the eighteenth and nineteenth centuries is reflected by changes in Arikara use of trade goods and native material assemblages. This theme is examined through the use of a series of proposed artifact processes defined in Chapter 6 and artifact categories defined in Chapter 7. The processes affecting the composition of artifact assemblages, as proposed in Chapter 6, are maintenance, replacement, addition, rejection, and transformation. There are three major archaeological contexts that are analyzed in relation to these five processes—domestic earthlodges, ceremonial earthlodges, and burials. The principal analysis is directed towards domestic earthlodges and burials, as the sample size for ceremonial earthlodges is too small for an effective consideration of the major proposition. Throughout the analy-

---

The epigraph that appears above is from Spaulding 1982:10.

sis of the three primary contexts, the principal objective is an examination of the artifact process expectations presented in Table 4.

In an analysis of this type, a major concern is the level at which differences between assemblages can be considered "real" or part of a valid trend. Rather than selecting a statistical definition of significant variability, the emphasis is on bringing together several different sources of information as a means of confirming or rejecting a specific argument. The strategy used here focuses on comparing simple relative differences, bolstered by percentages, trends, and other supporting arguments that may present a connection with the historically observed changes in the contact interaction process.

The actual comparisons to be made are based primarily on mean frequencies for domestic and ceremonial earthlodges (i.e., the total number of artifacts in a category at the N − 1 level for each period, divided by the number of domestic earthlodges or ceremonial earthlodges in the sample for that period) at the N − 1 level, or "combined" frequencies at the N level. The mean frequency is a measure of the quantity of each artifact category per earthlodge in each period. Although the use of frequencies in analyzing the contents of earthlodges may introduce biases resulting from the manner in which the deposits accumulated in the lodge (Cannon 1983:789–790), efforts were made to control these potential sources of error. The use of mean frequencies in effect standardizes the values for each period and in Chapter 7 strategies for dealing with length of occupation and sample size problems were discussed. Controlling for these problems eliminates much of the potential error that might be introduced into the analysis. While mean frequencies played the major role in the analysis of the domestic and ceremonial earthlodges, "richness," as an aspect of diversity, was also used.

For burials a presence/absence scale is used at the N − 1 level and a "combined" presence/absence scale at the N level for each period. The use of presence/absence burial data is, in part, a function of the relatively low quality of the available information. In several cases the quantity of items from a burial was not given in the archival sources, only whether an item was present. In a study of mortuary variability among the Pawnees, Arikaras, and Omahas, O'Shea (1984:62–63) also used presence/absence data. He noted that

> A preliminary analysis of attribute distribution showed that most types occur in a very uniform and limited number across the sample graves. This type of frequency distribution suggests that simple occurrence is the primary unit of variation.

Although presence/absence is a conservative measure, it may be more appropriate for a data set in which the frequency of objects is very low and in which numbers are dominated by such things as beads that may skew the distributions.

In addition to the analysis of the principal contexts, two additional sections are included in this chapter to provide a discussion of general trends in the data through time. The first of these sections discusses artifact category continuities. The second section examines the overall structure of the sets of relationships that exist between periods through the use of Q-Analysis.

DOMESTIC EARTHLODGES

The domestic earthlodge data set is considered the primary information set. This is the case despite inherent sampling problems and other factors that make the analysis of debris (i.e., usually objects left behind or deposited by the original inhabitants as part of the discard process) found in houses a difficult task. The information from domestic earthlodges (of the three contexts used in this study) represents the more complete expression of the everyday activities in an Arikara village, and for this reason is considered the most important context under study. The analysis is primarily based on a comparison of bar charts for each time period, measures of richness and diversity, and Q-Analysis. Each of the six periods is considered separately followed by a summary of overall changes through time.

Period I

Period I (late 1500s–1680) is by definition a pre-contact period assumed to be in a state of maintenance, as far as the introduction of European trade items is concerned. Although there were some effects of the European presence in North America already being felt on the Middle Missouri, there is virtually no evidence for the presence of Euro-goods. Period I therefore serves as the "aboriginal" baseline for considering changes in the material assemblage *after* the introduction of significant amounts of Euro-American goods.

The artifact inventories associated with each of the houses in Period I and the other time periods are listed by period (at the N − 1 level) and by individual earthlodge in the Appendix (Tables A-3, A-4, A-5, and A-6). Of the artifact inventories associated with the ten domestic earthlodges included in Period I, there are only three items of Euro-American origin (crockery sherds) recovered from one lodge (House 1E at the LaRoche site, 39ST9) and these are almost certainly intrusive from a later period (Hoffman 1968:37). Because of the large number of categories present at the N − 1 level, it is difficult to characterize the composition of the assemblage. At the N level, however, the smaller number of artifact sets (25) make it feasible to describe the "typical" assemblage for domestic earthlodges (Tables 13 and 14).

The most common material assemblage for domestic earthlodges in Period I includes a very high frequency of items belonging to the set, containing (primarily pot sherds), followed by the sets scraping, cutting, and piercing. Figure 14 shows the mean number of objects in each of the 25 N level sets, organized from left to right by relative frequency. The mean number of sherds in the containing set is off the scale in comparison to the other sets. Slightly less common than the first three sets are tools associated with the sets piercing, abrading, pounding, painting, knapping, perforating, and smoothing. Much less common are items that are part of the sets other personal appearance (e.g., beads), chopping, digging, worshiping, grinding, drilling, decorating, gaming, smoking, incising, and straightening. The sets fastening, wedging, scooping, and joining did not occur in any of the Period I earthlodges. The sets fastening, wedging, and joining are exclusively associated with Euro-American artifact categories and are not included with Arikara category sets. The basic composition of the Period I assemblage remains roughly characteristic of all later periods, although the incorporation of Euro-American goods provided some important changes.

TABLE 13. *Mean Number of Arikara Artifacts per Period for N Level Domestic Earthlodge Sets*

Set	Periods (with numbers of lodges)					
	I (10)	II (14)	III (14)	IV (14)	V (9)	VI (4)
Containing	1364.9	630.2	1099.7	653.4	506.3	75.0
Scraping	34.0	19.7	21.6	13.4	10.1	0.0
Cutting	31.0	21.9	30.3	14.4	10.8	0.5
Piercing	10.0	3.2	2.4	4.6	3.3	0.0
Abrading	8.8	5.9	12.1	2.9	6.1	0.0
Pounding	4.4	3.3	5.6	4.1	3.3	0.0
Painting	4.4	1.4	3.4	1.4	0.4	0.3
Knapping	3.9	3.1	2.1	3.6	0.1	0.0
Perforating	3.9	3.1	2.1	3.6	0.1	0.0
Smoothing	2.6	1.6	4.6	2.3	1.0	0.5
Other Personal Appearance	1.8	0.4	1.9	0.6	0.8	0.3
Chopping	1.1	3.8	1.4	2.2	0.0	0.0
Digging	0.9	1.9	3.7	8.4	2.6	0.0
Worshiping	0.8	0.6	2.2	0.3	1.1	0.0
Grinding	0.8	1.7	2.2	1.0	8.7	0.3
Drilling	0.7	0.6	0.5	0.4	0.0	0.0
Decorating	0.4	0.1	0.1	0.7	0.1	0.0
Gaming	0.3	0.2	0.4	0.7	1.9	0.3
Smoking	0.1	0.4	0.4	0.1	0.4	0.0
Incising	0.1	0.0	0.1	0.1	0.0	0.0
Straightening	0.1	0.6	0.8	0.7	1.4	0.0
Fastening	0.0	0.0	0.0	0.0	0.0	0.0
Wedging	0.0	0.0	0.0	0.0	0.0	0.0
Scooping	0.0	0.0	1.1	0.6	0.0	0.0
Joining	0.0	0.0	0.0	0.0	0.0	0.0

Period II

Period II (1681–1725) is the first post-contact period. In this period, Euro-American goods become part of the domestic earthlodge assemblage, with the first Euro-American goods showing up at the N level as

TABLE 14. *Mean Number of Euro-American Artifacts per Period for N Level Domestic Earthlodge Sets*

Set	Periods (with numbers of lodges)					
	I (10)	II (14)	III (14)	IV (14)	V (9)	VI (4)
Containing	0.3	0.1	0.1	0.1	2.7	4.3
Scraping	0.0	1.1	4.4	0.7	11.7	0.3
Cutting	0.0	1.1	5.0	1.1	12.1	7.5
Piercing	0.0	0.1	1.4	0.9	3.3	1.0
Abrading	0.0	0.0	0.0	0.0	0.0	0.3
Pounding	0.0	0.0	0.0	0.0	0.0	0.0
Painting	0.0	0.0	0.0	0.0	0.0	0.0
Knapping	0.0	0.0	0.1	0.1	0.0	0.0
Perforating	0.0	0.0	0.3	0.1	0.1	0.0
Smoothing	0.0	0.0	0.0	0.0	0.0	0.0
Other Personal Appearance	0.0	4.4	0.9	0.4	7.7	26.8
Chopping	0.0	0.0	0.0	0.0	0.0	0.0
Digging	0.0	0.0	0.0	0.0	0.1	0.0
Worshiping	0.0	0.0	0.1	0.0	0.4	0.0
Grinding	0.0	0.0	0.0	0.0	0.0	0.0
Drilling	0.0	0.0	0.0	0.0	0.0	0.3
Decorating	0.0	0.0	0.0	0.0	0.0	0.0
Gaming	0.0	0.0	0.0	0.0	0.0	0.0
Smoking	0.0	0.0	0.1	0.0	0.4	0.0
Incising	0.0	0.0	0.0	0.0	0.0	0.0
Straightening	0.0	0.0	0.0	0.0	0.0	0.0
Fastening	0.0	0.0	0.1	0.4	0.0	0.3
Wedging	0.0	0.0	0.0	0.0	0.3	0.0
Scooping	0.0	0.0	0.0	0.0	0.0	0.0
Joining	0.0	0.0	0.0	0.1	0.4	3.3

Fig. 14. Period I (late 1500s–1680) N level artifact count means from domestic earthblodges.

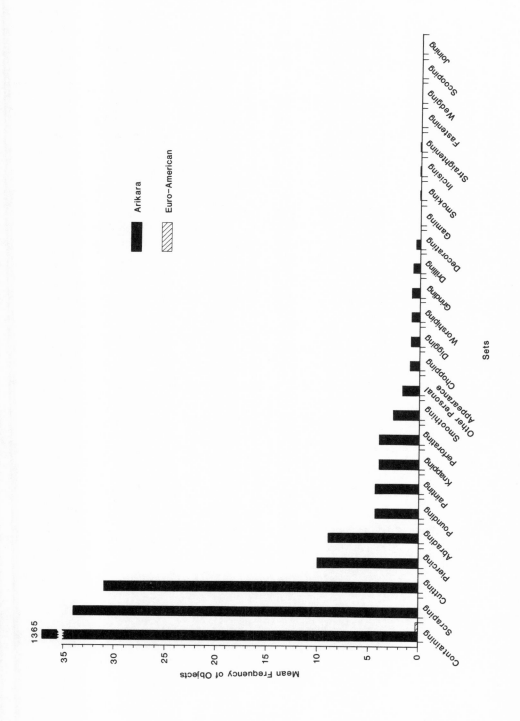

Arikara
Euro-American
1365
35
30
25
20
15
10
5
0
Mean Frequency of Objects
Containing
Scraping
Cutting
Piercing
Abrading
Pounding
Painting
Knapping
Perforating
Smoothing
Other Personal Appearance
Chopping
Digging
Worshiping
Grinding
Drilling
Decorating
Gaming
Smoking
Incising
Straightening
Fastening
Wedging
Scooping
Joining
Sets

items belonging to the containing, scraping, cutting, piercing, or other personal appearance sets (Table 14). When compared to the bar chart for Period I (Fig. 14), the bar chart for Period II (Fig. 15) shows some interesting changes. First, there is a general decline in artifact sets one to eleven. These eleven sets are, by-and-large, the principal groups that consistently occur in domestic lodges. In some categories the drop is very drastic. In the containing set (primarily pot sherds), the mean number of items occurring in a domestic earthlodge in Period II, compared to Period I, drops by 54 percent. The mean number of items in the scraping set drops by 43 percent. In the other nine sets, the mean reduction in frequency of occurrence is of a similar or greater proportion. It appears that the introduction of Euro-American goods is affecting the composition of the domestic earthlodge assemblage. This suggestion is further strengthened by the fact that all of the Euro-American goods that occurred in domestic earthlodges in this period fall within the same eleven sets that are reduced in terms of Arikara artifacts. The incorporated Euro-American goods, however, occupy only five of the eleven sets, including: containing, scraping, cutting, piercing, and other personal appearance. Probably the most obvious shift from Arikara to Euro-American goods occurs in the other personal appearance set (Fig. 15). Items, such as beads, belonging to this set become much more frequent. Although Euro-American goods seem to replace Arikara items, it is apparent that the frequency of introduced goods is still very low, especially in comparison to the number of items they seem to be displacing (Table 13).

There are three possible explanations for the relatively low frequency of Euro-American goods in contrast to the Arikara items they replace. First, it is probable that the greater use-life of metal tools, over that of stone and bone counterparts, means a lower discard rate and therefore fewer of these items enter the archaeological record over a comparable earthlodge occupation span. Second, metal fragments or

Fig. 15. Period II (1681–1725) N level artifact count means from domestic earthlodges.

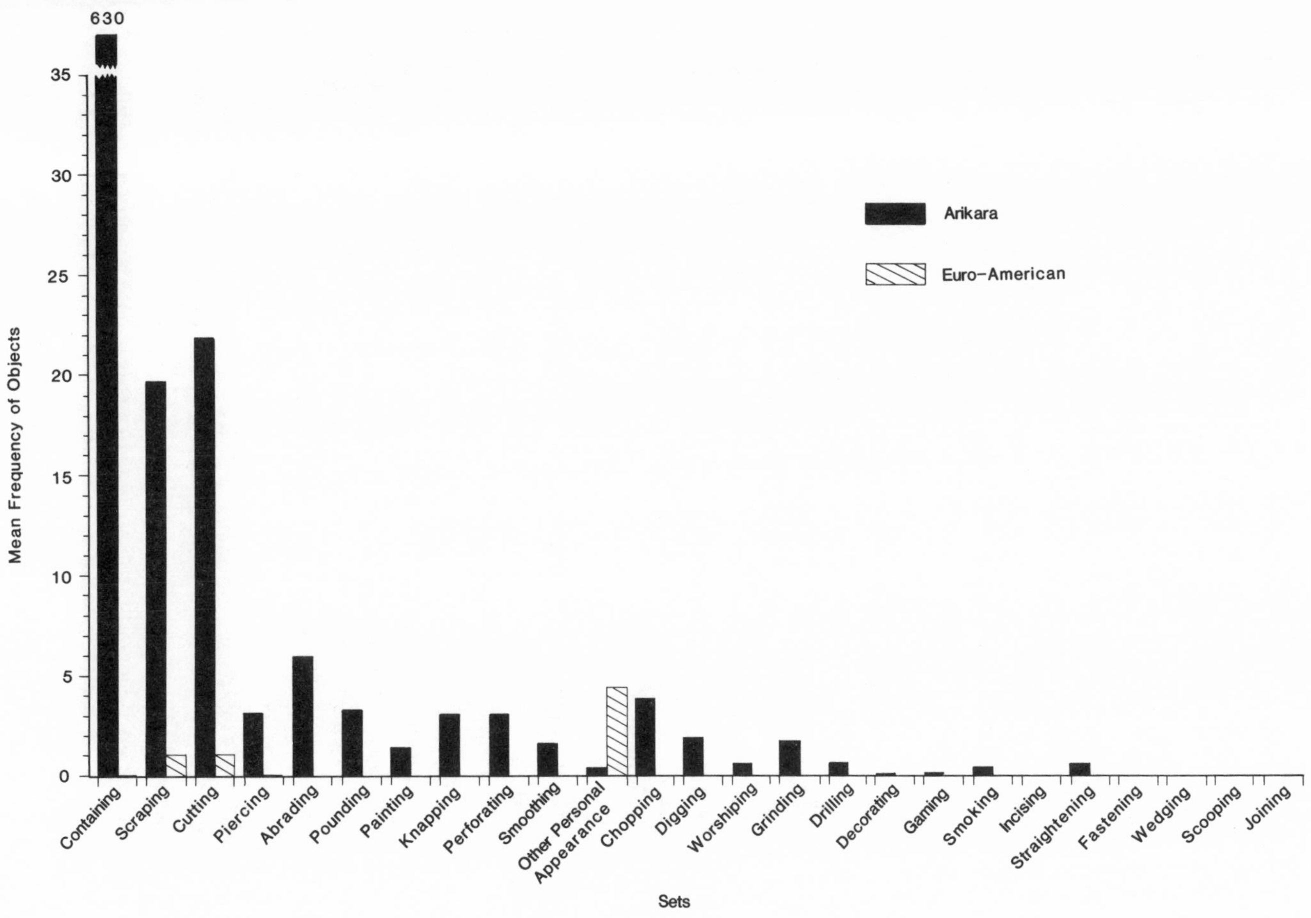

630
35
30
25
20
15
10
5
0
Mean Frequency of Objects
Arikara
Euro-American
Containing
Scraping
Cutting
Piercing
Abrading
Pounding
Painting
Knapping
Perforating
Smoothing
Other Personal Appearance
Chopping
Digging
Worshiping
Grinding
Drilling
Decorating
Gaming
Smoking
Incising
Straightening
Fastening
Wedging
Scooping
Joining
Sets

other sharp metal objects could be used to fulfill a number of tasks for which specialized tools were previously used (Oswalt 1976:211). In a study of contact period technological change on the Middle Missouri, Toom (1979:176–185, 197–198) noted a relatively steady decrease in the frequency of chipped stone tools, but a relatively uneven increase in metal tools. In the protohistoric and historic periods, metal tools continued to be underrepresented in the site material collections. He concluded that the relatively (compared to earlier frequencies of chipped stone tools) few metal tools in the historic period were a consequence of the greater efficiency of the Euro-American-introduced objects.

The third possible explanation involves the actual role of the Arikaras as middlemen in the fur trade. Ray (1978:26; see also Ray 1979; Tracy 1979) has argued that in the Canadian western Sub-Arctic "each trading post or point of contact was ringed with local, middleman, and indirect trade areas." From an archaeological point of view, the quantity of Euro-American goods represented in sites occupied by groups functioning as middlemen was probably underrepresented. The low representation of Euro-American goods would result from the movement of goods received by middlemen groups to groups in the indirect trade zone (Ray 1974:51–71). At least in the early protohistoric and historic periods, almost any Euro-American item had value, especially to groups with no easy access to the Euro-American outlets. Rather than discard a worn tool, middlemen groups probably traded used goods to groups in the indirect trade area. Since middlemen groups had better access to sources of Euro-goods, they could replenish their tool inventories with new goods. Naturally the location of the trading frontier fluctuated through time and many groups took their turn as middlemen, however, the general result was the underrepresentation of Euro-goods in middlemen groups at particular points in time. A major implication for archaeologists is that traditional means of dating contact period sites may actually be skewing the chronology. Generally, archaeologists assume that the more Euro-goods present on a site, the later in time that site is. However, with the middleman effect, sites appearing to be early may actually be later than expected.

Although the spatial arrangement of the system on the Upper Missouri was somewhat different, Toom (1979) has effectively used Ray's middleman hypothesis to examine the technological change from the late prehistoric through the early historic. Toom's analysis specifically dealt with the effects of the introduction of metal tools on the lithic technology of the Middle Missouri villagers. He found that lithic tools declined in frequencies while metal tools increased. But it was not a clear inverse relationship, and metal tools were underrepresented, presumably due to their greater durability (Toom 1979:197–198). For part of Toom's chronological sequence, the middleman effect also played a role.

The point to be made here is that the frequency of Euro-American goods in Period II sites may be underrepresented archaeologically due to the middleman trading behavior of the Arikaras. This is the third possible reason for low frequency of Euro-American goods, and the skewed inverse relationship between an increase in Euro-American goods and a decrease in Arikara goods. It may be concluded that, as far as the first eleven sets are concerned, the artifact process of replacement appears to be in operation. With regard to sets other than the first eleven, there is relatively little change, except for the chopping set. In this set the mean increases from 1.1 to 3.8. There is currently no explanation for this increase.

An additional measure useful in interpreting the relationship between artifact categories and the artifact processes is the relative "richness" of category ubiquity in each period. As applied here, "richness" simply means the number of different categories (at the N −1 level) present in each period. It is appropriate to compare the overall number of categories between Period I and Period II based on relative richness. This type of comparison has special application for discussion of the process of addition. Between Periods I and II there is a small decrease in the overall number of Arikara artifact categories—from 40 to 37. This decrease could easily be due to chance. Within the Euro-American categories a sharp increase occurs in the number of categories present (from one to nine), which is best interpreted as representing the process of addition. Overall, Period II seems, as expected, to be dominated by the processes of replacement and addition.

In Chapter 6 it was suggested that Period II (1681–1725) changes in domestic earthlodge material assemblages were dominated by the processes of replacement and addition, which most accurately reflect the material component of the social and historical trends operating in Period II. Based on the archaeological data discussed above, the artifact processes of replacement and addition *do* characterize the changes in Period II domestic earthlodge contexts. From an historical point of view, the Arikaras in Period II were just beginning their involvement in the economics of the fur trade. Very few Europeans had as yet made their way to the Arikaras and trade relations, and the entire interaction process, operated within the Arikara frame of reference. The Europeans and their goods were not a threat. In fact, Europeans were probably viewed as supernatural beings controlling special powers that could be acquired, in part, through acquisition of the exotic goods they offered for trade. Period II was also a time in which the Arikaras could easily supply the goods (principally furs) that interested Europeans. Although probably experiencing the impact of European-introduced disease, Arikara society was easily maintaining a coherent system of operation and was open to experimentation with the adoption of Euro-goods.

Period III

In Period III (1726–1775) the general pattern of trends in the material assemblages becomes less clear cut than in previous periods (Fig. 16). In comparison to Period II there is a rebounding of mean frequency for many of the Arikara material sets. The sets containing, scraping, cutting, abrading, pounding, painting, smoothing, other personal appearance, digging, worshiping, and grinding all show major increases in frequency. Only the piercing, knapping, perforating, and chopping sets show prominent decreases. The increase in mean frequency of so many of the Arikara sets suggests coherence of the Arikara material system and maintenance in the face of exogenous pressures. There is

Fig. 16. Period III (1726–1775) N level artifact count means from domestic earthlodges.

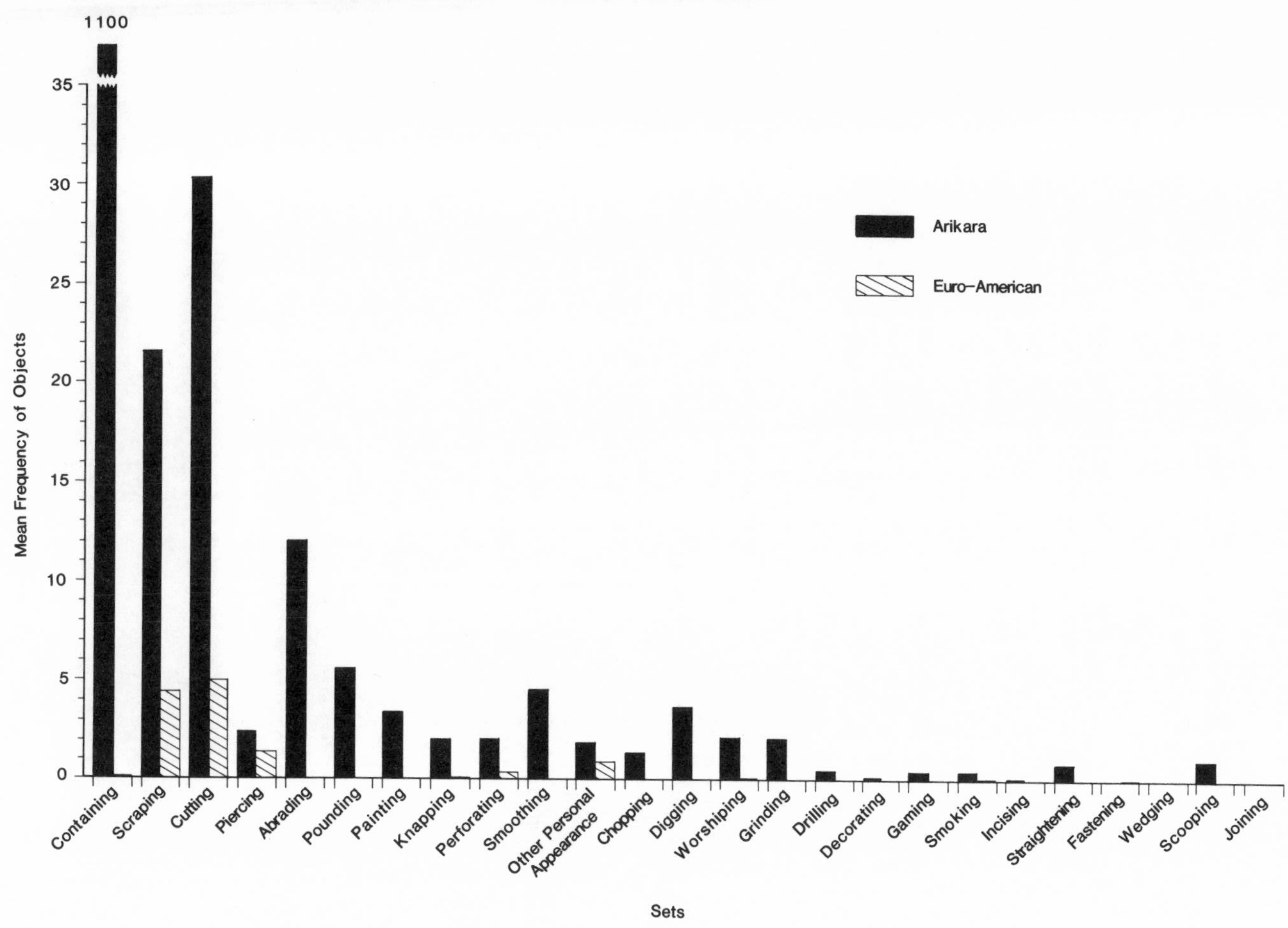

1100
35
30
25
20
15
10
5
0
Mean Frequency of Objects
Arikara
Euro-American
Containing
Scraping
Cutting
Piercing
Abrading
Pounding
Painting
Knapping
Perforating
Smoothing
Other Personal Appearance
Chopping
Digging
Worshiping
Grinding
Drilling
Decorating
Gaming
Smoking
Incising
Straightening
Fastening
Wedging
Scooping
Joining
Sets

some replacement going on in the painting and knapping sets, but this is relatively minor.

While coherence of the artifact system is implied by the increasing frequency of Arikara artifacts, the richness measure suggests that another process is dominant. At the N − 1 level, the number of Arikara categories found in Period III domestic earthlodges increases from 37 to 54. At the same time, the number of Euro-American categories also increases from 9 to 24. The mean number of Arikara categories per house increases from 15.9 to 22.5 and the mean number of Euro-American categories increases from 0.6 to 1.6 (Table 15). The richness indicator suggests that addition is a dominant process. Period III is apparently a major period of acceptance of Euro-American categories. It is also the period with the highest number of Arikara categories. It appears that the introduction of Euro-American goods is associated with a rebounding of Arikara category use.

In Chapter 6 it was hypothesized that maintenance, addition, and replacement would all be in operation among Period III Arikara domestic earthlodge assemblages. While the analysis suggests that this is true, addition was, to some extent, the dominant process. In most regards the historical explanations for Period III material changes can be seen as a continuation of those discussed for Period II, with only a few adjustments. Disease and warfare, in particular, were placing greater stresses

TABLE 15. *Mean Number of N −1 Level Artifact Category Occurrences in Domestic Earthlodges by Period*

Period	Arikara	Euro-American
I	17.1	0.1
II	15.9	0.6
III	22.5	1.6
IV	17.4	1.0
V	16.3	4.7
VI	4.3	4.8

on Arikara society. The Arikaras were, however, continuing to interact and trade with Europeans under favorable circumstances. But on the other hand, Period III is not as open to change, at least in the material realm, as Period II. Unlike Period II, replacement plays only a minor role in Period III, which may suggest a retrenchment in the social interactive scope of trade with Europeans. Although Europeans were maintaining their status as controllers of special powers and objects there seems to be less Arikara interest in modifying their own material systems. This may be a response to increasing social stress and perhaps a burgeoning recognition of Europeans as ordinary strangers.

Period IV

Period IV (1776–1805) illustrates a continuance of some trends seen in Period III and reverses others. There is a continued decline in the prevalence of Arikara scraping and cutting sets (Fig. 17). There is some increase in the piercing set, but a sharp decline in the Arikara abrading set. There is also some decline in Arikara sets pounding, painting, smoothing, and other personal appearance.

There are some general decreases in the Euro-American sets. Like the Arikara sets, the Euro-American scraping and cutting sets also decline. The piercing set also declines in frequency. Probably the most interesting trend is the continued decline of Euro-American goods in the other personal appearance set. The overall frequency of Euro-American items in this set is very low compared to earlier periods. It would seem that personal ornaments, like beads, are entering the archaeological record in domestic earthlodges less frequently. This may indicate a shift away from a demand for this type of good or it may indicate that these items are more commonly becoming a part of the offerings placed in burials.

The richness measure for Period IV indicates a decline of 17 percent in the number of Arikara categories at the N − 1 level, compared to Period III and a decline of 63 percent in the number of Euro-American categories. This drastic decline in the number of Euro-American categories implies the process of rejection is dominant in this period.

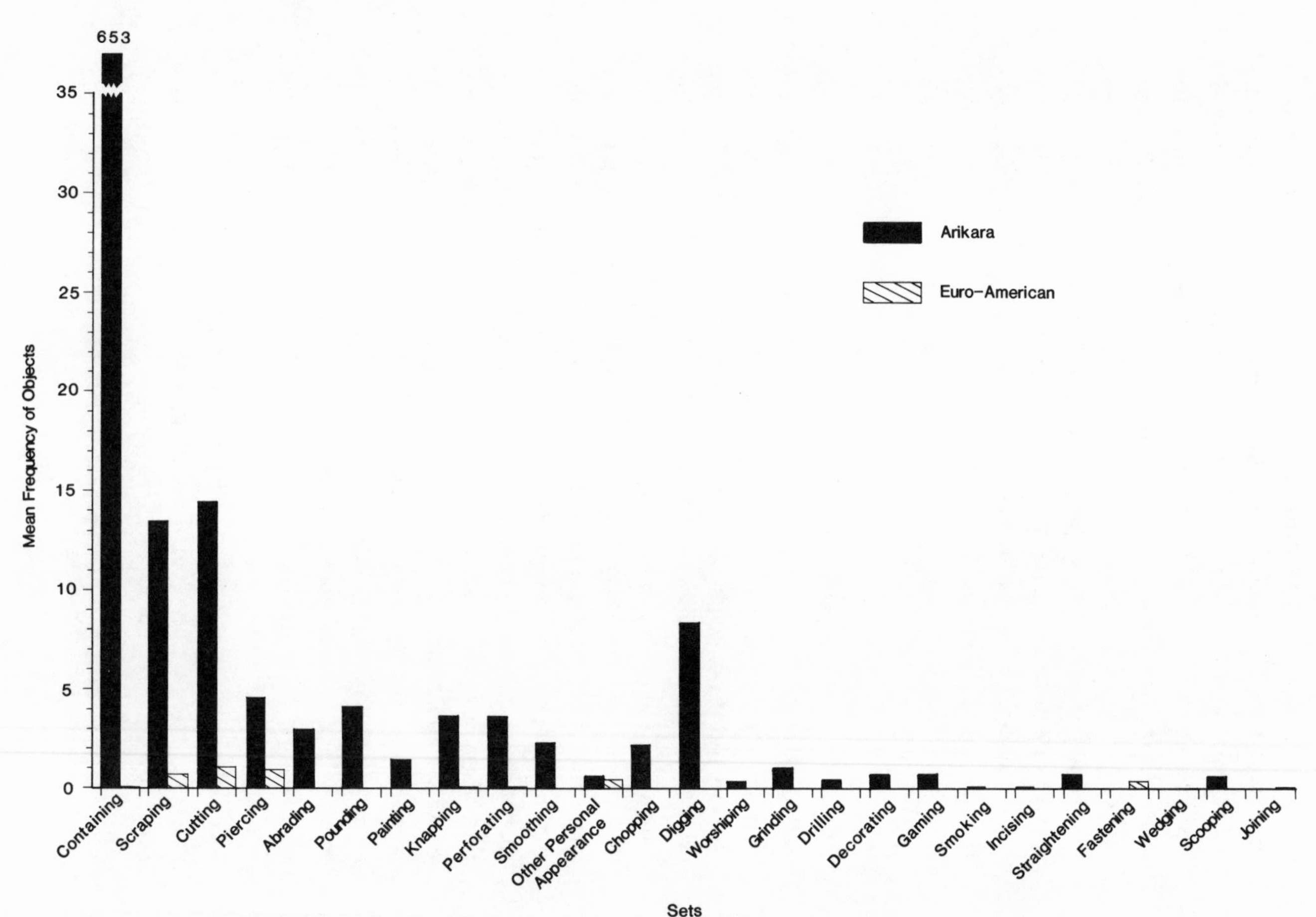
653
35
30
25
20
15
10
5
0
Mean Frequency of Objects
Arikara
Euro-American
Containing
Scraping
Cutting
Piercing
Abrading
Pounding
Painting
Knapping
Perforating
Smoothing
Other Personal Appearance
Chopping
Digging
Worshiping
Grinding
Drilling
Decorating
Gaming
Smoking
Incising
Straightening
Fastening
Wedging
Scooping
Joining
Sets

It is interesting to note that despite increasing Arikara access to Euro-American trade goods in this period, there is actually a major decline in the variety of Euro-goods that occur. On first appearance it might seem out of place that the Arikaras, who were increasingly involved in the economics of the fur trade, would apparently intentionally reject or exclude so many kinds of Euro-goods that were probably readily available and had even been used in times past. But it should be remembered that Period IV was a time of relative success for the Arikaras as middlemen traders. It was a time of good trade relations, yet a time in which the Arikaras were becoming increasingly aware that Europeans were not supernatural beings. While the Arikaras were certainly undergoing a variety of social pressures due to such things as epidemics and warfare, there is also evidence that the hierarchical diagrammatic icon (discussed in Chapter 5), which linked status rankings with a variety of social and cosmological structures, was still in operation and was functioning to maintain social coherence. The continued effectiveness of the diagrammatic icon, the success of Arikara exchange, and the desacralization of Europeans may have allowed the Arikaras to redefine Period IV artifact assemblages in terms of their own previous systems of usage, rather than shifting towards a more Europeanized set of tools. The archaeological data support this interpretation, in fact the trend towards a less Europeanized artifact inventory may have been presaged in Period III by the increasing number of native artifact categories in use and by the dominance of addition alone in Period III, rather than addition and replacement as in Period II.

Period IV represents a key component in understanding the extent to which interactions are structured by motivations and perspectives of the participants. Throughout this study it has been argued that cultural factors are important for understanding interaction and trade and that these factors are linked to material assemblages in a variety of ways. Period IV illustrates that the standard model of increasing Euro-

Fig. 17. Period IV (1776–1805) N level artifact count means from domestic earthlodges.

American artifact use and declining native artifact use does not explain all the variation. The Middleman Hypothesis of trading behavior (Ray 1978) likewise argues against a simple replacement model by pointing out that the material record is complexly organized on the basis of human motivation and behavior. But even more than a reflection of changing trading behavior, Period IV seems to indicate an Arikara realignment of perspectives on interaction with Euro-American traders.

Considering the importance of Period IV and the "unusual" material trends, several additional lines of evidence were considered as a means of substantiating the above interpretations and reiterating the validity of the data being used. The additional evidence to be considered includes potential sampling error and patterns of category replacement.

Overall, there is no reason to suspect sampling error as the cause of low Euro-American artifact category representation in Period IV. The Period IV sample consists of 14 domestic earthlodges from two different sites. The relative number of Euro-American categories from each site is roughly the same, indicating that one or the other of the sites is not skewing the distribution of material representation. The artifact inventories for several domestic earthlodges not used in the sample were examined to determine whether the use of different earthlodges would have produced dissimilar results. The comparison revealed that other earthlodges contained similar artifact and category frequencies to those earthlodges used in the analysis.

In Chapter 7 sources of variation within the samples for each period were expressed by a series of basic statistics, including mean, standard deviation, and range for domestic earthlodges and burials (Tables 8, 9, and 11). If the standard deviations for artifact and category frequencies were especially high for Period IV it might indicate that one or a few domestic earthlodges were unduly influencing the artifact means and category presence/absence data used to characterize changes in the material assemblages. Although all of the standard deviations can be considered "high," those for Period IV are within the range indicated for all periods, and in fact are relatively low for Arikara artifact and category frequencies (Tables 8 and 9). There is, therefore, no reason to suggest that artifact and category frequencies in Period IV exhibit more variation than in other periods.

Another potential source of variation, also discussed in Chapter 7, has to do with the differential size of domestic earthlodges. It might be expected that large diameter earthlodges would produce more artifacts because they were probably occupied by a larger number of individuals. The mean diameters for earthlodges from each period are listed in Table 7. The mean diameter for Period IV (9 m) is the smallest of all six periods, however, it differs by only 1.4 m from the mean diameter for Period III and is only 0.1 m smaller than the mean for Period II. As discussed in Chapter 7, there does not seem to be a strong correlation between earthlodge diameter and total frequency of artifacts recovered. For instance, although the Period III mean diameter is only 9 percent larger than the mean for Period IV, the Period III Arikara mean artifact frequency is almost 80 percent greater.

A potential explanation for the low artifact and category frequencies (especially among Euro-American artifacts) in Period IV lies in the specific N − 1 level artifact categories that were being excluded from the artifact inventories. If the differences in artifact frequencies between Periods III and IV were primarily restricted to artifact categories that occurred in small numbers (some categories at the N − 1 level occur only once in the entire data set), then the observed changes might only relate to chance fluctuations in these rarely occurring categories. Also, if the changes were primarily in the rarely occurring categories, and the consistently occurring categories were minimally affected, it would be reasonable to suggest that such change held little importance for the overall artifact assemblage for the period.

An analysis of the change in artifact categories documented in Periods III and IV indicate that most of the changes were taking place in the categories that occurred relatively consistently in the overall data set. The analysis was based on identifying Arikara sets at the N level that had no frequency values greater than 2 and Euro-American sets at the N level with frequency values no greater than 0.4. Once these sets were identified, their constituent N − 1 level categories were identified and tabulated for net changes between Periods III and IV. In the Arikara categories there was a net decrease of two categories in the rare sets and a net decrease of five categories in the consistently occurring sets. In the Euro-American categories there was no decrease in the rare sets, but there was a decrease of eleven categories in the consistently occurring sets. This indicates that rarely occurring categories were having little effect in the overall changes between Periods III and IV and that most change was taking place in sets that were generally consistent elements in most periods. These results lend support to the idea that the decrease in Euro-American categories in Period IV was not due to data error, but instead results from the artifact process of rejection.

There are two additional possible explanations for the apparent reduction in the use of Euro-American goods in Period IV. Both of these relate to the economics of the fur trade. The first is the possibility of lowered access to trade goods in Period IV. However, given the ethnohistorical evidence, it is apparent that if anything, there was an increase in the availability of Euro-goods. Period IV was the time of the first major trade expeditions from St. Louis coming up the Missouri River. There is no indication that trade goods were less available. There is also no indication that trade goods were becoming too costly for the Arikaras to purchase. However, it may have been the case that Arikara access to furs to be traded to Europeans was beginning to decline (see Fig. 5). This possible decline in access to furs might have meant a reduction in Arikara purchasing power. Such a possibility is of limited utility as an explanation, considering the events that took place in the next period. In Period V convincing evidence indicates that Arikara purchasing power did decline, but at the same time it is the period with the greatest quantities of Euro-goods recovered from earthlodges and burials. The Arikaras were apparently acquiring additional Euro-goods even as their ability to pay for them declined. Therefore, it is evident that in Period IV, as well as Period V, Arikara interests in Euro-goods were not linked solely to their economic ability to acquire these goods.

Period V

Evidence from Period V (1806–1835) illustrates a major shift in the trends observed in Period IV. In comparison to Period IV there are sharp declines in Arikara sets containing, scraping, cutting, piercing, pounding, painting, knapping, perforating, smoothing, chopping, and digging (Fig. 18). There is some increase in a few of the more rarely occurring Arikara sets, such as grinding, gaming, and straightening; however, these increases are relatively minor in comparison to the major declines in the more frequently occurring sets. There are three good examples of replacement. The Arikara set piercing, for instance, declines sharply while the Euro-American counterparts increase sharply. There is a continued decline in Arikara containing set associated with a major increase in the Euro-American containing set items. In the other personal appearance set, Euro-American items increase sharply while Arikara items remain at a low level.

The richness measure shows a minor decrease in the number of Arikara categories at the N −1 level (7 percent). For Euro-American categories, however, there is a tremendous increase (66 percent). This indicates that the process of addition is at work. The overall characterization for this period includes the artifact processes of replacement and addition, but is probably best described as a material system undergoing the process of transformation. Transformation is the most appropriate way to describe this period, considering the decline in frequency of Arikara items in several sets at the N level, the replacement of many items by Euro-American goods, and the large increase in Euro-American categories at the N −1 level.

The ethnohistorical evidence for Period V indicates that this was a time of major change for the Arikaras. During this period, Arikara ability to participate in the fur trade was hampered by lowered demand for furs and restricted access to fur resources. Hostilities with Euro-Americans increased and at one point the Arikaras even abandoned their villages on the Missouri River and moved to the Loup River in Nebraska to reside with the Pawnees (see Chapter 5 for additional details). From a conventional point of view, it might be expected that lowered access to Euro-American goods would indicate a reduction in frequency of such goods in Arikara contexts. In fact, the exact opposite was the case. Period V Arikara contexts (including domestic earthlodges *and* burials) contain more Euro-American goods than any other period, both in mean frequency of objects and total number of category occurrences.

The explanation for the seeming incongruity in Arikara use versus

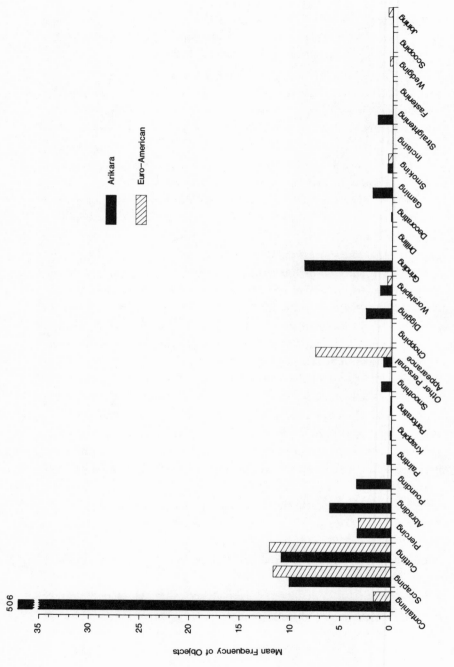
Mean Frequency of Objects
0
5
10
15
20
25
30
35
506
Arikara
Euro-American
Containing
Scraping
Cutting
Piercing
Abrading
Pounding
Painting
Knapping
Perforating
Smoothing
Other Personal Appearance
Chopping
Digging
Worshiping
Grinding
Drilling
Decorating
Gaming
Smoking
Incising
Straightening
Fastening
Wedging
Scooping
Joining
Sets

access to Euro-goods lies in the strategies adopted for dealing with the social disruptions of the time. In Period V the Arikaras were rapidly losing their status as middlemen traders, Euro-Americans were trapping fur animals without Indian assistance, depopulation from disease had forced realignments of some status categories, and Euro-American traders had slipped from their former supernatural status. Arikara society was on the verge of collapse. The loss of middleman status by the Arikaras might also have meant that fewer goods were being passed on to other groups and therefore the discard rate in domestic earthlodges would be greater. This possibility, however, does not explain the increased use of Euro-goods in burials or the redefinition of status indicators (O'Shea 1984:277–278).

In the previous Period (IV) the strategy for maintaining social coherence seems to have been, in part, to shore up at least the material component of social action by rejecting many kinds of Euro-goods to maintain a coherent material assemblage with closer ties to past systems of material expression. In Period V, however, it is argued that the social cohesiveness necessary to maintain continuity in material assemblages, and by implication, in the social system, had evaporated. Also, the lessened supernatural status of Euro-Americans meant that it was increasingly less necessary to take such connotations into account when trading for Euro-goods. Trade with Euro-Americans was becoming more "ordinary." The result of these changes in Arikara perspectives and ability to maintain their own social system was a rapid abandonment of "traditional" tool inventories in favor of the expedient and technologically sophisticated Euro-goods.

Period VI

Period VI (1836–1862) is the last time frame to be considered for domestic earthlodges. As indicated previously, the sample available for Period VI leaves much to be desired. There are only four structures available for analysis (all from Star Village, 32ME16), and these were

Fig. 18. Period V (1806–1835) N level artifact count means from domestic earthlodges.

only occupied for a few months in 1862. The total number of items in the artifact inventories for these earthlodges is very small compared to other earthlodges from earlier periods. Because of these factors it is inappropriate to assign artifact processes to Period VI. However, there are some trends worth noting.

All Arikara sets, except containing, occur in very low frequencies (Table 13 and Fig. 19). Even the containing set is very small compared to earlier periods, yet it does seem to reflect a trend towards a reduction in the use of native-made containers (primarily ceramics, although some wooden bowls may be included). At the same time there is a major increase in the mean frequency of items in the Euro-American containing set.

Period VI is the only period in which items in several Euro-American sets are actually more numerous than items in Arikara sets. In particular, the Euro-American sets cutting, piercing, joining, and especially other personal appearance contain more items than their Arikara counterparts. It does seem that these relationships reflect legitimate trends, but it is also apparent that a "functionally" complete artifact inventory is not represented by the sample. There are numerous unrepresented categories at the N − 1 level, and sets at the N level, that should normally be part of the inventory of every household. While the trends are by no means substantiated, it seems that in 1862 there was a growing shift away from the use of native manufactures. This is a tendency that seems to fit with the continued decline in Arikara social autonomy coupled with the greater reliance being placed on Euro-Americans, engendered by various forms of dependency generating factors, such as the increasingly frequent distribution of annuities.

CEREMONIAL EARTHLODGES

Because of the very small sample sizes available for ceremonial earthlodges, they are only discussed briefly, as a means of providing a

Fig. 19. Period VI (1836–1862) N level artifact count means from domestic earthlodges.

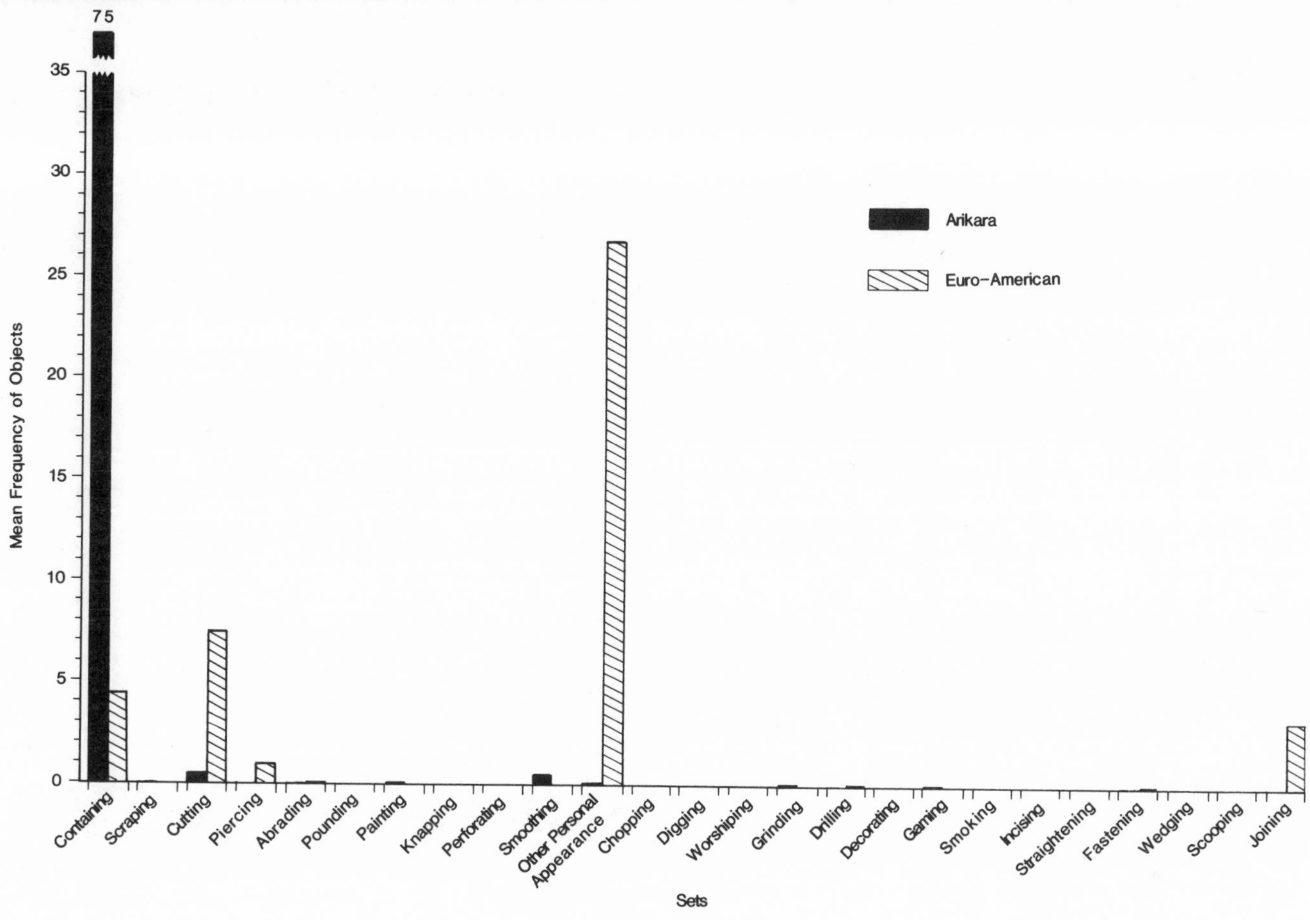
75
35
30
25
20
15
10
5
0
Mean Frequency of Objects
Arikara
Euro-American
Containing
Scraping
Cutting
Piercing
Abrading
Pounding
Painting
Knapping
Perforating
Smoothing
Other Personal Appearance
Chopping
Digging
Worshiping
Grinding
Drilling
Decorating
Gaming
Smoking
Incising
Straightening
Fastening
Wedging
Scooping
Joining
Sets

glimpse of the kinds of trends that may be part of this context. Mean frequencies of artifacts found in ceremonial earthlodges are presented at the N level in Tables 16 and 17. The entire sample consists of eight lodges: two from Period I, none from Period II, three from Period III, one from Period IV, one from Period V, and one from Period VI. After

TABLE 16. *Mean Number of Arikara Artifacts per Period for N Level Ceremonial Earthlodge Sets*

Set	Periods (with numbers of lodges)					
	I	II	III	IV	V	VI
	(2)	(0)	(3)	(1)	(1)	(1)
Containing	1367.5	0.0	411.7	67.0	1029.0	0.0
Scraping	38.5	0.0	1.0	12.0	1.0	2.0
Cutting	32.5	0.0	15.0	4.0	0.0	0.0
Piercing	0.1	0.0	0.7	2.0	0.0	0.0
Abrading	10.5	0.0	5.0	0.0	0.0	1.0
Pounding	2.0	0.0	4.3	0.0	0.0	0.0
Painting	0.5	0.0	2.3	0.0	0.0	1.0
Knapping	3.5	0.0	0.3	2.0	0.0	0.0
Perforating	3.5	0.0	0.3	2.0	0.0	0.0
Smoothing	1.5	0.0	0.7	0.0	0.0	0.0
Other Personal Appearance	1.5	0.0	0.3	3.0	1.0	0.0
Chopping	0.0	0.0	0.3	0.0	0.0	0.0
Digging	2.5	0.0	3.0	3.0	8.0	1.0
Worshiping	1.0	0.0	1.7	0.0	0.0	0.0
Grinding	2.0	0.0	2.0	0.0	0.0	0.0
Drilling	1.0	0.0	0.0	0.0	0.0	0.0
Decorating	0.0	0.0	0.7	0.0	0.0	0.0
Gaming	0.5	0.0	0.0	0.0	6.0	0.0
Smoking	0.0	0.0	0.0	0.0	0.0	0.0
Incising	0.0	0.0	0.0	0.0	0.0	0.0
Straightening	0.5	0.0	0.3	0.0	2.0	0.0
Fastening	0.0	0.0	0.0	0.0	0.0	0.0
Wedging	0.0	0.0	0.0	0.0	0.0	0.0
Scooping	0.0	0.0	0.0	0.0	0.0	1.0
Joining	0.0	0.0	0.0	0.0	0.0	0.0

examining the two tables, probably the most striking thing about them is the very low artifact frequencies in these buildings. In spite of the small sample sizes, the low frequencies indicate that ceremonial earthlodges generally contain fewer artifacts than domestic earthlodges, thus reflecting the differential function implied for these buildings. In domestic earthlodges most material remains are everyday tools

TABLE 17. *Mean Number of Euro-American Artifacts per Period for N Level Ceremonial Earthlodge Sets*

Set	Periods (with numbers of lodges)					
	I (2)	II (0)	III (3)	IV (1)	V (1)	VI (1)
Containing	0.0	0.0	0.0	0.0	1.0	2.0
Scraping	0.0	0.0	4.3	0.0	20.0	0.0
Cutting	0.0	0.0	4.3	0.0	20.0	0.0
Piercing	0.0	0.0	0.7	0.0	2.0	0.0
Abrading	0.0	0.0	0.0	0.0	0.0	0.0
Pounding	0.0	0.0	0.0	0.0	0.0	0.0
Painting	0.0	0.0	0.0	0.0	0.0	0.0
Knapping	0.0	0.0	0.0	0.0	0.0	0.0
Perforating	0.0	0.0	0.0	0.0	0.0	0.0
Smoothing	0.0	0.0	0.0	0.0	0.0	0.0
Other Personal Appearance	0.0	0.0	1.3	0.0	12.0	0.0
Chopping	0.0	0.0	0.0	0.0	0.0	0.0
Digging	0.0	0.0	0.0	0.0	0.0	0.0
Worshiping	0.0	0.0	0.0	0.0	1.0	0.0
Grinding	0.0	0.0	0.0	0.0	0.0	0.0
Drilling	0.0	0.0	0.0	0.0	0.0	0.0
Decorating	0.0	0.0	0.0	0.0	0.0	0.0
Gaming	0.0	0.0	0.0	0.0	0.0	0.0
Smoking	0.0	0.0	0.0	0.0	1.0	0.0
Incising	0.0	0.0	0.0	0.0	0.0	0.0
Straightening	0.0	0.0	0.0	0.0	0.0	0.0
Fastening	0.0	0.0	0.0	0.0	2.0	0.0
Wedging	0.0	0.0	0.0	0.0	0.0	0.0
Scooping	0.0	0.0	0.0	0.0	0.0	1.0
Joining	0.0	0.0	0.0	0.0	2.0	0.0

necessary for the livelihood of the household members. If it is indeed correct that ceremonial earthlodges were primarily not domestic residences, then it follows that the artifact inventory associated with these buildings would differ from the domestic earthlodges. This does not necessarily mean that a ceremonial earthlodge would only contain objects of primarily ceremonial usage. On the contrary, a ceremonial lodge might not contain any more of the objects that belong to such N level sets as worshiping, decorating, gaming, or smoking, than an ordinary domestic lodge. Yet it should be expected that the artifact inventory of a ceremonial lodge will differ considerably from that of a domestic lodge. The difference should lie not so much in the kind of sets represented, as in the proportion of the different sets.

The small sample size for ceremonial earthlodges precludes any conclusive statements, but it does appear that Arikara sets most common in domestic earthlodges are also common in ceremonial earthlodges. The containing set is the most common, as might be expected, considering that pot sherds are the primary component of this set. To some extent, the decline in the number of items in the containing set over time parallels that observed for domestic earthlodges. The principal exception is in Period V (1806–1835). The single ceremonial earthlodge in Period V has nearly as many containing set items as the lodges in Period I. Other common sets in ceremonial earthlodges include scraping and cutting. Other sets occur sporadically.

Euro-American N level sets also occur sporadically. Only containing, scraping, cutting, piercing, other personal appearance, worshiping, smoking, fastening, and joining sets are at all represented in the sample. Most of these items are found in the ceremonial lodges from Periods III and V. This fact tends to support the results of the Q-Analysis, which defines Periods III and V as the most "structurally" divergent in terms of both Arikara and Euro-American sets.

BURIALS

The third major context to be considered is burials. As discussed in Chapter 7, burials are a different sort of data set than either domestic or ceremonial earthlodges. First of all, burials and their associated artifacts are intentionally placed in the ground, whereas the artifacts found in the remains of domestic and ceremonial earthlodges consist of debris and trash deposits. Although trash may also be disposed of in a ritually prescribed manner and location (e.g., Moore 1982), it is nevertheless assumed that the meaning component in earthlodge residues is less significant than it is in a context such as burials.

The intentionality of the burial deposit, as a data set, must also take into consideration internally relevant variables, such as age and sex distinctions, that are known to structure the composition of the associated burial offerings. These considerations as well as potential sample size effect problems were evaluated prior to choosing the analysis sample (see Appendix, Table A-7). Of the over 2,000 excavated Arikara burials, most are associated with only two of the six time periods. This unfortunately meant the elimination of most of the burials from inclusion in the analysis. After considering the several criteria for selection of an appropriate sample, the final analysis sample included 74 burials from each of three periods (II, III, and V). While the final sample is small compared to the overall number of burials that might have been used, the criteria used in selecting the sample have helped insure its validity and comparability. It is, however, regrettable that only three periods are represented. This limits the scope of the interpretations and conclusions that might be made, although there are important trends evident in the sample.

Another characteristic of the burial sample is the extremely "sparse" nature of the data matrix. That is, most burials only have one or a few of the different categories of objects that represent the full range of observed inclusions. The mean and standard deviation for the number of categories of objects found in burials are listed in Table 11. Unlike the domestic earthlodge sample, there is really no basic artifact set found in most of the burials. There are, however, objects that do serve to distinguish age, sex, and status criteria (Orser 1980a; O'Shea 1984). Because of the rarity of occurrence of most artifact categories at the N − 1 level, analysis at the N level becomes even more important than was the case with domestic earthlodges.

Period II

Period II (1681–1725) is the first period under consideration. This is a post-contact period, therefore unlike the domestic earthlodge sample, there is no pre-contact, aboriginal "baseline" that can be defined. The absence of a pre-contact period makes it impossible to suggest the nature of the pre-contact burial association pattern. Burial itself may be a phenomenon that does not have a long pre-contact history in the Middle Missouri Coalescent tradition. As discussed in Chapter 3, there is virtually no early evidence for burial on the Middle Missouri, and in fact there is some evidence for above-ground exposure of the body. The absence of a precontact burial sample for use in this analysis is less a sampling problem and more a reflection of changing mortuary practices.

The Period II Arikara burial sample artifact inventory can be characterized as containing a relatively high occurrence of the N level

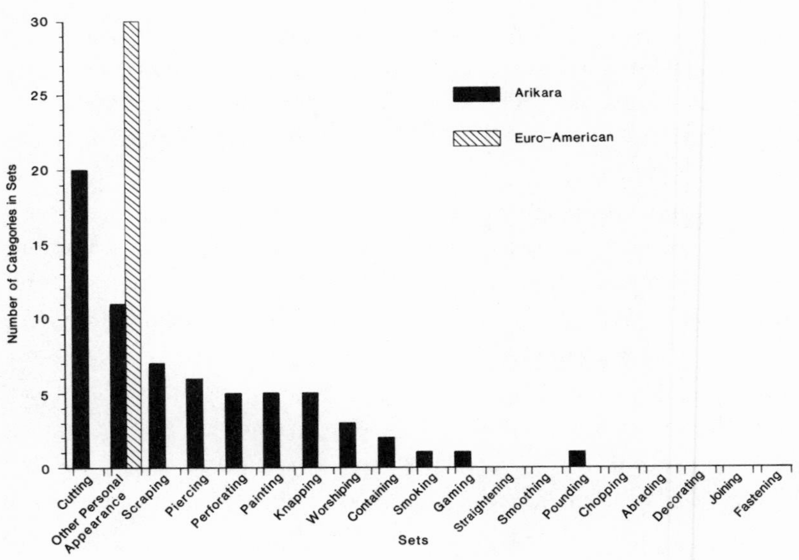

Fig. 20. Period II (1681–1725) N level artifact occurrence frequencies for burials.

sets cutting, other personal appearance, and scraping (Fig. 20 and Tables 18 and 19). Other N level Arikara sets occur five or fewer times in a sample of 74 burials. Of the 19 N level sets that occur in the entire burial sample (all three periods) only 12 occur in Period II. At the N -1 level, of the 53 categories present in the entire sample, only 23 occur in Period II (Table 20).

Although Period II is a post-contact period, there are relatively few Euro-American artifacts in the sample. Out of a total of 37 N -1 level Euro-American categories represented in the total sample for all three periods, there are only four present in Period II. At the N level,

TABLE 18. *Sums for Presence/Absence Occurrences of N Level Arikara Artifact Categories in Burials*

Set	Periods (with numbers of burials)		
	II (74)	III (74)	V (74)
Cutting	20	11	3
Other Personal Appearance	11	17	29
Scraping	7	7	4
Piercing	6	15	14
Perforating	5	3	2
Painting	5	29	24
Knapping	5	3	2
Worshiping	3	14	25
Containing	2	1	2
Smoking	1	2	2
Gaming	1	1	4
Straightening	0	2	4
Smoothing	0	1	3
Pounding	1	1	0
Chopping	0	1	0
Abrading	0	1	0
Decorating	0	1	0
Joining	0	0	0
Fastening	0	0	0

TABLE 19. *Sums for Presence/Absence Occurrences of N Level Euro-American Artifact Categories in Burials*

Set	Periods (with number of burials)		
	II (74)	III (74)	V (74)
Cutting	0	0	16
Other Personal Appearance	30	15	98
Scraping	0	0	9
Piercing	0	1	20
Perforating	0	0	1
Painting	0	0	0
Knapping	0	0	12
Worshiping	0	0	0
Containing	0	0	9
Smoking	0	0	0
Gaming	0	0	1
Straightening	0	0	0
Smoothing	0	0	0
Pounding	0	0	0
Chopping	0	0	1
Abrading	0	0	0
Decorating	0	0	0
Joining	0	0	1
Fastening	0	0	9

all of the Euro-American artifacts are part of the other personal appearance set. The Euro-American items in this set consist primarily of glass trade beads. The other personal appearance set is by far the most frequently occurring, whether concerning Arikara or Euro-American sets (Fig. 20).

In Period II the fact that all Euro-American artifact categories in the sample are part of the other personal appearance set demonstrates a very restricted case of addition to the burial artifact inventory. Whether this might also exemplify the process of replacement can not be determined due to the absence of a pre-contact sample. In the previous

TABLE 20. *Artifact Category Richness at N –1 Level for the Burial Sample*

Period	Arikara Categories	Euro-American Categories
II	23	4
III	34	5
V	35	35

Note: Richness is calculated as the number of different categories at the N –1 level in each period.

analysis of domestic earthlodges, however, Euro-American goods included a high proportion of other personal appearance items, yet there were several other N level sets also present. The presence of Euro-American items belonging to the containing, scraping, cutting, and piercing sets in domestic earthlodges was apparently associated with a reduction in prevalence of corresponding Arikara sets. This is a case of replacement in domestic earthlodges. By contrast, the very restricted use of Euro-American goods in burials does represent addition, but in general the process of maintenance is also in operation and appears to be dominant, considering that addition occurs in only one N level set.

The expectations outlined in Chapter 6 for Period II burials anticipated that there would be a considerable amount of addition to the burial assemblage. This did not turn out to be the case, instead maintenance was the dominant process. The conservative nature of burial associations seems to be related to the general social cohesiveness that characterized the Arikaras during this early period of direct contact. That is, the Arikaras did not simply adopt Euro-goods wholeheartedly, but instead conditioned their use of these new goods on the basis of preexisting cultural constraints. It could be argued that the reason most Euro-American goods used as burial offerings belonged to the other personal appearance set is because other kinds of items such as knives, hatchets, or even sheet metal pieces were scarce and too valuable for inclusion in burials. To put such things in graves would mean cutting off their worldly economic value and redefining value as spiritual and other-worldly. A strictly economic explanation, however, has limited value, as can be illustrated by the Period V burial data. In Period V, access to Euro-American goods was at a record low, but these items were being placed in burials in ever-increasing quantities. Clearly, economic value was not the only criteria for the use of Euro-American goods as burial associations.

Period III

In Period III (1726–1775) there are some major changes in the composition of the burial association assemblage (Fig. 21). At the N level, categories belonging to the cutting set are less numerous than in Period II, but in general there is an increase in several sets with only minor decreases in others. The painting set registers the greatest increase

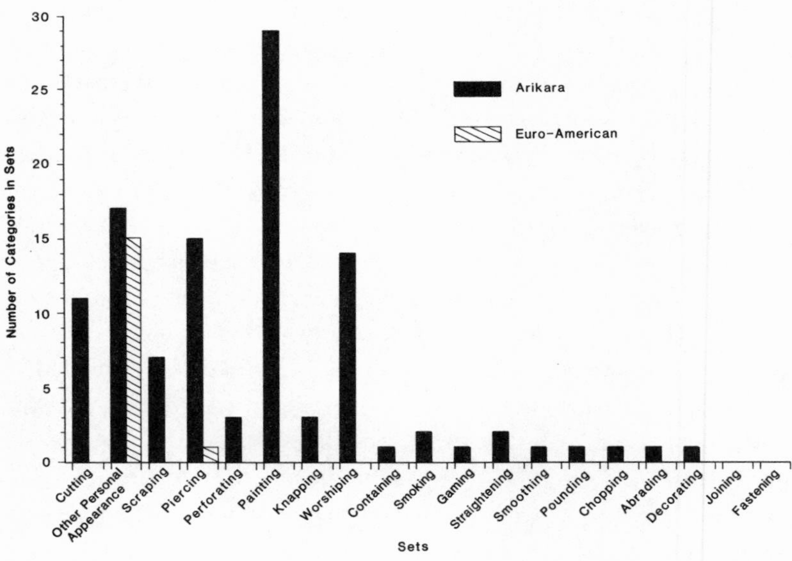

Fig. 21. Period III (1726–1775) N level artifact occurrence frequencies for burials.

among the Arikara sets. It becomes the most numerous set and occurs much more frequently than in Period II.

There are only two Euro-American sets (other personal appearance and piercing) represented at the N level in Period III. These two sets consist of five categories at the N −1 level (Table 20). The large number of other personal appearance set occurrences in Period II (30) was cut in half in Period III. The other Euro-American set represented in Period III (piercing) has only one occurrence at the N level. Clearly, the only important Euro-American artifact occurrences in Period III continue to be in the other personal appearance set. Period III continues to represent a restricted example of the addition process, especially considering that the number of Arikara category occurrences in the other personal appearance set has increased from 11 to 17 compared to Period II (i.e., the process of replacement is not represented). Even though addition is in operation, in a limited sense, the lack of a widespread occurrence of Euro-American goods suggests that maintenance continues to be the dominant process, as was the case in Period II.

An important trend, not necessarily related to the artifact processes, is the apparent move towards the more frequent occurrence of burial associations. The richness measure shows that 11 new N −1 level Arikara categories occur that were not part of the Period II sample. This trend continues in the next period and may be part of a general response of native peoples to Euro-American contact. The trend towards more associations has been noted elsewhere (Fitting 1976: 330–332) and has been attributed to a "saturation" of functional Euro-American goods in use inventories. When a group has all the Euro-American goods it can use or trade to other groups, it has been argued that the surplus becomes burial associations. This highly economic argument does not take into account other motivations, or even the potential effects of middleman trade. In a computer simulation of trade-good flow (based only on guns and kettles) to the Arikaras, Orser and Zimmerman (1984) found that, conservatively, within 15 or 20 years after the beginning of Euro-American trade, every Arikara adult at the Leavenworth site could have had access to a gun or metal container. They argue that a "saturation" of trade goods could have occurred soon after trade began. Yet the burial sample does not reflect this potential for early "saturation." Large amounts of Euro-American goods do not become part of the burial associations until Period V. Instead, only limited kinds of Euro-American goods find their way into the grave for at least the first 100 (and probably the first 125) years of direct contact.

The discrepancy between the "saturation-surplus" model and what seems to be occurring in the Arikara sample can be attributed to other aspects of trading behavior and cultural constraints. First, there is a strong indication that "conservatism" plays a role in structuring the composition of the artifact assemblage in ceremonial contexts. By "conservatism" I mean that ceremonial contexts are less likely to alter their material components rapidly. Conservatism is apparently a factor in the Arikara case, at least until Period V. Secondly, many factors such as depopulation were contributing to general social disruption and the redefinition of relative social status as well as the objects used to define social categories. Assuming that burial associations are a valid means of identifying relative social status, then increasing quantities of objects in graves may be a demonstration of the revaluation of status indicators and a reflection of the increasing numbers of individuals with access to wealth and who may have been attempting to bypass existing routes to status (see Chapter 5; Orser and Zimmerman 1984:207; O'Shea 1984: 256–279).

Period V

Period V (1806–1835) is the final period for which a burial sample is available for analysis and is the first period in which Euro-American goods become a major component of the assemblage (Fig. 22). There are also some major increases in Arikara N level sets. The most frequently occurring Arikara categories at the N level belong to the other personal appearance, piercing, painting, and worshiping sets. These four sets were also the most prevalent in Period III. There is continuity within the composition of the burial assemblage, but there is also replacement and addition. Replacement seems to be taking place in the cutting set. In comparison to Period III, the occurrence of categories in the Arikara cutting set has decreased sharply, while Euro-American category occurrences have increased.

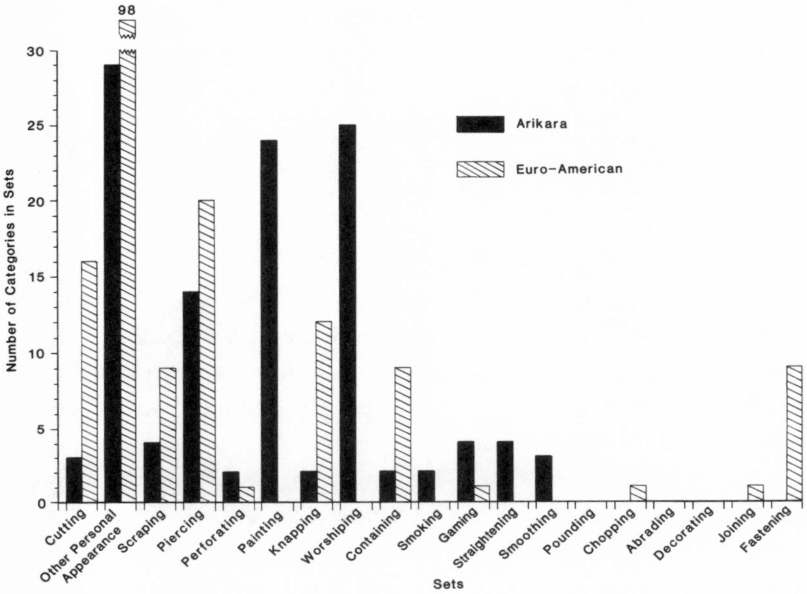

Fig. 22. Period V (1806–1835) N level artifact occurrence frequencies for burials.

More than replacement, the process of addition seems to be taking place within several different N level sets. The richness measure indicates a large increase in the number of Euro-American categories at the N − 1 level (from 5 to 35). The number of Arikara categories increases only slightly (from 34 to 35). The process of addition, as indicated by the category increases, is also suggested by the gain in occurrences at the N level. There are major increases in Euro-American category occurrence in the other personal appearance (interestingly paralleled by an increase in Arikara membership in the same set), scraping, piercing, knapping, containing, and fastening sets. Considering the major changes evidenced by the influx of so many Euro-American categories, and represented in the processes of addition and replacement, it is appropriate to refer to the changes in Period V as indicative of the process of transformation. The assignment of the process of transformation to Period V burials fits the expectation described in Chapter 6. The process of transformation has been described as characteristic of the domestic earthlodge context in Period V. The drastic changes taking place in both domestic and mortuary contexts correlate well with the extensive social and economic changes observed in the ethnohistorical record.

CATEGORY CONTINUITY IN DOMESTIC EARTHLODGES

In the previous discussions in this chapter the emphasis was placed on comparison of changes between one period and the next. In this section some basic trends in artifact change in domestic earthlodges will be examined in relation to all periods. Because domestic earthlodges are the only data set represented adequately in all time periods, other contexts will not be considered here.

The principal reason for examining trends in individual category occurrence through time is to understand in greater detail exactly where in the material assemblage change is actually taking place. As a basic premise, it may be suggested that Euro-American artifact categories that occur as consistent elements in the material assemblage in early periods will be perceived by the Arikaras as integrated and will be more likely to be consistently represented in later periods. The early post-contact periods (II and III) were characterized by replacement and addition to the native material assemblage. The later periods (IV and V) likewise experience addition and replacement, but rejection was also a major process. Periods IV and V are periods of increasing social disruption and increasingly strained trade relations with Euro-Americans. The less disruptive nature of the contact process in Periods II and III might have fostered an easier integration of Euro-goods into native material assemblages. In fact, integration is implied by the processes of addition and replacement. The question is then: Do Euro-American artifact categories that are introduced early tend to be maintained as consistent elements of the material system?

The other side of the above argument has to do with continuity in native artifact categories. Through Period V there are clearly many Arikara artifact categories that maintain continuity. This is to some extent expected considering that some Arikara artifacts have few or no effective Euro-American equivalents that occur regularly in the archaeological record (e.g., grinding stones or shaft abraders). As with Euro-American artifacts, the primary question here is which categories tend to be maintained through time. For the Arikara categories, Period I served as a baseline, therefore, if a category that occurred in Period I or II also occurred in Periods III, IV, and V, it was considered to have continuity. The principal data used to examine continuities in artifact categories are presented in Table 21. This table lists the presence or absence of each artifact category, tabulated by set membership.

To facilitate interpreting trends in category continuities, the N − 1 level categories were divided between basic production and nonproduction categories. Categories that belong to sets such as containing, scraping, and piercing were considered to be related to basic production activities. Other sets such as painting, other personal appearance, and decorating were assigned to the nonproduction group. In general, basic production sets tend to occur more consistently than nonproduction sets. It is therefore probable that continuities will be maintained more frequently in the basic production sets. This was certainly the case in the Arikara sets, but only slightly so in the Euro-American sets. For Arikara basic production categories, 26 showed continuity while 7 did not. For Euro-American basic production categories, 5 showed continuity while 13 did not.

In contrast to the basic production categories, the nonproduction categories, which generally occur less frequently, present a reversal of the continuity trends observed in the basic production categories. Of the Arikara nonproduction categories occurring in Periods I or II, 7 showed continuity while 17 did not. For Euro-American nonproduction categories, continuity was very low, only 2 categories occurring in Periods II or III showed continuity, while 8 categories did not.

In response to the questions posed above, it seems that early introduction of Euro-American categories is a poor indicator of which categories will be maintained through time. Of those categories that do show continuity, the largest proportion are related to basic production activities. This is especially true for the Arikara basic production categories, which overall show a much higher level of continuity than the Euro-American categories. These trends are probably at least partially related to the high frequency of Arikara artifacts and the low

TABLE 21. *Category Occurrences in Periods I–V Organized by N Level Set Membership*

Sets and Categories	Periods I	II	III	IV	V
Containing (Arikara)					
CER (sherds)	X	X	X	X	X
WBO (wood bowls)			X		
Containing (Euro-American)					
EAC (ceramics)	X				X
BGF (bottle glass)					X
OGF (other glass)		X	X		X
IRB (iron buckets)					X
MR (metal containers)				X	X
Scraping (Arikara)					
WKF (worked flakes)	X	X	X	X	X
SC (scrapers)	X	X	X	X	X
SS (shell scrapers)	X				
BOF (bone fleshers)		X	X	X	X
Scraping (Euro-American)					
IF (iron fragment)		X	X		X
CF (copper fragment)		X	X	X	X
BF (brass fragment)			X	X	X
ISC (iron scraper)			X	X	
Cutting (Arikara)					
SCK (scapula knives)	X	X	X	X	X
WKS (worked scapulas)		X	X	X	X
STK (stone knives)	X	X	X	X	X
BKH (bone knife handles)		X	X	X	X
WHA (wood handle)					X
WKF (worked flakes)	X	X	X	X	X
Cutting (Euro-American)					
IK (iron knives)			X	X	
CK (copper knives)		X	X		
BK (brass knives)			X	X	
OMK (other metal knives)					X
MKH (metal knife handles)					X
IF (iron fragments)		X	X		X
CF (copper fragments)		X	X	X	X
BF (brass fragments)			X	X	X

TABLE 21—*continued*

Sets and Categories	Periods				
	I	II	III	IV	V
IKH (iron knife handles)					X
Piercing (Arikara)					
SPP (stone projectile points)	X	X	X	X	X
BPP (bone projectile points)			X	X	X
WBW (wood bows)			X		
BOA (bone awls)	X	X	X	X	
BOP (bone punches)	X	X	X	X	X
NGF (native gun flints)			X	X	X
BFH (bone fishhooks)	X	X		X	
Piercing (Euro-American)					
MG (metal gun fragments)			X		X
IPP (iron projectile points)			X	X	X
CPP (copper projectile points)			X		
BPP (brass projectile points)			X	X	
EAF (Euro-American gun flints)					X
MTA (metal awls)			X	X	
Abrading (Arikara)					
SCSSA (sandstone abraders)	X	X	X	X	X
SCA (scoria abraders)	X	X	X	X	X
Pounding (Arikara)					
HS (hammer stones)	X	X	X	X	X
AS (anvil stones)		X	X		X
MA (mauls)	X	X	X	X	X
SCL (stone club heads)			X		
Painting (Arikara)					
PM (paint mortars)		X			
ST (stone tablets)			X	X	
GSD (ground stone discs)				X	X
BOB (bone brushes)	X		X	X	
BP (brown pigments)	X				
RP (red pigments)	X	X	X	X	X
YP (yellow pigments)	X	X	X	X	
WP (white pigments)	X		X		
GP (green pigments)	X				

Continued on next page

TABLE 21—*continued*

Sets and Categories	Periods I	II	III	IV	V
Knapping (Arikara)					
BOA (bone awls)	X	X	X	X	
BOP (bone punches)	X	X	X	X	X
Knapping (Euro-American)					
MTA (metal awls)			X	X	
Perforating (Arikara)					
BOA (bone awls)	X	X	X	X	
BOP (bone punches)	X	X	X	X	X
Perforating (Euro-American)					
MTA (metal awls)			X	X	
Smoothing (Arikara)					
BPA (bone paddles)		X	X	X	
BOG (bone grainers)	X	X	X	X	X
ULB (ulna beamers)			X		X
SMS (smoothing stones)		X	X	X	X
SHA (shaft sanders)	X	X	X	X	
QUF (quill flatteners)	X		X	X	X
Other Personal Appearance (Arikara)					
CEB (ceramic beads)					X
SP (stone pendants)				X	
BOT (bone tubes)	X	X	X		X
BOC (bone comb)			X		
BPE (bone pendants)		X		X	
DRC (drilled claws)					X
SHP (shell pendants)	X			X	X
SHB (shell beads)	X		X		
SB (stone beads)	X				
Other Personal Appearance (Euro-American)					
CT (copper tubes)		X	X		X
BT (brass tubes)					X
GTB (glass trade beads)			X	X	X
OTB (other trade beads)					X
IB (iron bangles)					X
CB (copper bangles)		X	X	X	X
BB (brass bangles)			X		X

Sets and Categories	Periods				
	I	II	III	IV	V
OMB (other metal bangles)					X
CBE (copper beads)		X	X		
BBE (brass beads)				X	
CC (copper cones)		X	X		
BD (brass discs)					X
SR (silver rings)					X
MER (metal rings)					X
LR (lead rings)					X
MMO (misc. metal ornaments)				X	
Chopping (Arikara)					
CE (celts)	X	X	X	X	
CH (choppers)	X	X	X	X	
Digging (Arikara)					
BFT (bison frontal-horn tool)			X	X	
Digging (Euro-American)					
MM (metal mattocks)					X
Worshiping (Arikara)					
CLP (clay pipes)			X		
STP (stone pipes)				X	X
FO (fossils)			X		X
CP (catlinite pipes)	X	X	X		X
OWC (other worked catlinite)	X		X	X	X
QC (quartz crystals)		X	X		
BSK (bison skull)				X	X
BES (bear skull)				X	
UOB (misc. unusual objects)			X		
Worshiping (Euro-American)					
EAP (ceramic pipes)			X		X
Grinding (Arikara)					
GS (grinding stones)	X	X	X	X	X
Drilling (Arikara)					
SD (stone drills)	X	X	X	X	
Decorating (Arikara)					
BSP (stamp paddles)	X				
BPA (bone paddle)		X	X	X	
QUF (quill flatteners)	X		X	X	X

Continued on next page

TABLE 21—*continued*

Sets and Categories	Periods I	II	III	IV	V
Gaming (Arikara)					
CGP (clay gaming pieces)					X
WKR (worked ribs)	X	X	X	X	X
BOW (bone whistles)			X	X	X
SHD (shell discs)	X		X		
SR (stone rings)	X				
STB (stone balls)			X	X	
Smoking (Arikara)					
CLP (clay pipes)			X		
STP (stone pipes)				X	X
CP (catlinite pipes)	X	X	X		X
Smoking (Euro-American)					
EAP (ceramic pipes)			X		X
Incising (Arikara)					
GR (gravers)	X		X	X	
Straightening (Arikara)					
BSW (bone shaft wrench)	X	X	X	X	X
Fastening (Euro-American)					
IBU (iron buttons)			X		
BBU (brass buttons)					X
OBU (other metal buttons)					X
CRC (copper ring clasps)			X		
Wedging (Euro-American)					
IW (iron wedges)					X
Scooping (Arikara)					
BFT (bison frontal-horn tool)			X	X	
Joining (Euro-American)					
INA (iron nails)				X	X
BRH (brass hinges)					X

frequency of Euro-American artifacts. In particular, the low frequency of Euro-American artifacts certainly makes it difficult to establish trends in artifact category continuities at the N − 1 level.

Another approach to examining artifact continuities can be undertaken at the N level by examining relative addition or deletion of N − 1 level categories in the N level sets. Tables 22 and 23 provide a listing of net changes between periods in the number of N − 1 level categories present in each period. Table 22 deals specifically with Arikara sets and Table 23 deals with Euro-American sets. In both tables, numbers preceded by a plus indicate the number of categories added to the set; those numbers preceded by a minus mark the number deleted from the set. Zeros indicate no change and dashes indicate that the set was not present in a particular period. In these tables, the clearest measure of continuity through time in a set is the presence of zeros in each of the period transitions. This would indicate that no change was taking place in the category membership in a particular set.

In the Arikara changes listed in Table 22, several sets show a high degree of continuity. The sets scraping, abrading, grinding, and straightening show complete continuity in the categories that make up these sets. The sets containing, knapping, perforating, and drilling also show continuity by the addition or subtraction of only one category in the entire chronological sequence. All of these sets fall into the basic production group. The sets that tend to show the greatest fluctuations in category membership occur in the nonproduction group. The relative changes in Arikara set membership tend to support the results of the N − 1 level category analysis discussed above. The greatest level of continuity occurs in the basic production sets, while the least continuity occurs in the nonproduction sets.

In the Euro-American set changes listed in Table 23, there is relatively little continuity indicated in any set. Most sets, whether basic production or nonproduction, show considerable fluctuation in set membership from one period to the next—a clear indication of less continuity in Euro-American sets than in Arikara sets. This observation also supports the results of the N − 1 level category continuity analysis presented above.

The lack of continuity in Euro-American sets probably reflects a

TABLE 22. *Net Changes in Arikara Categories (N –1 Level) Present in N Level Sets*

Sets	Periods			
	I–II	II–III	III–IV	IV–V
Basic Production				
Containing	0	0	0	+1
Scraping	0	0	0	0
Cutting	+2	0	0	+1
Piercing	0	+2	0	–2
Abrading	0	0	0	0
Pounding	+1	+1	–2	+1
Knapping	0	0	0	–1
Perforating	0	0	0	–1
Smoothing	+1	+2	–1	–1
Chopping	0	0	0	–2
Digging	0	+1	0	–1
Grinding	0	0	0	0
Drilling	0	0	0	–1
Straightening	0	0	0	0
Wedging	—	—	—	—
Scooping	0	+1	0	0
Nonproduction				
Painting	–3	+2	0	–3
Other Personal Appearance	–1	+1	0	+1
Worshiping	0	+4	–2	+1
Decorating	–1	+1	0	–1
Gaming	–2	+3	–1	0
Smoking	0	+2	–2	+2
Incising	–1	+1	0	–1
Fastening	—	—	—	—
Joining	—	—	—	—

Note: Those artifact activity sets that tend to show little or no change (0) from one period to the next are the sets illustrating the greatest amount of continuity. Dashes are left where set membership was zero for a particular period transition.

TABLE 23. *Net Changes in Euro-American Categories (N –1 Level) Present in N Level Sets*

Sets	Periods			
	I–II	II–III	III–IV	IV–V
Basic Production				
Containing	0	0	0	+4
Scraping	+2	+2	–1	0
Cutting	+3	+3	–1	0
Piercing	—	+5	–2	+1
Abrading	—	—	—	—
Pounding	—	—	—	—
Knapping	—	+1	0	–1
Perforating	—	+1	0	–1
Smoothing	—	—	—	—
Chopping	—	—	—	—
Digging	—	—	—	+1
Grinding	—	—	—	—
Drilling	—	—	—	—
Straightening	—	—	—	—
Wedging	—	—	—	+1
Scooping	—	—	—	—
Nonproduction				
Painting	—	—	—	—
Other Personal Appearance	+4	+2	–2	+11
Worshiping	—	+1	–1	+1
Decorating	—	—	—	—
Gaming	—	—	—	—
Smoking	—	+1	–1	+1
Incising	—	—	—	—
Fastening	—	+2	-2	+2
Joining	—	—	+1	+1

Note: Those artifact activity sets that tend to show little or no change (0) from one period to the next are the sets illustrating the greatest amount of continuity. Dashes are left where set membership was zero for a particular period transition.

series of factors relating to the process of interaction between the Arikaras and Euro-Americans. First, it should be anticipated that most fluctuations would occur in the Euro-American sets, considering that these sets are often being added to the existing, and more stable, Arikara artifact inventories. Secondly, most of the changes that were anticipated and analyzed in earlier sections of this chapter were inherently considered in relation to Euro-American categories. For instance, the artifact process of rejection, defined for Period IV, dealt principally with changes in Euro-American category prevalence.

CHRONOLOGICAL TRENDS AND Q-ANALYSIS

In the previous analytical sections changes in artifact inventories in Arikara contexts were described either in relation to the five artifact processes or in relation to changes in particular categories or sets through time. In this section the focus shifts towards a more encompassing view of change. Rather than considering change in individual artifact groupings at the N or N − 1 levels, the center of this discussion will be on the "structure" of the artifact inventories and how this structure changes. The principal method employed in this phase of the study is Q-Analysis, the basic ideas of which were introduced in Chapter 7.

There are a number of ways the overall structure of an artifact assemblage might be analyzed. If the objective is to look at change in artifact categories through time, then a simple correlation analysis can be very informative. In Table 15 the mean number of N − 1 level categories per domestic earthlodge are listed by time period, and by examining these changes in the relative richness of categories through time, it is apparent that the mean number of Arikara categories increases from Period I to III and then declines from Period III to VI. In contrast, the Euro-American categories show a more-or-less steady increase. As an example, a Spearman Rank correlation coefficient was calculated for the relationship between periods and the mean number of categories. The calculation produced a negative correlation of 0.314, which illustrates the mild inverse relationship between Arikara and Euro-American artifact categories. The moderate decline in Arikara categories and the steady increase in Euro-American categories parallels the sequence of replacement Toom (1979:176–185) found when comparing lithic tools with their metal counterparts. That Toom's results correspond to the observed relationships, even though he used a different categorical breakdown and different site samples (not all of which were Arikara), provides valuable support for the validity of the sample and methods used here.

From the results of the correlation analysis, the overall changes in Arikara category prevalence can be characterized by the process of Replacement (i.e., as Euro-American categories go up, Arikara categories go down). Although Euro-American categories appear to be replacing Arikara categories, the latter are not decreasing as fast as the former are increasing. The Euro-American sequence, taken by itself, can be characterized by the process of addition (i.e., there are more categories through time).

Although the overall trends presented in Table 15 are clear enough, a thorough analysis must consider the structure of other potential relationships. Spearman's, or other similar correlation coefficients, only look at the interplay of two variables. A multivariate approach to examining the structure of a set of relations would greatly increase the usefulness of an analysis of changing artifact trends. In Chapter 7, Q-Analysis was introduced as a means of explicitly defining the relationships between categories in a hierarchical model. Q-Analysis allows an examination of such complex and multiple relationships, while at the same time avoiding multivariate statistical techniques that may be inappropriate for the analysis of count or binary data. A Q-Analysis was conducted to explore the structure of relations that exist between N level artifact sets in domestic earthlodges. Before describing the results of the analysis, a brief discussion of the techniques and strategies involved in Q-Analysis will be presented.

Q-Analysis has as its principle concern the analysis of the "structure" of relations (Atkin 1978:493). Structure in this case refers to connectivities defined between variables. Q-Analysis has been used to analyze relations within sets of data as diverse as traffic flowing through road intersections (Johnson 1976), disease patterns (Chamberlain 1976), farming systems (Chapman 1984), periodic markets (Johnson and Wanmali 1981), and the game of chess (Atkin and Witten 1975). In archaeology, Aldenderfer (1987) has briefly discussed the use of cover set hierarchies; Evans (1978) has applied Q-Analysis, in a very preliminary way, to an application of Central Place Theory in a case study from the Valley of Mexico; and Gorenflo (1980) has also made a preliminary application of Q-Analysis to the problem of structure in archaeological mortuary data. By its very nature, Q-Analysis has wide application in the social sciences, as attested by these studies.

In its most basic form, Q-Analysis is concerned with the number of positive occurrences of something in an incidence matrix. The positive occurrences are termed vertices and multiple occurrences are viewed as being linked together to form simplicies. Therefore, the connectivity between two variables defines a simplex (σ) in an abstract complex; each simplex defined upon $q + 1$ vertices or points may in turn be characterized as a q-dimensional polyhedron. Thus, a one-simplex is a line connecting two vertices, a two-simplex is a triangle formed by three vertices, and so on (Atkin 1974:23).

A simple example of an incidence matrix and its connectivities may help illustrate the basic idea behind Q-Analysis. Figure 23 presents a hypothetical matrix with four time periods along the top and

		Periods (Verticies)			
		I	II	III	IV
Artifact Categories (Simplicies)	A_1	0	1	1	1
	A_2	1	0	1	1
	A_3	0	1	1	0

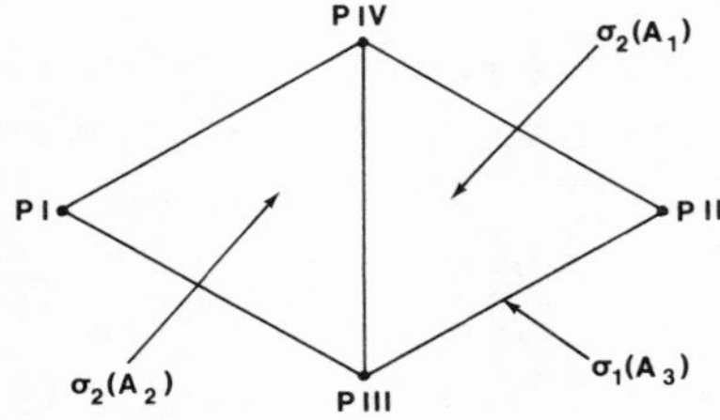

Fig. 23. Hypothetical incidence matrix and corresponding connectivity diagram.

three artifact categories along the side. Below the matrix is a diagram of the connectivities. In the matrix, artifact category A_1 occurs in Periods PII, PIII, and PIV. The connectivities for A_1 therefore define a two-simplex (σ_2) consisting of the PII, PIII, and PIV vertices, as illustrated by the joining lines in the diagram. Artifact category A_2 is also connected via a two-simplex (σ_2) with three periods (PI, PIII, and PIV), thus forming the triangle on the left side of the diagram. Artifact category A_3 is connected to two periods (PII and PIII), which results in a one-simplex (σ_1). Although the diagram does not illustrate this, double linkages occur between PII and PIII and between PIII and PIV. Period PI is the only period with no double linkages and is the least connected to the other periods. This is evident in the incidence matrix by the fact that PI contains only one artifact category (A_2) while the other periods contain two or three. Because PI is only connected by way of a single category (A_2), the period can be viewed as being the most dissimilar, although it does have secondary linkages with PIII and PIV through artifact category A_2. The geometrical diagram defined on the basis of the matrix in Figure 23 is often referred to as the backcloth. Patterns defined on this structural backcloth are termed traffic (Atkin 1978:494; P. Gould 1980:181). In the case of the above example, the traffic would be quantities of objects in each of the artifact categories. The addition of other periods or artifact categories would have an effect on the structure of the backcloth, potentially altering the entire relation.

In the example (Fig. 23), if the number of variables in the incidence matrix were increased, it would soon become impossible to represent graphically the n-dimensional polyhedron necessary to show the connectivities. Fortunately, there are other ways to display the structure of the matrix. To do this, the dimensionality of each simplex, as well as the dimensionality of the connectivities, must be defined. The dimension of a simplex, and the connectivities between simplicies, is referred to as Q. The Q value is one less than the number of vertices in the simplex (a single point is defined as a zero-simplex, σ_0). In Figure 24, the structure of the incidence matrix in Figure 23 is presented as a bar chart. This chart shows that PI has the least in common with the other periods and that PIII is the most interconnected. The

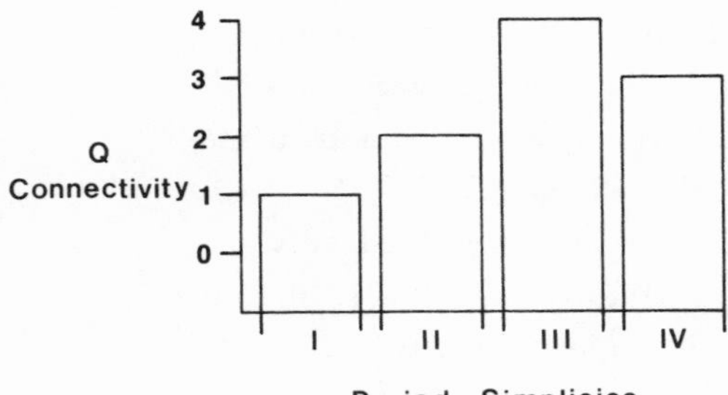

Fig. 24. Maximum Q-connectivities between simplicies for hypothetical incidence matrix.

use of a bar chart allows a quick graphic representation of the relationship between periods and can also be used with larger matrices (Chapman 1984:220). Alternatively, it is possible to provide a more detailed presentation by using a symmetrical matrix that shows the number of connectivities shared by each period.

The number of Q-connectivities displayed in the bar chart or a symmetrical matrix is one measure of the structure of the set of relations, in that it presents the number of connectivities for the principal variable. The bar chart does not, however, fully describe the pattern of connectivities on the backcloth. Another measure that aids in further describing the structure of the relation is the *eccentricity* of each simplex (Atkin 1974:33–35, 1981:90–91; Gatrell 1983:159; P. Gould 1981: 288–289):

$$\text{Ecc} = \frac{\hat{q} - \check{q}}{\check{q} + 1}$$

In this equation $\hat{q}$, (top q) is defined as the number of Q-connectivities for each simplex and $\check{q}$ (bottom q) is the level of the Q-connectivity at which the simplex joins another simplex. The lower the eccentricity of a simplex, the more interrelated it is. If the eccentricity value is zero, then the simplex is maximally connected and shares all its vertices with other simplicies. Higher eccentricity values, in turn, denote simplicies that are poorly connected.

With this brief digression on the methods of Q-Analysis, it is now possible to proceed to an application of the technique using the domestic earthlodge data. Within the data, contrasts have been drawn between changes in the relative proportion of the occurrence of Arikara

TABLE 24. *Euro-American Artifact Set Polyhedral Eccentricities for Time Periods*

Polyhedron	Top q	Bottom q	Eccentricity
Period I	0	0	0.00
Period II	4	4	0.00
Period III	9	7	0.25
Period IV	8	7	0.13
Period V	10	7	0.38

and Euro-American artifacts. These changes have been related to one or more of the five artifact processes in previous portions of this chapter. The objective will now be to consider some aspects of the interrelations (i.e., connectivities) between periods.

The following analysis is based on the N level Euro-American and Arikara artifact data set presented in Tables 13 and 14. Because of the small sample of domestic earthlodges from Period VI, it has been excluded from the analysis. The first part of the analysis was based on the Euro-American data set in Table 14. The results of this analysis are presented in Figure 25 and Table 24. Figure 25 shows the number of Q-connectivities that exist between the five periods. Period I is the least connected, as might be expected, since this is the precontact

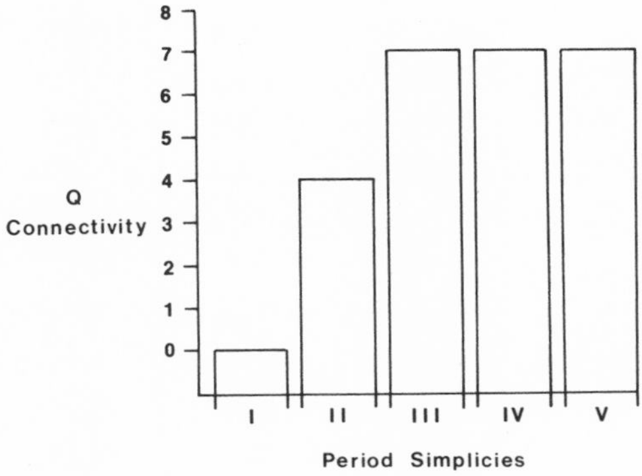

Fig. 25. Maximum Q-connectivities between simplicies for N level Euro-American artifact sets in domestic earthlodges.

period and there are almost no Euro-American artifacts. Period II is only moderately connected, but Periods III, IV, and V each exhibit seven connectivities. This means they are interrelated by way of eight N level artifact sets present in other periods. Considering there are a total of twelve possible connectivities, seven reflects only a moderate similarity between Periods III, IV, and V. The moderate similarity seems to be a function of the presence of some artifact sets that occur infrequently.

The eccentricities of the simplicies are presented in Table 24. As might be anticipated from Figure 25, Periods I and II have 0.0 eccentricities by virtue of their being "faces" of other simplicies. Periods III, IV, and V do show some moderate eccentricity with Periods III and V being the most eccentric or divergent.

This pattern of connectivities supports both the interpretations suggested by the bar chart, and the richness comparisons made for individual periods in the earlier part of this chapter. For Period III, it was suggested that addition was the dominant artifact process; for Period V, the processes of addition and replacement were subsumed under the process of transformation as the dominant means of characterizing the changes in artifact categories. Both Periods III and V were undergoing considerable Addition to their artifact inventories. Between these two periods, Period IV was undergoing rejection of Euro-American categories. The relatively high eccentricities for Periods III and V reflect addition to their artifact inventories, in that more sets are present that are not part of Period I, II, or IV. Periods III and V therefore reflect the greatest amount of divergence.

The structure of the Arikara N level sets is much more interrelated than that for the Euro-American sets. The eccentricities are presented in Table 25. The eccentricity values for all five periods are zero. This indicates that the Arikara sets are much more highly connected than were the Euro-American sets, and suggests that through all five periods there was a general continuity of many Arikara sets.

Although the high level of connectivity expressed by the zero eccentricities in Table 25 describes an important characteristic of the time periods, there is also a way of looking at relations that might be obscured at this general level. It may be remembered that the Q-Analy-

TABLE 25. *Arikara Artifact Set Polyhedral Eccentricities for Time Periods*

Polyhedron	Top q	Bottom q	Eccentricity
Period I	20	20	0.00
Period II	19	19	0.00
Period III	21	21	0.00
Period IV	21	21	0.00
Period V	17	17	0.00

sis is based on a binary matrix. This means that rarely occurring items carry the same importance as items that are found in every earthlodge. A Q-Analysis technique for examining relationships that might be expressed by a certain level of artifact occurrence is the introduction of a "slicing parameter" (Atkin 1974:34–35). The slicing parameter defines all values in the matrix below a certain number as absent and those above that number as present.

The Arikara data set was subdivided using a slicing parameter of one; thus, values above one were considered present and those below one were considered absent. This had the effect of eliminating some sets that were represented only rarely and focusing on those that were more frequently a consistent part of domestic artifact inventories. Figure 26 presents a bar chart showing the structure of the Q-connectivities. As was the case before application of the slicing parameter, the N level Arikara sets continue to be highly connected. The eccentricities for each period are presented in Table 26. Periods I, II, and IV show zero eccentricity, while Periods III and V show moderate amounts. This is similar to the results for the Euro-American sets, in which Periods III and V had the greatest level of eccentricity. Here too, Periods III and V are the most divergent in the composition of their artifact assemblages from the standpoint of the more frequently occurring sets. Period III was certainly a major period for the acceptance of Euro-American categories, but it was also the period with the greatest number of Arikara categories. The divergent nature of Period V also corresponds to a characterization of this period as undergoing the process of trans-

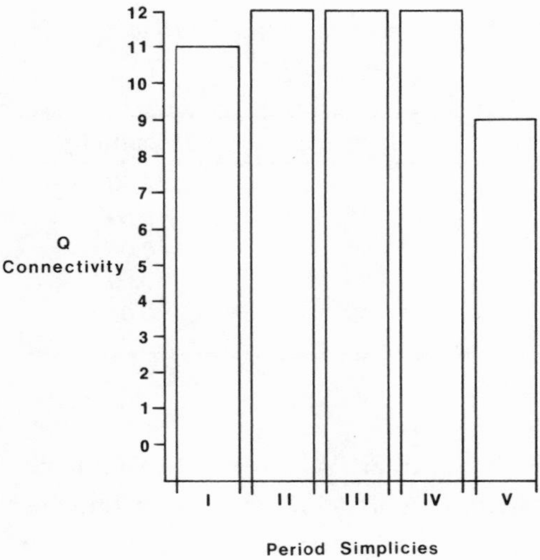

Fig. 26. Maximum Q-connectivities between simplicies for N level Arikara artifact sets in domestic earthblodges (slicing parameter = 1).

formation. In the case of Periods III and V, the use of a slicing parameter has helped identify the eccentricities of the Arikara sets for these periods and aided in linking them to similar relationships taking place in the Euro-American sets, as well as identifying patterns evident from other measures.

TABLE 26. ***Arikara Artifact Set Polyhedral Eccentricities for Time Periods with Application of a Slicing Parameter***

Polyhedron	Top q	Bottom q	Eccentricity
Period I	11	11	0.00
Period II	12	12	0.00
Period III	14	12	0.15
Period IV	12	12	0.00
Period V	11	9	0.20

EVALUATION

The objective of this chapter was to consider the evidence that might support or refute the expectations presented in Chapter 6 (summarized in Table 4). In Chapter 6 a series of five linking arguments (described as artifact processes) were defined as a means of specifying how Arikara material assemblages might change in correspondence with major shifts in the interaction process. The potential relationships are complex and several lines of evidence have been brought to bear.

The principal analysis results are presented in Table 27. Due to limited archaeological data available for ceremonial earthlodges, artifact processes were not assigned to this context, therefore ceremonial lodges are not represented in this table. The absence of burial samples for some periods also means that an artifact process was not identified for all periods. In most regards (excluding the discrepancies produced by gaps in the data sets), there is a close correspondence between the expectations developed from the ethnohistorical data and the analysis results based on the archaeological data.

The most consistent data set was the domestic earthlodge context, and the results fit the expectations for every period. Period I (late

TABLE 27. ***Relationship of Artifact Processes to Historical Sequence Based on Analysis Results***

Period	Maintain	Add	Replace	Reject	Transform
I	D, C, M				
II	M	D, M	D		
III	D, M	D, M	D		
IV	D			D	
V					D, M
VI					

Note: D = Domestic earthlodges; C = Ceremonial earthlodges; M = Mortuary (burials).

1500s–1680) is precontact and is assumed to be dominated by the process of maintenance, although it should also be recognized that complex interactions were also taking place between native groups prior to Euro-American contact. Period I does not enter into the analysis except as a point from which to consider the level of change in subsequent periods (from the point of view of direct Euro-American contact). Period II (1681–1725) was the first period evaluated in terms of the artifact process expectations. This period was found to be dominated by the process of addition of Euro-American artifact categories with some replacement of Arikara categories. Period III (1726–1775) was dominated by the process of addition, but maintenance and replacement were also important mechanisms. In Period IV (1776–1805), rejection of Euro-American categories dominated changes in the domestic artifact context. Period V (1806–1835) exhibited extensive addition and replacement and was characterized as being dominated by the process of transformation. Because of small sample size, no determination was made for Period VI (1836–1862).

The other primary archaeological data set was the burials. Cemetery samples were available for Periods II, III, and V. In Period II it was expected that the mortuary context would be dominated by the process of addition, as was the case for the domestic earthlodge context. Instead, addition played only a minor role in artifact inventory changes, while the dominant process was maintenance. Clearly the burial context was less susceptible to change in the composition of the material assemblage than was anticipated. The same pattern was observed in Period III (primarily maintenance with some addition), which matches the expectations for that period.

In Period V, the expectations were also confirmed. The relative continuity in the composition of the mortuary context continued through Period III (and perhaps Period IV), but the major shift in relations with Euro-Americans that occurred in Period V also correlated with a major shift in the archaeological context. In this respect, the Period V mortuary context was dominated by the process of transformation.

An analysis of continuities in individual artifact categories in domestic earthlodges indicated a relatively high level of continuity in

Arikara categories, but a relatively low level in Euro-American categories. In the Arikara categories, most of the continuity occurred in artifacts assigned to the basic production group, which is not too surprising considering that while economic patterns did change over the nearly 200 years encompassed by this study, the basic patterns of day-to-day life were not altered beyond recognition.

In addition to considering individual artifact categories or the processes affecting each period, the Q-Analysis of the structure of the artifact assemblages, among other things, pointed to the divergent character of Periods III and V in the domestic earthlodge context. These periods, in particular, can be viewed as times of major change in the composition of at least the domestic artifact assemblage.

The analysis of artifact categories has illustrated something of the relationship between social and material change. Although, to some extent, all of the artifact processes probably played a role in all periods, the goal has been the definition of dominant processes. The analysis has been successful in this goal.

9

CONCLUSIONS

> We must expect that for the offering, acceptance or refusal of every trait there are simultaneous causes of an economic, structural, sexual and religious nature.
>
> GREGORY BATESON

The basic question this study has attempted to address is: What is the nature of the relationship between changes in the Arikara archaeological material record and changes in the historic social interaction context? To answer this question a wide variety of ethnohistorical and archaeological data were brought into use. The results of the analyses indicate that there is, in fact, a clear and definable relationship between historical change and alterations in the composition of the material record, at least among the Arikaras.

DISCUSSION AND SUMMARY

In Chapter 1, it was argued that to understand the relationship between material change and social change in the contact period, it was of

---

The epigraph that appears above is from Bateson 1935:179.

utmost importance to consider the motivations and inherent cultural logic held by the groups coming into contact. The process of culture contact with Euro-Americans has often been described as native peoples *reacting* to the impositions of the dominant and powerful Euro-Americans. What is said about the native peoples is often in terms of their responses to circumstances largely beyond their control. This approach tends to obscure the validity of the native culture and limit the potential for understanding the causal structure of the interaction process, either from a native or an intruder point-of-view. In the Arikara case, contact with Euro-Americans was framed not only by the economics of the fur trade but also by Arikara perceptions and expectations about who the Euro-Americans were and how they might be anticipated to behave. For more than a century after direct contact with Euro-Americans the nature of the interaction continued to be largely controlled by Arikara views of exchange as a social process and Arikara notions of how to place Euro-Americans within a cultural context.

The attitudes and motivations of the Arikaras and Euro-Americans went through several changes in the eighteenth and first half of the nineteenth centuries. Perhaps more than anything, the nature of these changes tell the story of how and why the once numerous and powerful Arikara villages were reduced by 1862 to a single village fragment, clinging for protection to similar remnants of Mandan and Hidatsa villages. Considering the general archaeological orientation of this study it was important to link the cultural motivations and interactions of the contact period with an understanding of the role of goods as a part of the process of change. In many cases objects function in a social and symbolic way to define cultural categories by providing physical referents. To understand the process of adoption or exclusion of various kinds of goods requires considering the role objects play. From a technological standpoint, Euro-American goods were not always superior to native items. And even in cases in which the technical advantages of Euro-goods seems clear (at least from a eurocentric point of view), native peoples did not always beat a path to the traders' door (e.g., Elkin 1951:164–165). Trade goods were adopted and used in different contexts in different ways. Local cultural constraints worked to structure what was or was not a useful item, or one that might be readily incorporated. In order for an object to be adopted as part of a material inventory it must make some kind of cultural sense, and through time the Euro-goods that became part of Arikara material usage changed in conjunction with redefinitions of the interaction process itself.

The interaction process as it relates to material change is an integral aspect of Arikara society and culture. The Arikaras were a horticultural group who lived in semi-autonomous earthlodge villages on the Missouri River in South Dakota during protohistoric and historic times. The structure of Arikara culture was integrated by a complex set of status rankings. There was a hierarchical system of hereditary chiefs that not only had authority over the workings of each village, but also came together as a group council under the supervision of a single overall chief. Other social groupings included secular and medicine societies. The Arikaras were cultivators of maize, beans, squash, tobacco, and other crops, although they also conducted extensive bison hunts. The women did the cultivating and were the owners of the harvest. For generations before contact with Europeans, the Arikara villages had served as nodes on a vast intergroup trade network. This placed the Arikaras in the position of middlemen, a role they continued to enjoy for a considerable time after European contact.

The established role of the Arikaras as trade middlemen played an important part in their perceptions of the newly arrived Europeans. But even more important was the undeniable "otherness" of these strangers, and particularly of the goods they brought. Especially at first, the Arikaras saw the Europeans as spiritlike beings who owned many magical objects (for example, guns, magnifying glasses, and thermometers). Many of the strange objects were given as gifts to the chiefs, although most could be acquired by ordinary people through trade. In the time of initial contact, to acquire the goods of the Europeans meant also to acquire some of the power held by these strangers. During the eighteenth century the Arikaras acquired some familiarity with Europeans, and by the time of the major Spanish trade expeditions in the 1790s and Lewis and Clark in the first decade of the nineteenth century, Europeans and the newly arrived Americans had slipped earthward from their former spiritlike status. Even so, Lewis and Clark, for instance, were accorded high ranking considerations as representatives of the "Great Father" who lived in Washington. Supernatural powers were still ascribed to at least some Euro-Americans, although many traders behaved in a socially offensive and ignorant manner (from the Arikara perspective). The naturalist, Bradbury, for instance, while out collecting plants was mistaken for a medicine man. The painter Kurz was believed to have caused a major epidemic in the 1850s by painting the portraits of some individuals. Belief in supernatural powers held by Euro-Americans was maintained late into the nineteenth century. Through time, however, there was a more or less steady decline in the high estimation held of Euro-Americans.

As for the Euro-Americans, they had developed their own misunderstandings about the Arikaras. Much of it had to do with the disjuncture between Euro-American and Arikara perceptions of the nature of trade. For the traders, exchange was for profit and the desire for accumulation of wealth. While the Arikaras were shrewd and experienced traders, they tended to place trade in a social context tied to a complex set of obligations. The Arikaras were more interested in acquiring prestige and honor than in acquiring goods. The traders generally tried to extract themselves from social obligations, in order to keep exchange on a businesslike footing. By the early part of the nineteenth century, the Arikaras had become more hostile toward Euro-Americans. The traders and other visitors to the Upper Missouri were certainly not blind to the worsening relations, and as a result the Arikaras acquired a very unsavory reputation among many Euro-Americans. A good part of these hostile interactions were the result of events taking place on the other side of the Atlantic Ocean. Fluctuations in demands for furs were dictated by fashion and by such events as the War of 1812. The onset of hostile relations between the Arikaras and Euro-Americans corresponds closely to the drop in European demand for furs and the decreasing availability of fur resources in the Arikara area.

In earlier chapters fluctuations in fur trade economics were linked with the attitudes and motivations of the Arikaras and Euro-Americans as well as other economic, demographic, and social considerations, to construct a history of interaction for this particular segment of the Upper Missouri. This history of interaction was then used as an analytical framework for looking at changes in the archaeological record.

Six chronological periods were defined, dating from the late 1500s to 1862. Period I (late 1500s–1680) is the period immediately prior to direct contact. Archaeological material assemblages from this period contain virtually no European trade items. Period II (1681–1725) is the first period for which the presence of Europeans can be documented. During this period the number of Europeans making their way to the Upper Missouri was very small. The perception of Europeans as having spiritlike qualities was certainly an important factor in trade relations. The initial direct trade was almost certainly conducted under very amiable conditions. During Period III (1726–1775) there was a moderate increase in the amount of contact and the amount of Euro-goods available on the Upper Missouri and trade relations between the Arikaras and Europeans continued to be good. In Period IV (1776–1805) the availability of trade goods continued to increase and the Arikaras became firmly embroiled in the economics of the fur trade. Hyde (1952:48) considers this as a major time of crisis for the Arikaras, brought on by continued depopulation due to epidemics and warfare with the Dakotas. The decline in population and the subsequent amalgamation of village remnants produced a social crisis. The combination of village remnants meant that several village-level chiefs were now representing factions within a single village, resulting in the disruption of the social hierarchy. Archaeological evidence from a study of social ranking from burials points to a shift towards a less structured set of social distinctions with the loss of some rank categories (O'Shea 1984:271). Trade relations in Period IV continue to be good, but there is an increasing recognition that Europeans are not so supernatural after all.

As far as trade interactions were concerned, Period V (1806–1835) was a major period of change. There was a reversal of the generally good relations that had previously been the rule. It was a time in which Arikara access to furs was decreasing, international demand for furs was likewise in decline, and traders were consistently trying to bypass the Arikaras. Arikara hostilities towards Euro-Americans increased sharply.

The final time frame is Period VI (1836–1862). This is a period in which relations normalize to some extent, and the Arikaras increase their participation in trade by conducting extensive bison hunts and processing bison robes for sale.

The six time periods were compared to the archaeological data through the use of a series of five linking arguments. The five arguments or artifact processes are referred to as maintenance, replacement, addition, rejection, and transformation. Maintenance was linked to a cultural system maintaining coherence in the face of external pressures. Replacement involves the exchange of an Arikara artifact category for a Euro-American category of an equivalent functional nature. Replacement is related to maintenance, and is assumed to characterize a social context undergoing relatively little change, but open to the free exchange of goods. The process of addition, on the other hand, implies that new categories are being added and the overall composition or structure of the material assemblage is changing and is associated with a social system undergoing change. Rejection is just as the name implies, artifact categories available for inclusion, or that were once part of an assemblage, are no longer incorporated. A culture that is rejecting inclusion of new categories is assumed to be experiencing a high level of cultural coherence. Transformation is the final process. It is considered to be a drastic version of the combined characteristics of addition and replacement and indicates significant social changes are underway. Expected relationships between the five processes and each of the chronological periods are defined in Table 4.

The major part of the analysis conducted in Chapter 8 was a comparison of expected relationships with those evident from the archaeological data, which consisted of 22 sites divided among the six periods. The intention was to select sites that could be used to form data sets for an analysis of domestic earthlodges, ceremonial earthlodges, and burials. Because of the importance of context in determining the composition of an artifact assemblage, it was decided that the three contexts should be considered separately. In some cases the sample size was too small to make a valid comparison. For this reason, ceremonial earthlodges were not included in the major portion of the analysis. In all cases, the sample size for Period VI was inadequate, thus this period was excluded from most portions of the analysis.

The primary analysis consisted of comparing trends in occurrence of artifact categories between periods. A set of 164 categories was defined for inclusion in the analysis (Table 12). These categories formed the lowest level (N −1) in a hierarchical cover set model that was developed to explicitly present the relationships that exist in any hierarchical classification. The general strategy behind the development of this cover set model was a technique called Q-Analysis. Q-Analysis involves the use of cover sets to examine the "structure" of relationships. In the cover set model, it was recognized that sets have overlapping memberships, consequently at upper levels in the hierarchy, artifact categories may be counted more than once. That is, at higher order levels, referring to activities rather than objects, some items may function within more than one activity. Much of the analysis was conducted at the N level, which included a set of 25 activities, such as cutting, drilling, and grinding.

The results of the analysis for domestic earthlodges revealed a close correspondence between the expected relationships and those observed in the archaeological data. Period I (pre-contact) was assumed to be in a state of maintenance. In post-contact Period II, several artifact categories underwent addition to the existing inventory with some replacement of existing categories. Period II was a time of good trade relations in which the Arikaras viewed the Europeans as having supernatural powers, not only because of their actions and appearance, but also because of the exotic objects they had for trade. These factors helped produce an environment of open exchange in which the Arikaras readily accepted the unusual tools they were offered.

In Period III, addition was the dominant process, but maintenance and replacement were also at work. Period III is similar to Period II in that trade relations were good and the Arikaras were open to the acceptance of Euro-goods. There was, however, relatively little replacement of native categories. This shift towards adding to, but not altering, the composition of the basic artifact assemblage may have presaged what was to take place in the next period, namely rejection rather than addition of Euro-goods.

In Period IV there was a considerable rejection of Euro-American categories. The rejection of Euro-goods in Period IV is interpreted as part of a trend indicating a shift in Arikara interactions with Euro-Americans. The process of rejection defined in Period IV represents an important reversal of the normally expected trend in the adoption of Euro-American goods by native groups. It is often assumed that, through time, as access to trade goods increases, there will be a relatively steady increase of Euro-goods in native contexts, while items of local manufacture decrease. The results from Period IV indicate that the inverse relationship between native and Euro-goods does not hold true for the Arikaras in this time frame. The principal reason for Arikara rejection of Euro-American trade items in Period IV may be related to changing views of the traders and changing attitudes towards the interaction process itself. Traders were being viewed as less supernatural, the novelty of the goods they brought had faded, and the trade process itself was becoming less social and more businesslike. Although Arikara access to trade goods was probably increasing steadily, the socially motivated response was to adopt fewer Euro-goods and to even eliminate some goods that had been used in earlier times. The reduction in the use of European derived goods can be viewed as a strategy for mitigating the effects of European contact. By maintaining or returning to a more nearly native-based material assemblage, the material component of social action was normalized and strengthened at a time when the Arikaras were becoming less powerful and the Europeans were becoming more powerful and disruptive. In part, the trends observed may be thought of as a mechanism to maintain cultural boundaries. To be sure, not all European trade goods were eliminated and many kinds of trade items continued to be represented in domestic earthlodges. Such things as guns, knives, and many metal items had become routine aspects of Arikara material usage and were certainly not declining in usage. Furthermore, it is worth remembering that the domestic earthlodge context is not a complete picture of the Arikara material inventory, but the view from the earthlodge indicates a reduction in the use of Euro-goods and presumably, an attempt by the Arikaras, whether conscious or unconscious, to control change.

The next time frame is Period V. This period illustrated a major shift in the composition of the material assemblage. Unlike Period IV, this period was not characterized by rejection; instead, transformation was the dominant process and is assumed to be related to a social context undergoing redefinition. This seems to be what was happening to the Arikaras in Period V. The declining economics of the fur trade in Period V placed the Arikaras in an especially untenable position. They greatly increased hostilities towards Euro-Americans while at the same time attempting to maintain their status as trade middlemen. The strategy adopted by the Arikaras in Period V, as far as material usage was concerned, was the opposite of that employed in Period IV. Rather than removing Euro-American items from their material assemblages, they readily accepted many kinds of trade goods. Addition to the material assemblage and replacement of existing native artifact categories by Euro-American equivalents expanded to the point of significantly altering the composition of the artifact inventory. Period V may have been something of a point of no return for the Arikaras. Although, maintaining the semblance of an operating social system, they were in fact being manipulated by the ever-increasing Euro-American presence. The Arikaras were losing the ability to define their own course of action. It is suggested that the rapid adoption of many Euro-goods in Period V is an indication of the decline in Arikara autonomy.

Period VI is the final phase in the sequence. There was little archaeological information for this period, therefore it was not appropriate to assign artifact processes for this period. However, the expectations based on ethnohistorical information suggest that addition and replacement may also have been the dominant processes for domestic earthlodges in this period. The trend away from native manufactures evident in Period V seems to be continued in Period VI, along with further declines in Arikara autonomy and social cohesiveness.

The second major context for consideration in the analysis was burials. Burial samples were available only for Periods II, III, and V. In Period II there were very few European artifacts included as burial associations. Those that did occur were found exclusively in the other personal appearance set, and consisted entirely of glass, copper, and brass beads. The frequent occurrence of European beads in burials in Period II corresponded with a relatively high occurrence in domestic earthlodges. But subsistence-oriented tools found in domestic structures were not found in the burial sample for Period II. The obvious implication is that the criteria determining the nature of burial offerings were different than the criteria determining artifact usage in other contexts. For Period II there was little or no indication that Euro-goods played any important role in status distinctions (see Orser 1980a and O'Shea 1984 for extensive discussion of Arikara status markers in burials). The principal Period II artifact process was maintenance with addition as a minor process. Clearly a ceremonial context such as burials was less susceptible to change than a domestic context, which may be viewed as an indication of Arikara social cohesiveness in Period II.

For the Period III burials there were again relatively few Euro-goods in the sample; those that were present were again primarily in the other personal appearance set. As in Period II, maintenance was the dominant process and was also associated with some addition. It was expected that addition would be a major process, as was the case with Period II domestic earthlodges, but clearly the burial context was less susceptible to change than had been anticipated. The Arikaras were still operating as a autonomous system that had not experienced extensive social stress.

The final burial sample was representative of Period V. Unlike Periods II and III, Period V was not dominated by maintenance. There were instead major changes in the composition of the artifact assemblage, as was also the case in the domestic earthlodge sample. Transformation was the dominant process for Period V. O'Shea's study of status indicators in Arikara burials provides some insight to the significance of the transformation of the artifact assemblage in Period V (1984:276).

> Most of the types that do exhibit some association by age or sex in their occurrence at Leavenworth [Period V] are trade goods. During the span of time between the Larson [a site dating to Period II and early Period III] and Leavenworth sites, there is a weakening of the structured use of artifacts within the funerary complex and a partial replacement of native goods by trade materials as significant grave inclusions. . . . This pattern of change in artifact associations and usage belies the major impact of trade materials on Arikara culture and the perceptual shift that appears to have accompanied these goods.

It is interesting to note that O'Shea's study of burial practices and this analysis of changing artifact inventories essentially agree that the incorporation of Euro-goods in Period V was having an impact on the material expression of Arikara social categories. O'Shea's results also lend support to the identification of Period V as a time of change and redefinition of Arikara interactions with Euro-Americans. The social disruptions suggested by changes in the mortuary context are paralleled by changes in the domestic earthlodge context discussed above.

Following the analysis of artifact processes and contexts in Chapter 8, a brief consideration of trends in category continuities through time was presented. This analysis examined the manner in which change in each period was defined materially, by looking at what categories were making up the component of change. It was suggested that Euro-American artifact categories introduced early in the contact process would more readily be considered consistent aspects of the material assemblage. Therefore, change would occur more frequently in categories that had not been present in the earlier periods. It was found that Arikara basic production categories tended to show a high level of continuity, but Euro-American basic production categories did not. In Arikara and Euro-American nonproduction categories there was a low degree of continuity, probably because of the low frequency of occurrence for these artifacts. In general it did not seem that early introduction of Euro-American artifact categories was a good indicator of which categories would occur consistently through time.

In the final portion of Chapter 8, a Q-Analysis was conducted to examine the overall "structure" of the relationships that characterized the differences and similarities between each of the periods for the domestic earthlodge sample. Because of the comparatively incomplete representation of the chronological sequence in the burial samples, only domestic earthlodges were used. The results of the Q-Analysis show that the Euro-American artifact inventories for Periods III and V were relatively divergent or dissimilar from the other periods. That is, Periods III and V were least interconnected with the other periods. This seems to be a reflection of the fact that these were the major periods of addition, therefore, a number of categories were present that were not part of other periods.

For Arikara artifact sets at the same level of Q-Analysis as Euro-American sets, the results indicated native artifact inventories were highly interconnected and presented a relatively uniform pattern.

However, with the application of a slicing parameter of one (explained in Chapter 8), the structure of interconnectivities for Arikara artifact sets reflects a pattern similar to that for Euro-American sets. The measure of divergence indicated Periods III and V were once again the least connected. For Arikara artifact sets, it is apparent that these two periods were times of change in the artifact assemblages. Period III had the greatest number of artifact categories of any period and Period V has been repeatedly recognized as a period of major change. In this case, change in the material assemblage resulted in a less cohesive structure, as might be expected during a process of redefinition of the role of different kinds of artifacts.

IMPLICATIONS

The principal results of the analysis indicate that, at least in the case of the Arikaras, it is possible to construct a fairly strong link between certain kinds of historical processes and associated archaeological assemblages. This in itself is an encouraging indication that meaningful patterning does exist at this level of analysis in the archaeological record. It would, however, be premature to assume that the links defined here could be applied to other cases without first considering the nature of the social and historical contexts. Because different cultures operate under a variety of ideological and conceptual frameworks in the interaction process, it may be expected that an equally diverse set of potential responses exists. For instance, in Period III, Arikara domestic earthlodge material assemblages were undergoing a combination of the artifact processes maintenance, addition, and replacement. Addition was the dominant process for this period and was hypothesized as being related to a social system experiencing stress and change. There is, however, no reason to assume that addition is related to social stress in a different culture. The things that define social stress in a culture may, within limits, be culture specific, and are highly variable and largely undefined. In whatever way change or stress might be defined, at least the material correlates can almost certainly be expected to differ.

cited above, in that it is applied under limited and very controlled circumstances. Furthermore, it is not an attempt to correlate material and social change at a general undifferentiated level. From an individual artifact class point of view it would, for instance, be useful to establish the link between items known to be of consistent worth, or that were in demand on the basis of a cultural preference alone, with the observed archaeological usage of these objects. For example, do items that were known to be highly in demand continue to be used regardless of fluctuations in availability or other factors? The answer to such a question would be valuable, but of course it must also be recognized that it is incorrect to speak of an item as having been preferred on the basis of cultural factors alone, if by cultural factors, only ideological or symbolic constraints are considered. Economic considerations must also be taken into account as part of the mechanisms that control demand as well as the ability to purchase. A major point of this study has been to illustrate that both cultural and economic considerations are inseparable aspects of the interaction process.

Although it would be interesting to archaeologically trace specific kinds of objects that were known to be in demand, the ethnohistorical documentation tends to be vague, listing only the most general object categories, such as knives, hoes, beads, or vermilion. A potential source of more detailed information is the fur company trade inventories. Beginning with the first decade of the nineteenth century there are several sources that list goods being traded on the Upper Missouri (for example, Missouri Historical Society 1822). Some of the goods mentioned in these sources were probably traded to the Arikaras, but which ones or how much cannot be determined. During the same period that trade inventories become available as information sources, archaeological data are on the decline. Even if archaeological data were available, the trade inventories would only be useful for making general statements.

Along with examining variability in the demand or availability of individual types of artifacts, it is important to consider straightforward factors associated with material/social relations in a synchronic context. A study of modern material culture usage might provide insights unavailable in the ethnohistoric or archaeological record. A study by

Hayden and Cannon (1984) has examined a synchronic case in three present-day Maya Highland communities. Their study examined "how material items relate to social, economic and demographic characteristics of household inhabitants" (Hayden and Cannon 1984:1). While their study provides many important insights, probably their most consequential conclusion is the simple realization that material and socioeconomic relationships are extremely complex. This seems to be one of the principal ethnoarchaeological messages for the prehistorian. Other studies, such as Gelburd's (1978) study of Dobe !Kung San culture change or Robbins and Pollnac's (1977) analysis of the relationship between artifacts and cultural modernity in Buganda, point to the significance of such fine-grained considerations as the age makeup and economic pursuits of individuals living in a household. These studies, and many others have made important contributions to a theory of material change, but there is still a long way to go, for now the complexity of the issue is just beginning to come to light.

As Bateson observed in the epigraph to this chapter, material change in culture contact (but applicable to material change in general) is intertwined with a variety of human constraints. To find only one of these constraints on which to pin the bulk of causality is a task beyond the bounds of reality. The key to interpreting material change is in developing an approach that recognizes cultural relevance while also considering the interplay of economic, social, demographic, and other factors.

APPENDIX

TABULAR PRESENTATION OF ARIKARA AND EURO-AMERICAN DATA

TABLE A-1. *Arikara Artifact Counts per Period for N –1 Level Categories in Domestic Earthlodges*

Categories	Periods (with numbers of lodges)					
	I (10)	II (14)	III (14)	IV (14)	V (9)	VI (4)
CER	13649	8823	15396	9147	4556	300
CEB	0	0	0	0	1	0
CLP	0	0	3	0	0	0
CGP	0	0	0	0	1	0
SP	0	0	0	2	0	0
STP	0	0	0	1	2	0
SPP	59	62	98	37	22	1
SC	202	209	259	108	18	0
GR	1	0	2	2	0	0
SD	7	9	7	6	0	0
WKF	110	67	34	63	54	0
STK	177	121	108	85	29	2
MA	4	4	8	9	18	0
CE	1	3	2	2	0	0
SSA	44	50	122	18	14	0
SCA	44	33	47	23	41	0
SHA	22	14	26	6	0	0
BOA	35	38	18	47	0	0
BOF	0	1	9	16	19	0
BSW	1	8	11	10	13	0
BHS	0	0	0	0	0	0
BFT	0	0	15	8	0	0
SCH	9	25	37	109	23	0
SCK	33	18	7	39	2	0
WKS	0	97	256	10	10	0
BOP	4	6	12	3	1	0
BOG	2	5	23	11	4	0
BOT	14	3	20	0	3	0
BOB	2	0	9	2	0	1
BBE	0	2	3	2	1	0
BOC	0	0	1	0	0	0
BFH	2	1	0	11	0	0
BPA	0	1	1	4	0	0
BKH	0	4	19	3	2	0
WKR	1	3	2	6	15	1
QUF	2	0	1	6	1	0
BOW	0	0	1	2	1	0
BPE	0	1	0	2	0	0
BPP	0	0	5	4	1	0

TABLE A-1—*continued*

Categories	Periods (with numbers of lodges)					
	I (10)	II (14)	III (14)	IV (14)	V (9)	VI (4)
DRC	0	0	0	0	2	0
ULB	0	0	1	0	3	0
ULP	0	1	0	0	0	0
BSP	2	0	0	0	0	0
SS	28	0	0	0	0	0
SHP	1	0	0	3	1	1
SHB	2	0	2	0	0	0
SHD	1	0	1	0	0	0
SCL	0	0	1	0	0	0
HS	40	32	68	49	10	0
AS	0	10	2	0	2	0
PM	0	5	0	0	0	0
SB	1	0	0	0	0	0
ST	0	0	1	1	0	0
SR	1	0	0	0	0	0
GS	8	24	31	14	78	1
GSD	0	0	0	2	2	0
STB	0	0	1	2	0	0
CH	10	50	18	29	0	0
SMS	0	3	13	5	1	2
NGF	0	0	1	2	2	0
WBW	0	0	1	0	0	0
WBO	0	0	0	0	1	0
WHA	0	0	0	0	1	0
BP	2	0	0	0	0	0
RP	25	12	10	13	2	0
YP	11	3	17	1	0	0
WP	2	0	10	0	0	0
GP	2	0	0	0	0	0
FO	0	0	4	0	1	0
CP	1	5	3	0	2	0
OWC	7	0	5	1	4	0
CAP	0	0	0	0	0	0
QC	0	3	6	0	0	0
BSK	0	0	0	1	1	0
BES	0	0	0	1	0	0
UOB	0	0	10	0	0	0

Note: See TABLE 12 for key to abbreviations.

TABLE A-2. *Euro-American Artifact Counts per Period for N –1 Level Categories in Domestic Earthlodges*

Categories	Periods (with numbers of lodges)					
	I (10)	II (14)	III (14)	IV (14)	V (9)	VI (4)
EAC	3	0	0	0	1	1
EAP	0	0	1	0	4	0
MTA	0	0	2	1	0	0
IN	0	0	2	0	1	0
MG	0	0	1	0	6	0
EAH	0	0	0	0	0	1
IPP	0	0	7	2	13	1
CPP	0	1	6	0	0	0
BPP	0	0	2	10	0	0
MPP	0	0	0	0	3	0
IF	0	3	36	0	80	0
CF	0	12	9	3	17	0
BF	0	0	14	5	8	1
BGF	0	0	0	0	2	1
OGF	0	2	2	0	17	12
IT	0	0	0	0	1	0
CT	0	1	2	0	1	0
BT	0	0	0	0	1	0
EAF	0	0	0	0	5	3
GTB	0	0	5	2	26	104
OTB	0	0	0	0	2	0
INA	0	0	0	1	3	12
IS	0	0	0	0	0	1
IB	0	0	0	0	1	0
CB	0	1	1	1	2	0
BB	0	0	1	0	9	0
OMB	0	0	0	0	15	0
IK	0	0	6	1	0	0
CK	0	1	2	0	0	0
BK	0	0	3	7	0	0
OMK	0	0	0	0	2	1
MKH	0	0	0	0	1	0
IKH	0	0	0	0	1	0
IBU	0	0	1	0	0	0
BBU	0	0	0	0	3	0

TABLE A-2—*continued*

Categories	Periods (with numbers of lodges)					
	I (10)	II (14)	III (14)	IV (14)	V (9)	VI (4)
OBU	0	0	0	0	3	0
CBE	0	55	3	0	0	0
BBE	0	0	0	1	0	0
MF	0	0	0	0	0	1
MHA	0	0	0	0	0	1
IC	0	0	0	0	0	1
ICO	0	0	0	0	0	3
CC	0	4	1	0	0	0
MR	0	0	0	1	3	1
TC	0	0	0	0	0	2
IRB	0	0	0	0	1	0
BRB	0	0	0	0	0	0
CRC	0	0	1	0	0	0
BD	0	0	0	0	1	0
CD	0	0	0	0	1	0
BRR	0	0	0	0	1	0
IR	0	0	0	0	3	0
IRR	0	0	0	0	1	0
BR	0	0	0	0	1	0
SR	0	0	0	0	1	0
MER	0	0	0	0	1	0
LR	0	0	0	0	1	0
MMO	0	0	0	1	0	0
MM	0	0	0	0	1	0
MFH	0	0	0	0	2	0
IRC	0	0	0	0	0	0
ISC	0	0	2	2	0	0
IW	0	0	0	0	3	0
BRH	0	0	0	0	1	0

Note: See TABLE 12 for key to abbreviations.

TABLE A-3a. *Arikara Artifact Data for Domestic Earthlodges (Periods I–II)*

Record	Site	Name	Unit	OCCUP*	PERIOD	CER	CEB	CLP
1	39ST9	LaRoche	H1E	1	I	939	0	0
2	39ST9	LaRoche	H2E	2	I	940	0	0
3	39ST232	LaRoche (Bower's)	H1	2	I	1850	0	0
4	39DW234	Molstad	H1	1	I	1678	0	0
5	39DW234	Molstad	H2	1	I	1349	0	0
6	39ST9	LaRoche	H1C	1	I	94	0	0
7	39ST232	LaRoche (Bower's)	H5	1	I	725	0	0
8	39ST9	LaRoche	H4B	1	I	1142	0	0
9	39ST9	LaRoche	H3B	1	I	429	0	0
10	39ST9	LaRoche	H1A	1	I	4503	0	0
11	39LM26	Oacoma	F80	1	II	296	0	0
12	39LM26	Oacoma	F90	1	II	165	0	0
13	39LM26	Oacoma	F11	1	II	377	0	0
14	39WW7	Swan Creek	H3	1	II	953	0	0
15	39WW7	Swan Creek	H1	2	II	1185	0	0
16	39LM26	Oacoma	F2	1	II	317	0	0
17	39LM26	Oacoma	F70	1	II	766	0	0
18	39LM26	Oacoma	F60	2	II	321	0	0
19	39LM26	Oacoma	F35	1	II	197	0	0
20	39LM218	Black Partizan	F11	2	II	3083	0	0
21	39CH45	Hitchell	L2	1	II	431	0	0
22	39CH45	Hitchell	L1	1	II	196	0	0
23	39CH45	Hitchell	L3	1	II	214	0	0
24	39CH45	Hitchell	L5	1	II	322	0	0

* The variable OCCUP refers to whether an earthlodge is defined as long-term occupation (2) or short-term occupation (1).

Note: See TABLE 12 for key to abbreviations.

TABLE A-3a—*continued*

Variables															
CGP	SP	STP	SPP	SC	GR	SD	WKF	STK	MA	CE	SSA	SCA	SHA	BOA	BSW
0	0	0	1	20	0	0	6	10	0	0	2	2	0	0	0
0	0	0	7	5	0	0	6	9	1	1	3	2	0	2	0
0	0	0	6	40	0	3	18	35	1	0	6	9	4	5	0
0	0	0	10	25	1	0	0	12	0	0	0	0	1	6	1
0	0	0	7	7	0	1	0	16	0	0	0	4	1	9	0
0	0	0	1	4	0	0	3	3	1	0	1	1	2	0	0
0	0	0	0	14	0	0	8	14	0	0	1	2	0	0	0
0	0	0	12	21	0	0	13	14	0	0	8	4	0	3	0
0	0	0	0	12	0	0	9	10	0	0	11	6	0	1	0
0	0	0	15	54	0	3	47	54	1	0	12	14	14	9	0
0	0	0	0	13	0	0	4	0	0	0	7	2	0	1	1
0	0	0	0	5	0	0	2	2	0	0	1	0	0	1	0
0	0	0	2	11	0	3	30	5	0	0	11	2	2	4	0
0	0	0	7	10	0	1	3	7	0	0	0	9	0	9	0
0	0	0	11	16	0	4	6	12	1	1	0	8	5	3	0
0	0	0	3	1	0	0	7	1	0	0	1	1	0	0	0
0	0	0	3	8	0	0	3	2	0	0	2	1	0	1	1
0	0	0	2	13	0	0	5	0	0	0	10	1	0	5	0
0	0	0	1	4	0	0	0	0	0	0	1	1	0	0	2
0	0	0	25	87	0	0	7	78	0	2	2	4	7	8	4
0	0	0	0	3	0	1	0	2	1	0	7	0	0	0	0
0	0	0	4	9	0	0	0	2	1	0	3	1	0	3	0
0	0	0	0	5	0	0	0	4	1	0	4	0	0	1	0
0	0	0	4	24	0	0	0	6	0	0	1	3	0	2	0

Continued on next page

TABLE A-3a—*continued*

Record	Variables														
	BHS	BFT	SCH	SCK	WKS	BOP	BOG	BOT	BOB	BBE	BOC	BFH	BPA	BKH	WKR
1	0	0	1	2	0	0	0	0	0	0	0	1	0	0	0
2	0	0	1	2	0	0	0	4	0	0	0	0	0	0	0
3	0	0	3	8	0	0	1	10	0	0	0	1	0	0	0
4	0	0	0	2	0	2	0	0	0	0	0	0	0	0	0
5	0	0	0	3	0	1	0	0	0	0	0	0	0	0	0
6	0	0	1	0	0	0	0	0	0	0	0	0	0	0	0
7	0	0	0	4	0	0	0	0	0	0	0	0	0	0	0
8	0	0	1	4	0	0	0	0	0	0	0	0	0	0	0
9	0	0	0	3	0	1	0	0	0	0	0	0	0	0	0
10	0	0	2	5	0	0	1	0	2	0	0	0	0	0	1
11	0	0	1	0	8	0	0	0	0	0	0	1	0	2	0
12	0	0	0	0	0	0	0	0	0	0	0	0	0	0	0
13	0	0	1	1	11	0	0	0	0	0	0	0	0	2	0
14	0	0	6	3	3	0	0	0	0	0	0	0	0	0	0
15	0	0	4	4	8	0	0	2	0	0	0	0	0	0	3
16	0	0	0	0	0	0	0	0	0	0	0	0	0	0	0
17	0	0	2	0	2	0	1	0	0	1	0	0	0	0	0
18	0	0	5	0	11	0	0	0	0	0	0	0	0	0	0
19	0	0	0	0	0	0	0	0	0	0	0	0	0	0	0
20	0	0	0	5	51	6	4	1	0	1	0	0	1	0	0
21	0	0	1	1	1	0	0	0	0	0	0	0	0	0	0
22	0	0	5	3	0	0	0	0	0	0	0	0	0	0	0
23	0	0	0	1	1	0	0	0	0	0	0	0	0	0	0
24	0	0	0	0	1	0	0	0	0	0	0	0	0	0	0

TABLE A-3a—*continued*

Variables														
QUF	BOW	BPE	BPP	DRC	ULB	ULP	BSP	OWB	WKA	WMS	SS	SHP	SHB	SHD
1	0	0	0	0	0	0	0	1	0	0	0	0	1	0
0	0	0	0	0	0	0	1	0	0	1	2	0	0	0
0	0	0	0	0	0	0	0	2	0	0	6	0	0	1
0	0	0	0	0	0	0	0	1	0	0	2	0	0	0
0	0	0	0	0	0	0	0	0	0	0	0	0	0	0
0	0	0	0	0	0	0	0	1	0	1	7	0	0	0
0	0	0	0	0	0	0	0	0	0	0	1	0	0	0
0	0	0	0	0	0	0	0	0	0	0	3	0	1	0
1	0	0	0	0	0	0	0	0	0	4	0	0	0	0
0	0	0	0	0	0	0	1	1	0	10	7	1	0	0
0	0	0	0	0	0	0	0	0	0	0	0	0	0	0
0	0	0	0	0	0	0	0	1	2	0	0	0	0	0
0	0	0	0	0	0	0	0	1	6	0	0	0	0	0
0	0	1	0	0	0	0	0	1	1	0	0	0	0	0
0	0	0	0	0	0	0	0	2	0	0	0	0	0	0
0	0	0	0	0	0	0	0	0	0	0	0	0	0	0
0	0	0	0	0	0	0	0	0	1	0	0	0	0	0
0	0	0	0	0	0	0	0	2	2	0	0	0	0	0
0	0	0	0	0	0	0	0	0	0	0	0	0	0	0
0	0	0	0	0	0	1	0	15	6	2	0	0	0	0
0	0	0	0	0	0	0	0	0	0	0	0	0	0	0
0	0	0	0	0	0	0	0	0	0	0	0	0	0	0
0	0	0	0	0	0	0	0	2	1	0	0	0	0	0
0	0	0	0	0	0	0	0	1	0	0	0	0	0	0

Continued on next page

TABLE A-3a—*continued*

Record	Variables														
	SCL	HS	AS	PM	SB	ST	SR	GS	GSD	STB	CH	SMS	NGF	OWS	WBW
1	0	1	0	0	0	0	0	0	0	0	4	0	0	0	0
2	0	2	0	0	0	0	0	1	0	0	0	0	0	0	0
3	0	22	0	0	0	0	0	4	0	0	4	0	0	0	0
4	0	1	0	0	0	0	0	0	0	0	0	0	0	0	0
5	0	2	0	0	0	0	0	2	0	0	0	0	0	0	0
6	0	1	0	0	0	0	0	0	0	0	0	0	0	0	0
7	0	1	0	0	0	0	0	1	0	0	1	0	0	0	0
8	0	5	0	0	0	0	0	0	0	0	0	0	0	0	0
9	0	1	0	0	1	0	0	0	0	0	0	0	0	0	0
10	0	4	0	0	0	0	1	0	0	0	1	0	0	0	0
11	0	1	0	0	0	0	0	0	0	0	3	0	0	0	0
12	0	1	0	0	0	0	0	0	0	0	2	0	0	0	0
13	0	6	0	0	0	0	0	3	0	0	21	0	0	0	0
14	0	2	0	0	0	0	0	0	0	0	1	0	0	0	0
15	0	7	0	0	0	0	0	2	0	0	3	1	0	0	0
16	0	2	0	0	0	0	0	0	0	0	3	0	0	0	0
17	0	1	0	0	0	0	0	0	0	0	2	0	0	0	0
18	0	1	0	0	0	0	0	2	0	0	6	0	0	0	0
19	0	1	0	0	0	0	0	1	0	0	1	0	0	0	0
20	0	2	0	3	0	0	0	7	0	0	6	0	0	10	0
21	0	3	7	0	0	0	0	3	0	0	0	2	0	2	0
22	0	2	2	0	0	0	0	1	0	0	0	0	0	0	0
23	0	2	0	1	0	0	0	1	0	0	0	0	0	9	0
24	0	1	1	1	0	0	0	4	0	0	2	0	0	12	0

TABLE A-3a—*continued*

Variables															
WBO	WHA	WKW	BP	RP	YP	WP	GP	FO	CP	OWC	CAP	QC	BSK	BES	UOB
0	0	0	0	0	0	0	0	0	0	0	0	0	0	0	0
0	0	0	0	0	0	0	0	0	0	1	0	0	0	0	0
0	0	0	0	3	2	0	0	0	1	3	0	0	0	0	0
0	0	0	0	0	0	0	0	0	0	0	0	0	0	0	0
0	0	0	0	0	0	0	0	0	0	0	0	0	0	0	0
0	0	0	0	0	0	0	0	0	0	1	0	0	0	0	0
0	0	0	1	0	9	0	0	0	0	0	0	0	0	0	0
0	0	0	1	0	0	0	0	0	0	1	0	0	0	0	0
0	0	0	0	12	0	0	1	0	0	0	0	0	0	0	0
0	0	0	0	10	0	2	1	0	0	1	0	0	0	0	0
0	0	0	0	0	0	0	0	0	0	0	0	0	0	0	0
0	0	0	0	0	0	0	0	0	0	0	0	0	0	0	0
0	0	0	0	0	0	0	0	0	0	0	0	0	0	0	0
0	0	0	0	0	0	0	0	0	0	0	0	0	0	0	0
0	0	0	0	0	0	0	0	0	2	0	0	2	0	0	0
0	0	0	0	0	0	0	0	0	0	0	0	0	0	0	0
0	0	0	0	0	0	0	0	0	0	0	0	0	0	0	0
0	0	0	0	0	0	0	0	0	0	0	0	0	0	0	0
0	0	0	0	3	0	0	0	0	0	0	0	0	0	0	0
0	0	0	0	5	3	0	0	0	1	0	0	1	0	0	0
0	0	0	0	0	0	0	0	0	1	0	0	0	0	0	0
0	0	0	0	1	0	0	0	0	1	0	0	0	0	0	0
0	0	0	0	3	0	0	0	0	0	0	0	0	0	0	0
0	0	0	0	0	0	0	0	0	0	0	0	0	0	0	0

TABLE A-3b. *Arikara Artifact Data for Domestic Earthlodges (Periods III–IV)*

Record	Site	Name	Unit	Variables				
				OCCUP*	PERIOD	CER	CEB	CLP
25	39LM220	Crazy Bull	H1	1	III	213	0	0
26	39ST15	Indian Creek	F1	1	III	155	0	0
27	39ST6	Buffalo Pasture	F30	2	III	1843	0	0
28	39ST14	Phillips Ranch	F8	1	III	1905	0	1
29	39ST14	Phillips Ranch	F2	2	III	1404	0	0
30	39ST14	Phillips Ranch	F20	1	III	956	0	0
31	39ST6	Buffalo Pasture	F1	1	III	3278	0	0
32	39ST14	Phillips Ranch	F4	1	III	251	0	1
33	39ST6	Buffalo Pasture	F4	1	III	2570	0	1
34	39LM215	Peterson	F1	1	III	949	0	0
35	39ST17	Fort George	H6	1	III	395	0	0
36	39ST17	Fort George	H3	2	III	645	0	0
37	39ST1	Cheyenne River	F60	1	III	504	0	0
38	39ST17	Fort George	H4	1	III	328	0	0
39	39HU26	Spotted Bear	H1	1	IV	844	0	0
40	39CO34	Red Horse Hawk	L8	1	IV	1097	0	0
41	39CO34	Red Horse Hawk	L11	2	IV	497	0	0
42	39CO34	Red Horse Hawk	L6	2	IV	449	0	0
43	39CO34	Red Horse Hawk	L13	1	IV	388	0	0
44	39CO34	Red Horse Hawk	L10	1	IV	875	0	0
45	39HU26	Spotted Bear	H4	2	IV	1674	0	0
46	39CO34	Red Horse Hawk	L12	1	IV	603	0	0
47	39CO34	Red Horse Hawk	L14	1	IV	490	0	0
48	39HU26	Spotted Bear	H5	1	IV	211	0	0
49	39CO34	Red Horse Hawk	L4	1	IV	190	0	0
50	39HU26	Spotted Bear	H3	1	IV	907	0	0
51	39HU26	Spotted Bear	H2	1	IV	315	0	0
52	39CO34	Red Horse Hawk	L15	1	IV	607	0	0

* The variable OCCUP refers to whether an earthlodge is defined as long-term occupation (2) or short-term occupation (1).

Note: See TABLE 12 for key to abbreviations.

TABLE A-3b—*continued*

Variables															
CGP	SP	STP	SPP	SC	GR	SD	WKF	STK	MA	CE	SSA	SCA	SHA	BOA	BSW
0	0	0	4	16	0	0	0	5	0	0	0	2	1	0	0
0	0	0	1	8	0	0	0	1	0	0	1	0	0	0	0
0	0	0	28	37	1	0	1	13	0	0	26	7	6	0	2
0	0	0	3	10	0	0	4	8	1	1	2	7	3	0	1
0	0	0	0	4	0	0	1	5	0	0	0	2	2	0	0
0	0	0	10	38	0	0	1	13	0	0	3	1	3	2	1
0	0	0	11	20	0	5	1	6	0	0	22	5	1	6	4
0	0	0	7	13	0	0	0	3	2	0	4	2	2	2	0
0	0	0	16	26	0	0	6	11	0	0	23	8	7	2	2
0	0	0	10	63	0	1	0	16	1	0	11	5	0	1	0
0	0	0	0	2	0	0	2	3	2	0	7	3	0	1	0
0	0	0	2	15	0	0	15	16	1	0	12	2	0	1	0
0	0	0	3	2	0	1	1	3	0	1	2	1	1	0	1
0	0	0	3	5	1	0	2	5	1	0	9	2	0	3	0
0	0	0	6	18	0	1	0	14	0	0	2	3	0	4	1
0	0	0	5	11	0	1	11	7	2	0	1	4	0	2	0
0	1	0	1	4	0	0	3	3	4	0	1	4	0	1	0
0	0	0	1	4	0	2	8	6	0	0	0	2	0	0	0
0	1	0	2	3	0	0	5	1	0	1	0	1	0	0	0
0	0	0	1	5	0	0	3	2	0	0	0	0	0	3	0
0	0	0	2	22	0	1	15	16	0	0	6	1	6	8	5
0	0	0	0	2	1	0	2	3	0	0	0	0	0	0	0
0	0	0	0	5	1	0	2	4	2	0	0	0	0	0	0
0	0	0	1	3	0	0	0	1	0	0	0	0	0	4	0
0	0	0	2	0	0	0	1	1	0	0	0	1	0	3	0
0	0	0	8	19	0	1	7	20	0	1	7	5	0	13	4
0	0	0	7	9	0	0	5	6	0	0	1	1	0	8	0
0	0	1	1	3	0	0	1	1	1	0	0	1	0	1	0

Continued on next page

TABLE A-3b—*continued*

Record	BHS	BFT	SCH	SCK	WKS	BOP	BOG	BOT	BOB	BBE	BOC	BFH	BPA	BKH	WKR
25	0	0	0	1	2	1	0	0	0	0	0	0	0	0	0
26	0	0	2	0	3	0	0	0	0	0	0	0	0	0	0
27	0	1	1	0	33	3	3	1	2	0	0	0	0	3	0
28	0	3	0	2	57	1	0	1	1	0	0	0	0	0	0
29	0	0	0	1	4	1	0	0	0	1	0	0	0	1	0
30	0	0	0	0	21	0	0	1	0	0	0	0	0	1	0
31	0	7	2	0	54	1	4	5	2	2	0	0	0	5	0
32	0	0	0	0	9	0	0	0	0	0	0	0	0	0	0
33	0	2	1	1	72	4	13	10	1	0	1	0	0	8	0
34	0	0	6	1	0	1	2	1	0	0	0	0	0	0	0
35	0	1	1	0	0	0	1	0	3	0	0	0	0	0	0
36	0	1	18	0	0	0	0	0	0	0	0	0	0	0	0
37	0	0	1	0	1	0	0	0	0	0	0	0	0	0	0
38	0	0	5	1	0	0	0	1	0	0	0	0	1	1	2
39	0	1	18	6	0	0	0	0	1	0	0	9	0	0	0
40	0	1	14	1	0	1	1	0	0	1	0	0	1	0	1
41	0	3	5	7	5	0	1	0	0	0	0	0	2	1	1
42	0	0	4	4	0	0	1	0	0	0	0	0	0	0	0
43	0	0	6	2	0	1	0	0	0	0	0	0	0	0	0
44	0	2	13	1	0	0	5	0	0	0	0	0	0	2	1
45	0	0	9	1	0	0	0	0	0	0	0	1	0	0	0
46	0	1	7	3	0	0	0	0	0	0	0	0	1	0	1
47	0	0	2	1	0	0	2	0	0	0	0	0	0	0	1
48	0	0	2	0	0	0	0	0	0	0	0	0	0	0	0
49	0	0	3	7	5	1	0	0	0	0	0	0	0	0	0
50	0	0	11	2	0	0	0	0	0	0	0	1	0	0	0
51	0	0	6	0	0	0	0	0	0	0	0	0	0	0	0
52	0	0	9	4	0	0	1	0	1	1	0	0	0	0	1

TABLE A-3b—*continued*

Variables														
QUF	BOW	BPE	BPP	DRC	ULB	ULP	BSP	OWB	WKA	WMS	SS	SHP	SHB	SHD
0	0	0	0	0	0	0	0	0	0	0	0	0	1	0
0	0	0	0	0	0	0	0	0	0	0	0	0	1	0
0	0	0	2	0	0	0	0	14	5	0	0	0	0	0
0	0	0	1	0	1	0	0	22	1	0	0	0	0	0
0	0	0	0	0	0	0	0	4	2	0	0	0	0	0
0	0	0	0	0	0	0	0	0	1	0	0	0	0	0
0	1	0	1	0	0	0	0	21	5	0	0	0	0	0
0	0	0	0	0	0	0	0	3	1	0	0	0	0	0
0	0	0	1	0	0	0	0	46	3	0	0	0	0	0
1	0	0	0	0	0	0	0	0	0	0	0	0	0	0
0	0	0	0	0	0	0	0	0	1	0	0	0	0	0
0	0	0	0	0	0	0	0	1	2	0	0	0	0	0
0	0	0	0	0	0	0	0	8	1	0	0	0	0	1
0	0	0	0	0	0	0	0	2	0	0	0	0	0	0
0	0	0	1	0	0	0	0	0	0	0	0	0	0	0
4	0	0	0	0	0	0	0	1	0	0	0	0	0	0
0	1	0	0	0	0	0	0	1	4	0	0	0	0	0
1	0	0	0	0	0	0	0	1	0	0	0	0	0	0
0	0	0	0	0	0	0	0	4	8	0	0	0	0	0
0	0	0	0	0	0	0	0	2	0	0	0	2	0	0
0	0	0	0	0	0	0	0	0	0	1	0	0	0	0
1	0	0	0	0	0	0	0	1	0	0	0	1	0	0
0	0	0	0	0	0	0	0	2	1	0	0	0	0	0
0	1	0	1	0	0	0	0	0	0	0	0	0	0	0
0	0	1	0	0	0	0	0	0	0	0	0	0	0	0
0	0	0	2	0	0	0	0	0	3	3	0	0	0	0
0	0	0	0	0	0	0	0	0	3	0	0	0	0	0
0	0	1	0	0	0	0	0	0	1	0	0	0	0	0

Continued on next page

TABLE A-3b—*continued*

Record	Variables														
	SCL	HS	AS	PM	SB	ST	SR	GS	GSD	STB	CH	SMS	NGF	OWS	WBW
25	0	0	0	0	0	0	0	0	0	0	1	0	0	0	0
26	0	1	0	0	0	0	0	0	0	0	0	0	0	1	0
27	0	7	1	0	0	0	0	2	0	0	4	0	0	29	1
28	0	2	0	0	0	0	0	6	0	0	2	7	0	20	0
29	0	0	0	0	0	0	0	0	0	0	1	1	0	7	0
30	0	2	0	0	0	0	0	0	0	0	1	4	0	23	0
31	0	21	0	0	0	0	0	4	0	0	4	0	0	32	0
32	0	3	0	0	0	0	0	0	0	0	0	1	0	22	0
33	1	18	1	0	0	0	0	6	0	0	3	0	0	32	0
34	0	4	0	0	0	0	0	0	0	0	0	0	0	0	0
35	0	1	0	0	0	1	0	5	0	0	0	0	0	0	0
36	0	3	0	0	0	0	0	3	0	1	0	0	1	0	0
37	0	3	0	0	0	0	0	0	0	0	2	0	0	6	0
38	0	3	0	0	0	0	0	5	0	0	0	0	0	0	0
39	0	6	0	0	0	0	0	2	0	0	3	0	0	0	0
40	0	3	0	0	0	0	0	6	0	2	0	0	0	0	0
41	0	1	0	0	0	0	0	2	0	0	0	0	0	0	0
42	0	0	0	0	0	1	0	0	0	0	0	0	1	0	0
43	0	0	0	0	0	0	0	2	0	0	0	0	0	0	0
44	0	0	0	0	0	0	0	0	0	0	0	0	0	0	0
45	0	15	0	0	0	0	0	0	0	0	9	0	0	0	0
46	0	1	0	0	0	0	0	0	2	0	0	0	0	0	0
47	0	0	0	0	0	0	0	0	0	0	0	0	0	0	0
48	0	2	0	0	0	0	0	1	0	0	1	0	0	0	0
49	0	0	0	0	0	0	0	0	0	0	0	0	1	0	0
50	0	11	0	0	0	0	0	1	0	0	9	3	0	0	0
51	0	10	0	0	0	0	0	0	0	0	7	2	0	0	0
52	0	0	0	0	0	0	0	0	0	0	0	0	0	0	0

TABLE A-3b—*continued*

Variables															
WBO	WHA	WKW	BP	RP	YP	WP	GP	FO	CP	OWC	CAP	QC	BSK	BES	UOB
0	0	0	0	0	0	0	0	0	2	0	0	4	0	0	0
0	0	0	0	0	0	0	0	0	0	0	0	0	0	0	0
0	0	0	0	2	2	3	0	1	0	3	0	0	0	0	4
0	0	0	0	0	0	0	0	0	0	0	0	0	0	0	2
0	0	0	0	0	0	0	0	0	0	0	0	0	0	0	0
0	0	0	0	3	1	1	0	0	0	0	0	0	0	0	1
0	0	0	0	0	2	0	0	0	0	0	0	0	0	0	0
0	0	0	0	0	0	0	0	0	0	0	0	0	0	0	1
0	0	0	0	2	9	3	0	0	0	1	0	0	0	0	1
0	0	0	0	0	0	0	0	0	0	0	0	0	0	0	0
0	0	2	0	1	1	1	0	2	0	1	0	0	0	0	0
0	0	0	0	1	1	1	0	0	0	0	0	1	0	0	0
0	0	0	0	0	0	0	0	1	0	0	0	0	0	0	0
0	0	0	0	1	1	1	0	0	1	0	0	1	0	0	1
0	0	0	0	2	0	0	0	0	0	1	0	0	0	0	0
0	0	0	0	0	0	0	0	0	0	0	0	0	0	0	0
0	0	0	0	0	0	0	0	0	0	0	0	0	0	0	0
0	0	0	0	1	0	0	0	0	0	0	0	0	0	0	0
0	0	0	0	0	0	0	0	0	0	0	0	0	0	0	0
0	0	0	0	0	0	0	0	0	0	0	0	0	0	0	0
0	0	0	0	2	0	0	0	0	0	0	0	0	0	0	0
0	0	0	0	0	0	0	0	0	0	0	0	0	0	0	0
0	0	0	0	1	0	0	0	0	0	0	0	0	0	0	0
0	0	0	0	1	0	0	0	0	0	0	0	0	0	0	0
0	0	0	0	1	0	0	0	0	0	0	0	0	1	1	0
0	0	0	0	4	1	0	0	0	0	0	0	0	0	0	0
0	0	0	0	0	0	0	0	0	0	0	0	0	0	0	0
0	0	0	0	1	0	0	0	0	0	0	0	0	0	0	0

TABLE A-3C. *Arikara Artifact Data for Domestic Earthlodges (Periods V–VI)*

Record	Site	Name	Unit	Variables				
				OCCUP*	PERIOD	CER	CEB	CLP
53	39CO9	Leavenworth	L20	1	V	1067	0	0
54	39ST50	None	F3	2	V	415	0	0
55	39CO9	Leavenworth	L3	1	V	1095	1	0
56	39CO9	Leavenworth	L23	1	V	559	0	0
57	39CO9	Leavenworth	L47	1	V	241	0	0
58	39CO9	Leavenworth	L40	1	V	303	0	0
59	39ST50	None	F13	2	V	413	0	0
60	39CO9	Leavenworth	L7	1	V	268	0	0
61	39CO9	Leavenworth	L2	1	V	195	0	0
62	32ME16	Star Village	F1	1	VI	291	0	0
63	32ME16	Star Village	F5	1	VI	0	0	0
64	32ME16	Star Village	F8	1	VI	9	0	0
65	32ME16	Star Village	F3	1	VI	0	0	0

* The variable OCCUP refers to whether an earthlodge is defined as long-term occupation (2) or short-term occupation (1).

Note: See TABLE 12 for key to abbreviations.

TABLE A-3c—*continued*

Variables															
CGP	SP	STP	SPP	SC	GR	SD	WKF	STK	MA	CE	SSA	SCA	SHA	BOA	BSW
0	0	1	1	4	0	0	0	0	2	0	0	3	0	0	4
0	0	0	0	2	0	0	0	7	1	0	6	6	0	0	2
0	0	0	16	9	0	0	47	19	3	0	0	0	0	0	0
0	0	1	0	1	0	0	2	0	3	0	0	2	0	0	1
0	0	0	1	0	0	0	2	0	1	0	3	14	0	0	3
0	0	0	2	2	0	0	2	0	4	0	0	3	0	0	3
0	0	0	1	0	0	0	0	3	1	0	1	10	0	0	0
0	0	0	1	0	0	0	0	0	0	0	0	0	0	0	0
1	0	0	0	0	0	0	1	0	3	0	4	3	0	0	0
0	0	0	1	0	0	0	0	2	0	0	0	0	0	0	0
0	0	0	0	0	0	0	0	0	0	0	0	0	0	0	0
0	0	0	0	0	0	0	0	0	0	0	0	0	0	0	0
0	0	0	0	0	0	0	0	0	0	0	0	0	0	0	0

Continued on next page

TABLE A-3c—*continued*

Record	Variables														
	BHS	BFT	SCH	SCK	WKS	BOP	BOG	BOT	BOB	BBE	BOC	BFH	BPA	BKH	WKR
53	0	0	3	0	1	0	1	0	0	0	0	0	0	0	3
54	0	0	3	0	5	1	0	0	0	0	0	0	0	1	1
55	0	0	0	0	0	0	0	0	0	0	0	0	0	0	0
56	0	0	1	0	0	0	1	1	0	0	0	0	0	0	0
57	0	0	4	0	2	0	0	0	0	0	0	0	0	0	7
58	0	0	7	0	0	0	0	0	0	1	0	0	0	0	1
59	0	0	4	2	2	0	1	1	0	0	0	0	0	1	0
60	0	0	1	0	0	0	1	1	0	0	0	0	0	0	2
61	0	0	0	0	0	0	0	0	0	0	0	0	0	0	1
62	0	0	0	0	0	0	0	0	0	0	0	0	0	0	1
63	0	0	0	0	0	0	0	0	0	0	0	0	0	0	0
64	0	0	0	0	0	0	0	0	0	0	0	0	0	0	0
65	0	0	0	0	0	0	0	0	1	0	0	0	0	0	0

TABLE A-3c—*continued*

Variables														
QUF	BOW	BPE	BPP	DRC	ULB	ULP	BSP	OWB	WKA	WMS	SS	SHP	SHB	SHD
1	1	0	0	0	2	0	0	17	2	0	0	0	0	0
0	0	0	0	0	0	0	0	1	3	0	0	0	0	0
0	0	0	0	0	0	0	0	18	1	0	0	0	0	0
0	0	0	0	0	0	0	0	3	3	0	0	0	0	0
0	0	0	1	1	0	0	0	0	0	0	0	0	0	0
0	0	0	0	0	0	0	0	8	2	1	0	0	0	0
0	0	0	0	0	0	0	0	0	0	0	0	0	0	0
0	0	0	0	1	1	0	0	7	0	0	0	1	0	0
0	0	0	0	0	0	0	0	0	0	0	0	0	0	0
0	0	0	0	0	0	0	0	0	0	0	0	1	0	0
0	0	0	0	0	0	0	0	0	0	0	0	0	0	0
0	0	0	0	0	0	0	0	1	0	1	0	0	0	0
0	0	0	0	0	0	0	0	2	0	0	0	0	0	0

Continued on next page

TABLE A-3c—*continued*

Record	Variables														
	SCL	HS	AS	PM	SB	ST	SR	GS	GSD	STB	CH	SMS	NGF	OWS	WBW
53	0	0	0	0	0	0	0	0	0	0	0	0	0	23	0
54	0	1	1	0	0	0	0	0	0	0	0	0	0	1	0
55	0	1	0	0	0	0	0	7	0	0	0	0	1	56	0
56	0	1	0	0	0	0	0	13	0	0	0	0	0	0	0
57	0	2	0	0	0	0	0	32	0	0	0	0	0	7	0
58	0	2	0	0	0	0	0	21	2	0	0	1	1	0	0
59	0	2	1	0	0	0	0	0	0	0	0	0	0	2	0
60	0	0	0	0	0	0	0	0	0	0	0	0	0	5	0
61	0	1	0	0	0	0	0	5	0	0	0	0	0	1	0
62	0	0	0	0	0	0	0	0	0	0	0	1	0	3	0
63	0	0	0	0	0	0	0	0	0	0	0	0	0	2	0
64	0	0	0	0	0	0	0	1	0	0	0	1	0	2	0
65	0	0	0	0	0	0	0	0	0	0	0	0	0	2	0

TABLE A-3c—*continued*

Variables															
WBO	WHA	WKW	BP	RP	YP	WP	GP	FO	CP	OWC	CAP	QC	BSK	BES	UOB
0	0	0	0	1	0	0	0	0	0	2	0	0	1	0	0
1	0	3	0	0	0	0	0	0	0	0	0	0	0	0	0
0	0	0	0	0	0	0	0	0	0	0	0	0	0	0	0
0	0	0	0	0	0	0	0	0	0	0	0	0	0	0	0
0	0	0	0	0	0	0	0	1	0	1	0	0	0	0	0
0	0	0	0	0	0	0	0	0	1	0	0	0	0	0	0
0	1	0	0	1	0	0	0	0	0	0	0	0	0	0	0
0	0	0	0	0	0	0	0	0	1	0	0	0	0	0	0
0	0	0	0	0	0	0	0	0	0	1	0	0	0	0	0
0	0	0	0	0	0	0	0	0	0	0	0	0	0	0	0
0	0	0	0	0	0	0	0	0	0	0	0	0	0	0	0
0	0	0	0	0	0	0	0	0	0	0	0	0	0	0	0
0	0	0	0	0	0	0	0	0	0	0	0	0	0	0	0

TABLE A-4a. *Euro-American Artifact Data for Domestic Earthlodges (Periods I–II)*

Record	Site	Name	Unit	OCCUP*	PERIOD	EAC	EAP	MTA	IN
				Variables					
1	39ST9	LaRoche	H3B	1	I	0	0	0	0
2	39ST9	LaRoche	H1C	1	I	0	0	0	0
3	39ST9	LaRoche	H4B	1	I	0	0	0	0
4	39ST232	LaRoche (Bower's)	H1	2	I	0	0	0	0
5	39ST9	LaRoche	H1A	1	I	0	0	0	0
6	39DW234	Molstad	H1	1	I	0	0	0	0
7	39ST9	LaRoche	H1E	1	I	3	0	0	0
8	39ST232	LaRoche (Bower's)	H5	1	I	0	0	0	0
9	39DW234	Molstad	H2	1	I	0	0	0	0
10	39ST9	LaRoche	H2E	2	I	0	0	0	0
11	39LM26	Oacoma	F35	1	II	0	0	0	0
12	39LM26	Oacoma	F80	1	II	0	0	0	0
13	39LM218	Black Partizan	F11	2	II	0	0	0	0
14	39LM26	Oacoma	F60	2	II	0	0	0	0
15	39WW7	Swan Creek	H1	2	II	0	0	0	0
16	39LM26	Oacoma	F90	1	II	0	0	0	0
17	39CH45	Hitchell	L3	1	II	0	0	0	0
18	39WW7	Swan Creek	H3	1	II	0	0	0	0
19	39LM26	Oacoma	F70	1	II	0	0	0	0
20	39LM26	Oacoma	F11	1	II	0	0	0	0
21	39CH45	Hitchell	L5	1	II	0	0	0	0
22	39CH45	Hitchell	L1	1	II	0	0	0	0
23	39CH45	Hitchell	L2	1	II	0	0	0	0
24	39LM26	Oacoma	F2	1	II	0	0	0	0

* The variable OCCUP refers to whether an earthlodge is defined as long-term occupation (2) or short-term occupation (1).

Note: See TABLE 12 for key to abbreviations.

TABLE A-4a—*continued*

Variables																
BN	MG	EAH	IPP	CPP	BPP	MPP	IF	CF	BF	ZF	LF	OMF	BGF	OGF	IT	CT
0	0	0	0	0	0	0	0	0	0	0	0	0	0	0	0	0
0	0	0	0	0	0	0	0	0	0	0	0	0	0	0	0	0
0	0	0	0	0	0	0	0	0	0	0	0	0	0	0	0	0
0	0	0	0	0	0	0	0	0	0	0	0	0	0	0	0	0
0	0	0	0	0	0	0	0	0	0	0	0	0	0	0	0	0
0	0	0	0	0	0	0	0	0	0	0	0	0	0	0	0	0
0	0	0	0	0	0	0	0	0	0	0	0	0	0	0	0	0
0	0	0	0	0	0	0	0	0	0	0	0	0	0	0	0	0
0	0	0	0	0	0	0	0	0	0	0	0	0	0	0	0	0
0	0	0	0	0	0	0	0	0	0	0	0	0	0	0	0	0
0	0	0	0	0	0	0	1	0	0	0	0	0	0	0	0	0
0	0	0	0	0	0	0	1	2	0	0	0	0	0	0	0	0
0	0	0	0	0	0	0	0	0	0	0	0	0	0	0	0	0
0	0	0	0	0	0	0	1	4	0	0	0	0	0	0	0	0
0	0	0	0	1	0	0	0	2	0	0	0	0	0	0	0	0
0	0	0	0	0	0	0	0	0	0	0	0	0	0	0	0	1
0	0	0	0	0	0	0	0	0	0	0	0	0	0	0	0	0
0	0	0	0	0	0	0	0	0	0	0	0	0	0	0	0	0
0	0	0	0	0	0	0	0	0	0	0	0	0	0	0	0	0
0	0	0	0	0	0	0	0	0	0	0	0	0	0	1	0	0
0	0	0	0	0	0	0	0	0	0	0	0	0	0	0	0	0
0	0	0	0	0	0	0	0	0	0	0	0	0	0	0	0	0
0	0	0	0	0	0	0	0	0	0	0	0	0	0	0	0	0
0	0	0	0	0	0	0	0	4	0	0	0	0	0	1	0	0

Continued on next page

TABLE A-4a—*continued*

Record	BT	EAF	BU	GTB	OTB	INA	IS	IB	CB	BB	OMB	IK	CK	BK	OMK	MKH
1	0	0	0	0	0	0	0	0	0	0	0	0	0	0	0	0
2	0	0	0	0	0	0	0	0	0	0	0	0	0	0	0	0
3	0	0	0	0	0	0	0	0	0	0	0	0	0	0	0	0
4	0	0	0	0	0	0	0	0	0	0	0	0	0	0	0	0
5	0	0	0	0	0	0	0	0	0	0	0	0	0	0	0	0
6	0	0	0	0	0	0	0	0	0	0	0	0	0	0	0	0
7	0	0	0	0	0	0	0	0	0	0	0	0	0	0	0	0
8	0	0	0	0	0	0	0	0	0	0	0	0	0	0	0	0
9	0	0	0	0	0	0	0	0	0	0	0	0	0	0	0	0
10	0	0	0	0	0	0	0	0	0	0	0	0	0	0	0	0
11	0	0	0	0	0	0	0	0	0	0	0	0	0	0	0	0
12	0	0	0	0	0	0	0	0	0	0	0	0	0	0	0	0
13	0	0	0	0	0	0	0	0	0	0	0	0	0	0	0	0
14	0	0	0	0	0	0	0	0	0	0	0	0	0	0	0	0
15	0	0	0	0	0	0	0	0	1	0	0	0	1	0	0	0
16	0	0	0	0	0	0	0	0	0	0	0	0	0	0	0	0
17	0	0	0	0	0	0	0	0	0	0	0	0	0	0	0	0
18	0	0	0	0	0	0	0	0	0	0	0	0	0	0	0	0
19	0	0	0	0	0	0	0	0	0	0	0	0	0	0	0	0
20	0	0	0	0	0	0	0	0	0	0	0	0	0	0	0	0
21	0	0	0	0	0	0	0	0	0	0	0	0	0	0	0	0
22	0	0	0	0	0	0	0	0	0	0	0	0	0	0	0	0
23	0	0	0	0	0	0	0	0	0	0	0	0	0	0	0	0
24	0	0	0	0	0	0	0	0	0	0	0	0	0	0	0	0

TABLE A-4a—*continued*

Variables																	
IKH	IBU	BBU	OBU	CBE	BBE	MF	MHA	IC	ICO	CC	MR	TC	IRB	BRB	OIO	OCO	CRC
0	0	0	0	0	0	0	0	0	0	0	0	0	0	0	0	0	0
0	0	0	0	0	0	0	0	0	0	0	0	0	0	0	0	0	0
0	0	0	0	0	0	0	0	0	0	0	0	0	0	0	0	0	0
0	0	0	0	0	0	0	0	0	0	0	0	0	0	0	0	0	0
0	0	0	0	0	0	0	0	0	0	0	0	0	0	0	0	0	0
0	0	0	0	0	0	0	0	0	0	0	0	0	0	0	0	0	0
0	0	0	0	0	0	0	0	0	0	0	0	0	0	0	0	0	0
0	0	0	0	0	0	0	0	0	0	0	0	0	0	0	0	0	0
0	0	0	0	0	0	0	0	0	0	0	0	0	0	0	0	0	0
0	0	0	0	0	0	0	0	0	0	0	0	0	0	0	0	0	0
0	0	0	0	0	0	0	0	0	0	4	0	0	0	0	0	0	0
0	0	0	0	0	0	0	0	0	0	0	0	0	0	0	0	0	0
0	0	0	0	0	0	0	0	0	0	0	0	0	0	0	0	0	0
0	0	0	0	0	0	0	0	0	0	0	0	0	0	0	0	0	0
0	0	0	0	55	0	0	0	0	0	0	0	0	0	0	0	0	0
0	0	0	0	0	0	0	0	0	0	0	0	0	0	0	0	0	0
0	0	0	0	0	0	0	0	0	0	0	0	0	0	0	0	0	0
0	0	0	0	0	0	0	0	0	0	0	0	0	0	0	0	0	0
0	0	0	0	0	0	0	0	0	0	0	0	0	0	0	0	0	0
0	0	0	0	0	0	0	0	0	0	0	0	0	0	0	0	0	0
0	0	0	0	0	0	0	0	0	0	0	0	0	0	0	0	0	0
0	0	0	0	0	0	0	0	0	0	0	0	0	0	0	0	0	0
0	0	0	0	0	0	0	0	0	0	0	0	0	0	0	0	0	0
0	0	0	0	0	0	0	0	0	0	0	0	0	0	0	0	0	0

Continued on next page

TABLE A-4a—*continued*

Record	Variables															
	BD	CD	BRR	IR	IRR	BR	SR	MER	LR	MMO	MM	MFH	IRC	ISC	IW	BRH
1	0	0	0	0	0	0	0	0	0	0	0	0	0	0	0	0
2	0	0	0	0	0	0	0	0	0	0	0	0	0	0	0	0
3	0	0	0	0	0	0	0	0	0	0	0	0	0	0	0	0
4	0	0	0	0	0	0	0	0	0	0	0	0	0	0	0	0
5	0	0	0	0	0	0	0	0	0	0	0	0	0	0	0	0
6	0	0	0	0	0	0	0	0	0	0	0	0	0	0	0	0
7	0	0	0	0	0	0	0	0	0	0	0	0	0	0	0	0
8	0	0	0	0	0	0	0	0	0	0	0	0	0	0	0	0
9	0	0	0	0	0	0	0	0	0	0	0	0	0	0	0	0
10	0	0	0	0	0	0	0	0	0	0	0	0	0	0	0	0
11	0	0	0	0	0	0	0	0	0	0	0	0	0	0	0	0
12	0	0	0	0	0	0	0	0	0	0	0	0	0	0	0	0
13	0	0	0	0	0	0	0	0	0	0	0	0	0	0	0	0
14	0	0	0	0	0	0	0	0	0	0	0	0	0	0	0	0
15	0	0	0	0	0	0	0	0	0	0	0	0	0	0	0	0
16	0	0	0	0	0	0	0	0	0	0	0	0	0	0	0	0
17	0	0	0	0	0	0	0	0	0	0	0	0	0	0	0	0
18	0	0	0	0	0	0	0	0	0	0	0	0	0	0	0	0
19	0	0	0	0	0	0	0	0	0	0	0	0	0	0	0	0
20	0	0	0	0	0	0	0	0	0	0	0	0	0	0	0	0
21	0	0	0	0	0	0	0	0	0	0	0	0	0	0	0	0
22	0	0	0	0	0	0	0	0	0	0	0	0	0	0	0	0
23	0	0	0	0	0	0	0	0	0	0	0	0	0	0	0	0
24	0	0	0	0	0	0	0	0	0	0	0	0	0	0	0	0

TABLE A-4b. *Euro-American Artifact Data for Domestic Earthlodges (Periods III–IV)*

Record	Site	Name	Unit	Variables					
				OCCUP*	PERIOD	EAC	EAP	MTA	IN
25	39LM220	Crazy Bull	H1	1	III	0	0	0	0
26	39ST6	Buffalo Pasture	F4	1	III	0	1	1	1
27	39ST6	Buffalo Pasture	F1	1	III	0	0	0	0
28	39ST14	Phillips Ranch	F4	1	III	0	0	0	1
29	39ST15	Indian Creek	F1	1	III	0	0	0	0
30	39ST6	Buffalo Pasture	F30	2	III	0	0	0	0
31	39ST14	Phillips Ranch	F8	1	III	0	0	0	0
32	39ST14	Phillips Ranch	F20	1	III	0	0	0	0
33	39ST14	Phillips Ranch	F2	2	III	0	0	0	0
34	39LM215	Peterson	F1	1	III	0	0	0	0
35	39ST1	Cheyenne River	F60	1	III	0	0	0	0
36	39ST17	Fort George	H4	1	III	0	0	1	0
37	39ST17	Fort George	H3	2	III	0	0	0	0
38	39ST17	Fort George	H6	1	III	0	0	0	0
39	39HU26	Spotted Bear	H1	1	IV	0	0	0	0
40	39HU26	Spotted Bear	H2	1	IV	0	0	0	0
41	39HU26	Spotted Bear	H4	2	IV	0	0	0	0
42	39CO34	Red Horse Hawk	L10	1	IV	0	0	0	0
43	39CO34	Red Horse Hawk	L11	2	IV	0	0	0	0
44	39CO34	Red Horse Hawk	L15	1	IV	0	0	1	0
45	39CO34	Red Horse Hawk	L4	1	IV	0	0	0	0
46	39CO34	Red Horse Hawk	L6	2	IV	0	0	0	0
47	39HU26	Spotted Bear	H3	1	IV	0	0	0	0
48	39CO34	Red Horse Hawk	L14	1	IV	0	0	0	0
49	39HU26	Spotted Bear	H5	1	IV	0	0	0	0
50	39CO34	Red Horse Hawk	L13	1	IV	0	0	0	0
51	39CO34	Red Horse Hawk	L12	1	IV	0	0	0	0
52	39CO34	Red Horse Hawk	L8	1	IV	0	0	0	0

* The variable OCCUP refers to whether an earthlodge is defined as long-term occupation (2) or short-term occupation (1).

Note: See TABLE 12 for key to abbreviations.

TABLE A-4b—*continued*

Record	BN	MG	EAH	IPP	CPP	BPP	MPP	IF	CF	BF	ZF	LF	OMF	BGF	OGF	IT
25	0	0	0	0	0	0	0	0	0	1	0	0	0	0	0	0
26	0	0	0	2	1	0	0	4	0	2	0	0	0	0	0	0
27	0	0	0	0	0	0	0	4	0	2	0	0	0	0	0	0
28	0	0	0	0	0	0	0	3	0	0	0	0	0	0	0	0
29	0	0	0	0	0	0	0	1	0	0	0	0	0	0	0	0
30	0	0	0	2	5	0	0	3	0	1	0	0	0	0	2	0
31	0	0	0	0	0	1	0	1	0	2	0	0	0	0	0	0
32	0	0	0	0	0	0	0	4	0	0	0	0	0	0	0	0
33	0	0	0	0	0	0	0	3	0	2	0	0	0	0	0	0
34	0	0	0	0	0	0	0	0	6	0	0	0	0	0	0	0
35	0	0	0	1	0	0	0	7	3	0	0	0	0	0	0	0
36	0	0	0	1	0	0	0	2	0	0	0	0	0	0	0	0
37	0	0	0	0	0	0	0	2	0	1	0	0	0	0	0	0
38	0	1	0	1	0	1	0	2	0	3	0	0	0	0	0	0
39	0	0	0	0	0	0	0	0	0	0	0	0	0	0	0	0
40	0	0	0	0	0	0	0	0	0	0	0	0	0	0	0	0
41	1	0	0	0	0	0	0	0	0	0	0	0	0	0	0	0
42	0	0	0	0	0	2	0	0	0	1	0	0	0	0	0	0
43	0	0	0	0	0	0	0	0	0	0	0	0	0	0	0	0
44	0	0	0	0	0	0	0	0	0	0	0	0	0	0	0	0
45	0	0	0	0	0	0	0	0	0	4	0	0	0	0	0	0
46	0	0	0	0	0	2	0	0	0	0	0	0	0	0	0	0
47	0	0	0	0	0	0	0	0	0	0	0	0	0	0	0	0
48	0	0	0	0	0	0	0	0	0	0	0	0	0	0	0	0
49	0	0	0	1	0	0	0	0	3	0	0	0	0	0	0	0
50	0	0	0	0	0	1	0	0	0	0	0	0	0	0	0	0
51	0	0	0	0	0	1	0	0	0	0	0	0	0	0	0	0
52	0	0	0	1	0	4	0	0	0	0	0	0	0	0	0	0

TABLE A-4b—*continued*

Variables																
CT	BT	EAF	BU	GTB	OTB	INA	IS	IB	CB	BB	OMB	IK	CK	BK	OMK	MKH
0	0	0	0	0	0	0	0	0	0	0	0	0	0	0	0	0
1	0	0	0	3	0	0	0	0	0	0	0	2	0	1	0	0
0	0	0	0	0	0	0	0	0	0	0	0	0	0	0	0	0
0	0	0	0	0	0	0	0	0	0	0	0	0	0	0	0	0
0	0	0	0	0	0	0	0	0	0	0	0	0	0	0	0	0
0	0	0	0	2	0	0	0	0	1	0	0	0	1	1	0	0
0	0	0	0	0	0	0	0	0	0	0	0	0	0	0	0	0
0	0	0	0	0	0	0	0	0	0	0	0	0	0	0	0	0
0	0	0	0	0	0	0	0	0	0	0	0	0	0	0	0	0
0	0	0	0	0	0	0	0	0	0	0	0	2	0	0	0	0
1	0	0	0	0	0	0	0	0	0	0	0	0	1	0	0	0
0	0	0	0	0	0	0	0	0	0	1	0	0	0	0	0	0
0	0	0	0	0	0	0	0	0	0	0	0	1	0	0	0	0
0	0	0	0	0	0	0	0	0	0	0	0	1	0	1	0	0
0	0	0	0	0	0	0	0	0	0	0	0	0	0	0	0	0
0	0	0	0	0	0	0	0	0	0	0	0	0	0	0	0	0
0	0	0	0	0	0	1	0	0	0	0	0	0	0	0	0	0
0	0	0	0	1	0	0	0	0	0	0	0	0	0	1	0	0
0	0	0	0	0	0	0	0	0	0	0	0	0	0	3	0	0
0	0	0	0	0	0	0	0	0	0	0	0	0	0	0	0	0
0	0	0	0	0	0	0	0	0	0	0	0	0	0	1	0	0
0	0	0	0	0	0	0	0	0	0	0	0	0	0	1	0	0
0	0	0	0	0	0	0	0	0	0	0	0	0	0	0	0	0
0	0	0	0	0	0	0	0	0	0	0	0	0	0	0	0	0
0	0	0	0	0	0	0	0	0	1	0	0	0	0	0	0	0
0	0	0	0	0	0	0	0	0	0	0	0	0	0	0	0	0
0	0	0	0	1	0	0	0	0	0	0	0	0	0	0	0	0
0	0	0	0	0	0	0	0	0	0	0	0	1	0	1	0	0

TABLE A-4b—*continued*

Record	Variables															
	IKH	IBU	BBU	OBU	CBE	BBE	MF	MHA	IC	ICO	CC	MR	TC	IRB	BRB	OIO	OCO
25	0	0	0	0	0	0	0	0	0	0	0	0	0	0	0	0	0
26	0	0	0	0	0	0	0	0	0	0	0	0	0	0	0	2	0
27	0	0	0	0	1	0	0	0	0	0	0	0	0	0	0	0	0
28	0	0	0	0	0	0	0	0	0	0	0	0	0	0	0	1	0
29	0	1	0	0	0	0	0	0	0	0	0	0	0	0	0	0	0
30	0	0	0	0	0	0	0	0	0	0	0	0	0	0	0	0	0
31	0	0	0	0	0	0	0	0	0	0	0	0	0	0	0	1	0
32	0	0	0	0	0	0	0	0	0	0	0	0	0	0	0	0	0
33	0	0	0	0	0	0	0	0	0	0	0	0	0	0	0	0	0
34	0	0	0	0	2	0	0	0	0	0	1	0	0	0	0	0	0
35	0	0	0	0	0	0	0	0	0	0	0	0	0	0	0	0	0
36	0	0	0	0	0	0	0	0	0	0	0	0	0	0	0	0	0
37	0	0	0	0	0	0	0	0	0	0	0	0	0	0	0	0	0
38	0	0	0	0	0	0	0	0	0	0	0	0	0	0	0	0	0
39	0	0	0	0	0	0	0	0	0	0	0	0	0	0	0	0	0
40	0	0	0	0	0	0	0	0	0	0	0	0	0	0	0	0	0
41	0	0	0	0	0	0	0	0	0	0	0	0	0	0	0	0	0
42	0	0	0	0	0	0	0	0	0	0	0	0	0	0	0	0	0
43	0	0	0	0	0	0	0	0	0	0	0	0	0	0	0	0	0
44	0	0	0	0	0	0	0	0	0	0	0	0	0	0	0	0	0
45	0	0	0	0	0	0	0	0	0	0	0	0	0	0	0	0	0
46	0	0	0	0	0	0	0	0	0	0	0	0	0	0	0	0	0
47	0	0	0	0	0	0	0	0	0	0	0	0	0	0	0	0	0
48	0	0	0	0	0	0	0	0	0	0	0	0	0	0	0	0	0
49	0	0	0	0	0	0	0	0	0	0	0	0	0	0	0	0	0
50	0	0	0	0	0	0	0	0	0	0	0	0	0	0	0	0	0
51	0	0	0	0	0	1	0	0	0	0	0	1	0	0	0	0	0
52	0	0	0	0	0	0	0	0	0	0	0	0	0	0	0	0	0

TABLE A-4b—*continued*

Variables																
CRC	BD	CD	BRR	IR	IRR	BR	SR	MER	LR	MMO	MM	MFH	IRC	ISC	IW	BRH
0	0	0	0	0	0	0	0	0	0	0	0	0	0	0	0	0
0	0	0	0	0	0	0	0	0	0	0	0	0	0	0	0	0
0	0	0	0	0	0	0	0	0	0	0	0	0	0	0	0	0
0	0	0	0	0	0	0	0	0	0	0	0	0	0	0	0	0
0	0	0	0	0	0	0	0	0	0	0	0	0	0	0	0	0
0	0	0	0	0	0	0	0	0	0	0	0	0	0	0	0	0
0	0	0	0	0	0	0	0	0	0	0	0	0	0	0	0	0
1	0	0	0	0	0	0	0	0	0	0	0	0	0	0	0	0
0	0	0	0	0	0	0	0	0	0	0	0	0	0	0	0	0
0	0	0	0	0	0	0	0	0	0	0	0	0	0	0	0	0
0	0	0	0	0	0	0	0	0	0	0	0	0	0	0	0	0
0	0	0	0	0	0	0	0	0	0	0	0	0	0	0	0	0
0	0	0	0	0	0	0	0	0	0	0	0	0	0	0	0	0
0	0	0	0	0	0	0	0	0	0	0	0	0	0	2	0	0
0	0	0	0	0	0	0	0	0	0	0	0	0	0	0	0	0
0	0	0	0	0	0	0	0	0	0	0	0	0	0	0	0	0
0	0	0	0	0	0	0	0	0	0	0	0	0	0	0	0	0
0	0	0	0	0	0	0	0	0	0	0	0	0	0	1	0	0
0	0	0	0	0	0	0	0	0	0	0	0	0	0	0	0	0
0	0	0	0	0	0	0	0	0	0	0	0	0	0	0	0	0
0	0	0	0	0	0	0	0	0	0	0	0	0	0	0	0	0
0	0	0	0	0	0	0	0	0	0	0	0	0	0	0	0	0
0	0	0	0	0	0	0	0	0	0	0	0	0	0	0	0	0
0	0	0	0	0	0	0	0	0	0	0	0	0	0	0	0	0
0	0	0	0	0	0	0	0	0	0	0	0	0	0	0	0	0
0	0	0	0	0	0	0	0	0	0	1	0	0	0	0	0	0
0	0	0	0	0	0	0	0	0	0	0	0	0	0	0	0	0
0	0	0	0	0	0	0	0	0	0	0	0	0	0	1	0	0

TABLE A-4C. *Euro-American Artifact Data for Domestic Earthlodges (Periods V–VI)*

Record	Site	Name	Unit	Variables					
				OCCUP*	PERIOD	EAC	EAP	MTA	IN
53	39ST50	None	F13	2	V	0	0	0	0
54	39ST50	None	F3	2	V	0	0	0	0
55	39CO9	Leavenworth	L20	1	V	0	2	0	0
56	39CO9	Leavenworth	L47	1	V	0	0	0	0
57	39CO9	Leavenworth	L2	1	V	0	0	0	0
58	39CO9	Leavenworth	L23	1	V	0	1	0	1
59	39CO9	Leavenworth	L3	1	V	0	0	0	0
60	39CO9	Leavenworth	L7	1	V	1	0	0	0
61	39CO9	Leavenworth	L40	1	V	0	1	0	0
62	32ME16	Star Village	F8	1	VI	1	0	0	0
63	32ME16	Star Village	F5	1	VI	0	0	0	0
64	32ME16	Star Village	F1	1	VI	0	0	0	0
65	32ME16	Star Village	F3	1	VI	0	0	0	0

* The variable OCCUP refers to whether an earthlodge is defined as long-term occupation (2) or short-term occupation (1).

Note: See TABLE 12 for key to abbreviations.

TABLE A-4c—*continued*

Variables																
BN	MG	EAH	IPP	CPP	BPP	MPP	IF	CF	BF	ZF	LF	OMF	BGF	OGF	IT	CT
0	0	0	0	0	0	0	3	0	0	0	0	0	0	0	0	0
0	0	0	0	0	0	0	3	0	0	0	0	1	1	0	0	0
0	3	0	0	0	0	3	0	0	0	0	0	158	0	9	0	0
0	1	0	4	0	0	0	10	1	2	0	0	0	0	2	1	0
0	0	0	0	0	0	0	1	0	0	0	0	0	0	0	0	0
0	0	0	2	0	0	0	3	0	1	0	0	1	1	3	0	0
0	0	0	3	0	0	0	3	0	1	0	1	8	0	0	0	0
0	2	0	2	0	0	0	3	3	0	0	0	0	0	2	0	0
0	0	0	2	0	0	0	54	13	4	0	0	0	0	1	0	1
0	0	0	1	0	0	0	0	0	0	1	0	0	1	6	0	0
0	0	0	0	0	0	0	0	0	0	0	0	0	0	2	0	0
0	0	1	0	0	0	0	0	0	0	1	0	0	0	0	0	0
0	0	0	0	0	0	0	0	0	1	0	0	0	0	4	0	0

Continued on next page

TABLE A-4c—*continued*

Record	BT	EAF	BU	GTB	OTB	INA	IS	IB	CB	BB	OMB	IK	CK	BK	OMK	MKH
53	1	0	0	0	0	0	0	0	0	1	0	0	0	0	0	0
54	0	0	0	0	0	0	0	0	0	1	0	0	0	0	0	0
55	0	2	0	19	0	0	0	0	0	0	10	0	0	0	0	0
56	0	0	0	3	0	1	0	0	0	1	0	0	0	0	0	1
57	0	0	0	0	0	0	0	0	0	0	0	0	0	0	0	0
58	0	1	0	2	2	1	0	0	0	0	5	0	0	0	1	0
59	0	0	0	0	0	0	0	0	0	0	0	0	0	0	0	0
60	0	0	0	0	0	1	0	0	0	0	0	0	0	0	0	0
61	0	2	0	2	0	0	0	1	2	6	0	0	0	0	1	0
62	0	1	0	0	0	6	1	0	0	0	0	0	0	0	0	0
63	0	0	0	1	0	4	0	0	0	0	0	0	0	0	1	0
64	0	0	1	7	0	2	0	0	0	0	0	0	0	0	0	0
65	0	2	0	96	0	0	0	0	0	0	0	0	0	0	0	0

TABLE A-4c—*continued*

Variables																	
IKH	IBU	BBU	OBU	CBE	BBE	MF	MHA	IC	ICO	CC	MR	TC	IRB	BRB	OIO	OCO	CRC
0	0	1	0	0	0	0	0	0	0	0	0	0	0	0	0	0	0
0	0	0	0	0	0	0	0	0	0	0	0	0	0	0	0	0	0
0	0	0	2	0	0	0	0	0	0	0	0	0	0	0	0	0	0
0	0	0	0	0	0	0	0	0	0	0	2	0	0	0	0	0	0
0	0	0	0	0	0	0	0	0	0	0	0	0	0	0	0	0	0
0	0	0	0	0	0	0	0	0	0	0	1	0	1	0	0	0	0
0	0	2	1	0	0	0	0	0	0	0	0	0	0	0	0	0	0
0	0	0	0	0	0	0	0	0	0	0	0	0	0	0	0	0	0
1	0	0	0	0	0	0	0	0	0	0	0	0	0	0	0	2	0
0	0	0	0	0	0	0	1	1	3	0	1	2	0	0	0	0	0
0	0	0	0	0	0	0	0	0	0	0	0	0	0	0	0	0	0
0	0	0	0	0	0	0	0	0	0	0	0	0	0	0	0	0	0
0	0	0	0	0	0	1	0	0	0	0	0	0	0	0	0	0	0

Continued on next page

TABLE A-4c—*continued*

Record	Variables															
	BD	CD	BRR	IR	IRR	BR	SR	MER	LR	MMO	MM	MFH	IRC	ISC	IW	BRH
53	0	0	0	0	0	0	0	0	0	0	0	0	0	0	0	0
54	0	0	0	0	0	0	0	0	0	0	0	0	0	0	0	0
55	0	0	0	0	0	0	0	1	0	0	1	0	0	0	0	0
56	0	0	0	1	0	0	0	0	0	0	0	1	0	0	0	0
57	0	0	1	0	0	0	0	0	1	0	0	0	0	0	0	0
58	0	0	0	0	0	1	0	0	0	0	0	0	0	0	2	1
59	1	0	0	0	0	0	0	0	0	0	0	1	0	0	1	0
60	0	0	0	0	1	0	0	0	0	0	0	0	0	0	0	0
61	0	1	0	2	0	0	1	0	0	0	0	0	0	0	0	0
62	0	0	0	0	0	0	0	0	0	0	0	0	0	0	0	0
63	0	0	0	0	0	0	0	0	0	0	0	0	0	0	0	0
64	0	0	0	0	0	0	0	0	0	0	0	0	0	0	0	0
65	0	0	0	0	0	0	0	0	0	0	0	0	0	0	0	0

TABLE A-5. *Arikara Artifact Data for Ceremonial Earthlodges*

Variables	Molstad (39DW234) H7	LaRoche (39ST9) H3A	Indian Creek (39ST15) F3	Phillips Ranch (39ST14) F15	Fort George (39ST17) F34	Red Horse Hawk (39CO34) L7	Leavenworth (39CO9) L34	Star Village (32ME16) F12
	Site and Unit							
OCCUP*	2	1	1	1	1	1	1	1
PERIOD	I	I	III	III	III	IV	V	VI
CER	1610	1125	583	289	363	67	1029	0
CEB	0	0	0	0	0	0	0	0
CLP	0	0	0	0	0	0	0	0
CGP	0	0	0	0	0	0	0	0
SP	0	0	0	0	0	0	0	0
STP	0	0	0	0	0	0	0	0
SPP	13	13	10	5	3	3	0	0
SC	47	17	21	12	1	8	1	2
GR	0	0	0	0	0	0	0	0
SD	1	1	0	0	0	0	0	0
WKF	0	7	1	1	0	4	0	0
STK	27	22	8	6	0	0	0	0
MA	1	0	0	1	0	0	0	0
CE	0	0	0	0	0	0	0	0
SSA	0	7	1	3	3	0	0	1
SCA	5	9	5	1	2	0	0	0
SHA	1	2	1	0	0	0	0	0
BOA	5	2	1	0	0	2	0	0
BOF	0	0	0	1	0	0	2	0
BSW	1	0	0	1	0	0	2	0
BHS	0	0	0	0	0	0	0	1
BFT	0	0	0	0	0	0	0	0
SCH	3	2	1	0	8	3	8	0
SCK	6	3	0	0	0	1	0	0
WKS	0	0	1	28	0	0	0	0
BOP	0	0	0	0	0	0	0	0
BOG	0	0	0	0	0	0	0	0
BOT	0	1	0	1	0	0	0	0

Continued on next page

Note: See TABLE 12 for key to abbreviations.

TABLE A-5—*continued*

Variables	Site and Unit							
	Molstad (39DW234) H7	LaRoche (39ST9) H3A	Indian Creek (39ST15) F3	Phillips Ranch (39ST14) F15	Fort George (39ST17) F34	Red Horse Hawk (39CO34) L7	Leavenworth (39CO9) L34	Star Village (32ME16) F12
BOB	0	0	0	0	0	0	0	0
BBE	0	0	0	0	0	0	0	0
BOC	0	0	0	0	0	0	0	0
BFH	0	0	0	0	0	0	0	0
BPA	0	0	1	0	0	0	0	0
BKH	0	0	0	0	0	0	0	0
WKR	0	0	0	0	0	0	6	0
QUF	0	0	0	0	0	0	0	0
BOW	0	0	0	0	0	0	0	0
BPE	0	0	0	0	0	0	0	0
BPP	1	0	0	0	0	0	0	0
DRC	0	0	0	0	0	2	1	0
ULB	0	0	0	0	0	0	0	0
ULP	0	0	0	0	0	0	0	0
BSP	0	0	0	0	1	0	0	0
OWB	0	0	2	1	0	0	16	0
WKA	0	0	0	0	1	0	2	0
WMS	0	3	0	0	0	0	0	0
SS	5	1	0	0	0	0	0	0
SHP	1	0	0	0	0	1	0	0
SHB	0	0	0	0	0	0	0	0
SHD	1	0	0	0	0	0	0	0
SCL	0	0	0	0	0	0	0	0
HS	1	2	3	1	8	0	0	0
AS	0	0	0	0	0	0	0	0
PM	0	0	0	0	0	0	0	0
SB	0	0	0	0	0	0	0	0
ST	0	0	0	0	1	0	0	0
SR	0	0	0	0	0	0	0	0
GS	4	0	1	0	5	0	0	0
GSD	0	0	0	0	0	0	0	0

TABLE A-5—*continued*

Variables	Site and Unit							
	Molstad (39DW234) H7	LaRoche (39ST9) H3A	Indian Creek (39ST15) F3	Phillips Ranch (39ST14) F15	Fort George (39ST17) F34	Red Horse Hawk (39CO34) L7	Leavenworth (39CO9) L34	Star Village (32ME16) F12
STB	0	0	0	0	0	0	0	0
CH	0	0	1	0	0	0	0	0
SMS	0	0	0	0	0	0	0	0
NGF	0	0	0	0	1	0	0	0
OWS	0	0	1	3	0	0	0	0
WBW	0	0	0	0	0	0	0	0
WBO	0	0	0	0	0	0	0	0
WHA	0	0	0	0	0	0	0	0
WKW	0	0	0	0	0	0	0	0
BP	0	0	0	0	0	0	0	0
RP	0	1	2	1	1	0	0	0
YP	0	0	0	0	1	0	0	0
WP	0	0	0	0	1	0	0	1
GP	0	0	0	0	0	0	0	0
FO	0	0	1	0	1	0	0	0
CP	0	0	0	0	0	0	0	0
OWC	0	1	1	0	0	0	0	0
CAP	0	1	0	0	0	0	0	0
QC	0	0	0	0	0	0	0	0
BSK	0	0	1	0	0	0	0	0
BES	0	0	0	0	0	0	0	0
UOB	0	1	0	0	1	0	0	0

*The variable OCCUP refers to whether an earthlodge is defined as long-term occupation (2) or short-term occupation (1).

TABLE A-6. *Euro-American Artifact Data for Ceremonial Earthlodges*

Variables	Site and Unit							
	Molstad (39DW234) H7	LaRoche (39ST9) H3A	Indian Creek (39ST15) F3	Phillips Ranch (39ST14) F15	Fort George (39ST17) F34	Red Horse Hawk (39CO34) L7	Leavenworth (39CO9) L34	Star Village (32ME16) F12
OCCUP*	2	1	1	1	1	1	1	1
PERIOD	I	I	III	III	III	IV	V	VI
EAC	0	0	0	0	0	0	0	0
EAP	0	0	0	0	0	0	1	0
MTA	0	0	0	0	0	0	0	0
IN	0	0	0	0	0	0	0	0
BN	0	0	0	0	0	0	0	0
MG	0	0	0	0	0	0	2	0
EAH	0	0	0	0	0	0	0	0
IPP	0	0	0	0	0	0	0	0
CPP	0	0	0	0	0	0	0	0
BPP	0	0	0	0	2	0	0	0
IF	0	0	0	4	2	0	14	0
CF	0	0	0	6	0	0	6	0
BF	0	0	0	0	1	0	0	0
ZF	0	0	0	0	0	0	0	0
LF	0	0	0	0	0	0	0	0
OMF	0	0	0	0	0	0	0	0
BGF	0	0	0	0	0	0	0	0
OGF	0	0	0	0	0	0	1	0
IT	0	0	0	0	0	0	0	0
CT	0	0	0	0	0	0	0	0
BT	0	0	0	0	0	0	0	0
EAF	0	0	0	0	0	0	0	0
BU	0	0	0	0	0	0	0	0
GTB	0	0	1	0	0	0	6	0
OTB	0	0	0	0	0	0	1	0
INA	0	0	0	0	0	0	1	0
IS	0	0	0	0	0	0	0	0
IB	0	0	0	0	0	0	0	0
CB	0	0	0	0	0	0	0	0

Note: See TABLE 12 for key to abbreviations.

TABLE A-6—*continued*

Variables	Site and Unit							
	Molstad (39DW234) H7	LaRoche (39ST9) H3A	Indian Creek (39ST15) F3	Phillips Ranch (39ST14) F15	Fort George (39ST17) F34	Red Horse Hawk (39CO34) L7	Leavenworth (39CO9) L34	Star Village (32ME16) F12
BB	0	0	0	0	1	0	1	0
OMB	0	0	0	0	0	0	0	0
IK	0	0	0	0	0	0	0	0
CK	0	0	0	0	0	0	0	0
BK	0	0	0	0	0	0	0	0
OMK	0	0	0	0	0	0	0	0
MKH	0	0	0	0	0	0	0	0
IKH	0	0	0	0	0	0	0	0
IBU	0	0	0	0	0	0	0	0
BBU	0	0	0	0	0	0	2	0
OBU	0	0	0	0	0	0	0	0
CBE	0	0	0	2	0	0	0	0
BBE	0	0	0	0	0	0	0	0
MF	0	0	0	0	0	0	0	0
MHA	0	0	0	0	0	0	0	0
IC	0	0	0	0	0	0	0	0
ICO	0	0	0	0	0	0	0	0
CC	0	0	0	0	0	0	1	0
MR	0	0	0	0	0	0	0	0
TC	0	0	0	0	0	0	0	1
IRB	0	0	0	0	0	0	0	1
BRB	0	0	0	0	0	0	1	0
OIO	0	0	0	0	0	0	0	0
OCO	0	0	1	0	0	0	0	0
CRC	0	0	0	0	0	0	0	0
BD	0	0	0	0	0	0	0	0
CD	0	0	0	0	0	0	0	0
BRR	0	0	0	0	0	0	0	0
IR	0	0	0	0	0	0	1	0
IRR	0	0	0	0	0	0	0	0
BR	0	0	0	0	0	0	1	0
SR	0	0	0	0	0	0	0	0

Continued on next page

TABLE A-6—*continued*

Variables	Site and Unit							
	Molstad (39DW234) H7	LaRoche (39ST9) H3A	Indian Creek (39ST15) F3	Phillips Ranch (39ST14) F15	Fort George (39ST17)	Red Horse Hawk (39CO34) L7	Leavenworth (39CO9) L34	Star Village (32ME16) F12
MER	0	0	0	0	0	0	0	0
LR	0	0	0	0	0	0	0	0
MMO	0	0	0	0	0	0	0	0
MM	0	0	0	0	0	0	0	0
MFH	0	0	0	0	0	0	0	0
IRC	0	0	0	0	0	0	1	0
ISC	0	0	0	0	0	0	0	0
IW	0	0	0	0	0	0	0	0
BRH	0	0	0	0	0	0	0	0

*The variable OCCUP refers to whether an earthlodge is defined as long-term occupation (2) or short-term occupation (1).

TABLE A-7. *Arikara and Euro-American Artifact Data for Burials*

Site	Name	Burial	Period	Sex*	Age[†]	Categories
39SL4	Sully	F115-5	II	0	1	GTB
39SL4	Sully	F115-6A	II	2	4	WKS
39SL4	Sully	F116-4A	II	2	4	BIS
39SL4	Sully	F116-10	II	0	2	SHB
39SL4	Sully	F116-12A	II	0	2	GTB
39SL4	Sully	F117-5	II	0	1	POT, WMS
39SL4	Sully	F218-1	II	0	1	GTB
39SL4	Sully	F218-2B	II	0	4	GSD
39SL4	Sully	F218-12	II	1	4	WKS
39SL4	Sully	F218-14	II	1	6	BKH
39SL4	Sully	F218-24A	II	2	4	BOP, WKF
39SL4	Sully	F218-28A	II	0	2	SHB
39SL4	Sully	F218-29A	II	0	1	CBE
39SL4	Sully	F218-30	II	0	1	GTB
39SL4	Sully	F218-32	II	0	1	WKS
39SL4	Sully	F218-36	II	0	2	CBE
39SL4	Sully	F220-4A	II	1	5	WKR
39SL4	Sully	F220-9B	II	0	1	WKF
39SL4	Sully	F220-15A	II	1	4	SMA, BOB
39SL4	Sully	F220-16	II	0	1	CBE
39SL4	Sully	F220-25	II	1	6	OWB
39SL4	Sully	F220-27A	II	1	6	BOA
39SL4	Sully	F220-28B	II	0	1	CT, OWS
39SL4	Sully	F220-33	II	0	1	WMS
39SL4	Sully	F320-8	II	0	1	GTB, CBE
39SL4	Sully	F320-14	II	1	6	CP
39SL4	Sully	F320-19B	II	2	5	BOA
39SL4	Sully	F320-21	II	0	3	WMS
39SL4	Sully	F320-22A	II	1	5	CBE
39SL4	Sully	F320-27	II	2	6	BOA, WKF
39SL4	Sully	F418-4A	II	0	2	GPD
39SL4	Sully	F420-5	II	2	6	BOA, RP
39SL4	Sully	F420-8B	II	2	4	STK
39SL4	Sully	F420-9	II	2	6	OWB
39SL4	Sully	F420-11A	II	2	6	STK
39SL4	Sully	F420-11B	II	2	4	SC
39SL4	Sully	F420-12	II	0	1	GTB
39SL4	Sully	F421-2B	II	1	4	BOT, SPP

Continued on next page

TABLE A-7—*continued*

Site	Name	Burial	Period	Sex*	Age†	Categories
39SL4	Sully	F421-3	II	2	6	SCK
39SL4	Sully	F421-7A	II	2	4	WKS
39SL4	Sully	F421-17	II	2	4	HS
39SL4	Sully	F421-28C	II	1	4	WKS
39SL4	Sully	F421-36A	II	2	4	GTB
39SL4	Sully	F421-36B	II	0	1	GTB, OCO
39SL4	Sully	F421-37A	II	1	4	RP
39SL4	Sully	F421-39	II	1	4	GTB, BIS
39SL4	Sully	F421-45A	II	0	2	SHB
39SL4	Sully	F421-47	II	0	2	STK
39SL4	Sully	F421-48B	II	0	1	POT
39SL4	Sully	F421-49	II	0	2	BPE
39SL4	Sully	F421-60B	II	0	2	GTB, WMS
39SL4	Sully	F421-63D	II	1	5	STK, OWB
39SL4	Sully	F421-66D	II	1	5	STK, OWB
39SL4	Sully	F421-68B	II	0	3	GTB
39SL4	Sully	F421-69	II	2	4	GTB
39SL4	Sully	F421-71	II	0	1	STK
39SL4	Sully	F421-76	II	0	1	GTB
39SL4	Sully	F421-79	II	1	4	GTB
39SL4	Sully	F421-87B	II	0	2	SHP
39SL4	Sully	F421-88A	II	0	2	WKS
39SL4	Sully	F421-92	II	0	1	SHB
39SL4	Sully	F421-96	II	1	4	CBE
39SL4	Sully	F421-97B	II	0	3	GTB
39SL4	Sully	F421-100	II	1	6	GPD, WKW
39SL4	Sully	F421-101	II	0	1	CBE, WKS
39SL4	Sully	F421-102	II	0	2	GTB, CBE, BBE, SHB
39SL4	Sully	F421-105C	II	0	3	OWB
39SL4	Sully	F421-111A	II	1	6	BPE, SHB
39SL4	Sully	F421-113	II	0	3	SC, BIC
39SL4	Sully	F421-116A	II	1	5	WKS
39SL4	Sully	F421-119A	II	0	1	GTB
39SL4	Sully	F421-119D	II	0	2	GTB
39SL4	Sully	F421-127A	II	0	1	CT
39SL4	Sully	F421-129	II	0	4	CT
39WW1	Mobridge	F101-6B	III	0	1	SHB
39WW1	Mobridge	F101-12B	III	1	5	CP
39WW1	Mobridge	F101-20B	III	2	6	CP, SCA, BOA, SC, STK
39WW1	Mobridge	F101-24	III	0	1	BBE, SHB

TABLE A-7—*continued*

Site	Name	Burial	Period	Sex*	Age[†]	Categories
39WW1	Mobridge	F101-25D	III	1	4	BBR, BOT
39WW1	Mobridge	F101-27F	III	1	4	SPP
39WW1	Mobridge	F101-28B	III	0	2	RP
39WW1	Mobridge	F101-29B	III	0	1	SHB
39WW1	Mobridge	F201-2B	III	2	5	STK
39WW1	Mobridge	F201-8C	III	1	5	BIS
39WW1	Mobridge	F201-10B	III	2	4	RP
39WW1	Mobridge	F201-11F	III	2	5	SCH
39WW1	Mobridge	F201-15	III	0	1	SHB
39WW1	Mobridge	F201-19	III	0	2	SHB
39WW1	Mobridge	F201-20A	III	0	1	SHB
39WW1	Mobridge	F201-22	III	0	2	BOT
39WW1	Mobridge	F201-23	III	0	1	SHB
39WW1	Mobridge	F201-33D	III	2	5	STK
39WW1	Mobridge	F201-39A	III	0	2	BSK
39WW1	Mobridge	F301-1B	III	0	2	RP
39WW1	Mobridge	F301-4G	III	2	4	STK
39WW1	Mobridge	F301-5C	III	0	1	RP
39WW1	Mobridge	F301-10	III	1	5	BP, WP
39WW1	Mobridge	F301-12A	III	2	6	SHB, RP, BIB
39WW1	Mobridge	F301-12C	III	1	4	POT
39WW1	Mobridge	F301-19	III	0	4	STK
39WW1	Mobridge	F301-20	III	0	1	OBE
39WW1	Mobridge	F301-21	III	0	2	OBE
39WW1	Mobridge	F301-22A	III	0	4	BSW
39WW1	Mobridge	F301-26A	III	2	4	SPP
39WW1	Mobridge	F301-27C	III	0	1	SHB
39WW1	Mobridge	F302-1A	III	0	3	GTB
39WW1	Mobridge	F302-2	III	0	1	POT, GTB, WMS
39WW1	Mobridge	F302-5A	III	0	1	BIB
39WW1	Mobridge	F302-5B	III	1	6	BBR,,CBE
39WW1	Mobridge	F302-9	III	1	5	TUS
39WW1	Mobridge	F302-10	III	0	2	RAB, SPP
39WW1	Mobridge	F302-14	III	0	2	GTB, CBE
39WW1	Mobridge	F302-15	III	0	2	GTB
39WW1	Mobridge	F302-21A	III	2	4	SPP
39WW1	Mobridge	F302-22	III	2	5	STK, SC, SPP, BOA
39WW1	Mobridge	F302-23C	III	0	2	GTB, BBE
39WW1	Mobridge	F302-25B	III	0	3	GTB
39WW1	Mobridge	F302-27C	III	1	5	SPP
39WW1	Mobridge	F302-33A	III	2	4	QUF, OMF

Continued on next page

TABLE A-7—*continued*

Site	Name	Burial	Period	Sex*	Age†	Categories
39WW1	Mobridge	F302-37A	III	0	4	YP
39WW1	Mobridge	F302-44F	III	1	6	AS
39WW1	Mobridge	F303-1A	III	2	6	BIB, WKS
39WW1	Mobridge	F303-2C	III	1	4	POT, BFH
39WW1	Mobridge	F303-2D	III	2	3	RP
39WW1	Mobridge	F303-2E	III	0	4	RP
39WW1	Mobridge	F303-3D	III	0	2	BU
39WW1	Mobridge	F303-6	III	0	1	STK
39WW1	Mobridge	F402-2	III	0	2	RP
39WW1	Mobridge	F402-19D	III	0	2	RP
39WW1	Mobridge	F402-25A	III	0	1	SHB
39WW1	Mobridge	F402-26	III	0	1	RP
39WW1	Mobridge	F402-30	III	0	1	RP
39WW1	Mobridge	F402-34A	III	1	4	DUB, OMF
39WW1	Mobridge	F402-34B	III	2	4	SHB, SC
39WW1	Mobridge	F402-46A	III	1	4	RP, YP, GP, SC, WKF, SPP, CH, STK, BOF, BOW, BIC
39WW1	Mobridge	F402-62A	III	0	4	WP, RP, YP, STK, SPP, OWS, SC, BOA, OMF, BSW, ANT
39WW1	Mobridge	F402-66J	III	1	4	RP, SHP
39WW1	Mobridge	F402-70B	III	1	4	RP
39WW1	Mobridge	F402-70C	III	1	4	RP
39WW1	Mobridge	F402-71C	III	1	4	BIS, RP
39WW1	Mobridge	F402-74	III	0	1	BBR, BBE
39WW1	Mobridge	F402-76B	III	0	3	RP
39WW1	Mobridge	F402-84A	III	2	4	RP
39WW1	Mobridge	F402-94A	III	1	4	BIS
39WW1	Mobridge	F402-95A	III	0	1	GTB, SPP
39WW1	Mobridge	F402-95B	III	0	2	GTB, BIS, RP
39WW1	Mobridge	F402-99B	III	0	2	BON
39WW1	Mobridge	F402-110A	III	1	4	BIS, SPP, RP, YP
39CO9	Leaven-worth	F101-7	V	1	5	GTB, BSW, SP
39CO9	Leaven-worth	F101-9	V	2	3	MBR, YP, GTB, CB, SHP
39CO9	Leaven-worth	F101-12	V	2	4	GTB

TABLE A-7—*continued*

Site	Name	Burial	Period	Sex*	Age[†]	Categories
39CO9	Leaven-worth	F101-14	V	0	2	GPD, GTB
39CO9	Leaven-worth	F101-15	V	1	6	MAX, BOT, GPD, GTB, BIC, SPP, MG, OCO
39CO9	Leaven-worth	F101-17	V	0	2	GTB, CB, MR
39CO9	Leaven-worth	F101-18A	V	1	5	MAR, CB, RP, ANE, ANT
39CO9	Leaven-worth	F101-19	V	0	1	MBR, CB
39CO9	Leaven-worth	F101-24	V	1	4	MER, CB, GTB, OCO, RP, ANT
39CO9	Leaven-worth	F101-26	V	2	4	MER, CT, MR, OCO, RP, BOC, SPP
39CO9	Leaven-worth	F101-30	V	1	6	GTB
39CO9	Leaven-worth	F101-31A	V	2	5	MER, OCO, CB, BOB
39CO9	Leaven-worth	F101-32	V	0	1	GPD
39CO9	Leaven-worth	F101-34	V	0	1	OMF, BPE, BOB
39CO9	Leaven-worth	F101-35	V	2	6	MPP, MFH, MMO, SC, DUB, BSW, SPP, OWB, NGF, BIC, STK
39CO9	Leaven-worth	F101-36	V	0	3	GTB
39CO9	Leaven-worth	F101-46	V	0	2	OGF, CBU, GTB
39CO9	Leaven-worth	F101-47	V	0	1	GTB
39CO9	Leaven-worth	F101-48A	V	2	4	GTB, WKR
39CO9	Leaven-worth	F101-51	V	0	1	GTB

Continued on next page

TABLE A-7—*continued*

Site	Name	Burial	Period	Sex*	Age†	Categories
39CO9	Leaven-worth	F101-54A	V	2	6	GTB, MBR, ANE, WMS, SPP, BSW
39CO9	Leaven-worth	F101-59	V	0	1	GTB, OCO, CB, MCC, RP, GPD, ANE
39CO9	Leaven-worth	F101-60	V	0	1	GTB, BIC, BOT
39CO9	Leaven-worth	F101-61	V	0	2	GTB, MBR, POT
39CO9	Leaven-worth	F101-63	V	0	1	GTB, MBP, MER
39CO9	Leaven-worth	F101-64	V	0	1	GTB
39CO9	Leaven-worth	F101-65	V	1	5	GTB, CF, OMF, CK, CBU, BU, LF, INA, OMK, MER, OCO, SC, RP, BOB, NGF
39CO9	Leaven-worth	F101-66	V	0	1	GTB, CBU, GPD
39CO9	Leaven-worth	F101-67	V	0	1	GTB
39CO9	Leaven-worth	F101-69	V	2	4	GTB, GPD, BPE
39CO9	Leaven-worth	F101-73	V	2	5	OBE
39CO9	Leaven-worth	F201-1	V	2	4	GTB, BSW, RP
39CO9	Leaven-worth	F201-3	V	0	1	GTB, MPP, GPD
39CO9	Leaven-worth	F201-4	V	2	5	GTB, CB, BPE
39CO9	Leaven-worth	F201-5B	V	0	3	GTB, CBU, OGF, BU, MBR, WMS, NGF, BOB, TUS, GPD

TABLE A-7—*continued*

Site	Name	Burial	Period	Sex*	Age†	Categories
39CO9	Leaven-worth	F201-8	V	0	1	GTB
39CO9	Leaven-worth	F201-10	V	1	4	GTB, RP
39CO9	Leaven-worth	F201-11	V	0	3	GTB, BU
39CO9	Leaven-worth	F201-12	V	0	1	GTB, OCO
39CO9	Leaven-worth	F201-13	V	2	4	GTB, CBU, BOF
39CO9	Leaven-worth	F102-3D	V	1	4	GTB, MBR, MPP, GPD, WMS, RP
39CO9	Leaven-worth	F102-4	V	2	4	GTB
39CO9	Leaven-worth	F102-17	V	1	4	GTB, CF, GPD, BOT, BIC
39CO9	Leaven-worth	F102-18D	V	1	4	GTB, SCI, BRB, MER, OCO, GPD, RP, SCK
39CO9	Leaven-worth	F102-22	V	1	5	GTB, MER, NGF
39CO9	Leaven-worth	F102-27	V	0	1	GTB, MPP, EAF, DRC, SC, BOW, OWB, BIS, BIC
39CO9	Leaven-worth	F102-28	V	0	2	GTB, CF, LF
39CO9	Leaven-worth	F102-31	V	0	2	GTB, CBU, SHA
39CO9	Leaven-worth	F102-42	V	1	6	GTB, OMF, MR, BRB, BU, MTA, MBR, TUS, RP, GP, OWC, BIS, SPP, BIC
39CO9	Leaven-worth	F102-51	V	0	1	GTB, OMF, MBR, MFH, IRB, ANT, STK
39CO9	Leaven-worth	F102-52	V	0	1	GTB, CB

Continued on next page

TABLE A-7—*continued*

Site	Name	Burial	Period	Sex*	Age[†]	Categories
39CO9	Leaven-worth	F102-53A	V	0	2	GTB
39CO9	Leaven-worth	F102-55	V	1	4	BIC
39CO9	Leaven-worth	F202-1	V	0	2	GTB, ANT
39CO9	Leaven-worth	F202-3	V	1	5	GTB, GPD, DRC
39CO9	Leaven-worth	F202-4	V	0	1	GTB, SCI, HOS, IF, MPP, BGF, MG, OMK, MR, GPD, DRC, SHA, RP, STP, RAB, SHB, WKR, NGF, SPP
39CO9	Leaven-worth	F202-5C	V	0	2	GTB, IF, RAB, BOA
39CO9	Leaven-worth	F202-7	V	0	2	DRC, RP, BOW, BOB
39CO9	Leaven-worth	F202-9	V	0	1	GTB, RAB
39CO9	Leaven-worth	F202-10A	V	0	2	GTB, OBU, GPD, SMA
39CO9	Leaven-worth	F202-10B	V	2	3	GTB, CB, MBR, BOA
39CO9	Leaven-worth	F202-13	V	1	5	MPP, OMB, CB
39CO9	Leaven-worth	F203-1	V	1	5	GTB, OMK, CF, MG, SHA, CP, RP
39CO9	Leaven-worth	F203-6	V	0	1	GTB, GBU, IK, MPP, MR, RP, YP
39CO9	Leaven-worth	F203-7	V	0	1	GTB, RP
39CO9	Leaven-worth	F203-9	V	1	5	GTB, GP
39CO9	Leaven-worth	F203-23	V	1	4	NGF
39CO9	Leaven-worth	F203-25	V	0	1	POT

TABLE A-7—*continued*

Site	Name	Burial	Period	Sex*	Age†	Categories
39CO9	Leaven-worth	F203-26	V	2	5	GTB
39CO9	Leaven-worth	F203-27	V	1	6	GTB, OMF, MPP
39CO9	Leaven-worth	F203-30	V	0	1	GTB, IB, GPD
39CO9	Leaven-worth	F203-31	V	0	1	GTB
39CO9	Leaven-worth	F203-32	V	0	4	GTB, CF
39CO9	Leaven-worth	F120-5	V	0	2	GTB, MBR, CBU

*Codes for the sex variable are: 0 = indeterminate, 1 = male, and 2 = female.
†Codes for the age variable are: 1 = infant (0–2 years), 2 = child (3–12 years), 3 = adolescent (13–17 years), 4 = adult (18–30 years), 5 = mature adult (31–40 years), and 6 = old adult (41–50+ years).

REFERENCES CITED

Abel, Annie H. (editor)

1932 *Chardon's Journal at Fort Clark, 1834–1839.* South Dakota State Department of History, Pierre.

1939 *Tabeau's Narrative of Loisel's Expedition to the Upper Missouri.* University of Oklahoma Press, Norman.

Adams, Marie J.

1973 Structural Aspects of a Village Art. *American Anthropologist* 75:265–279.

Adams, William Y.

1979 On the Argument from Ceramics to History: A Challenge Based on Evidence from Medieval Nubia. *Current Anthropology* 20:727–734.

Aldenderfer, Mark S.

1987 On the Structure of Archaeological Data. In *Quantitative Research in Archaeology: Progress and Prospects,* edited by Mark S. Aldenderfer, pp. 89–113. Sage, Newbury Park, California.

Anderson, Keith M.

1969 Ethnographic Analogy and Archaeological Interpretation. *Science* 163(3863):113–114, 135–138.

Ascher, Robert

1961 Analogy in Archaeological Interpretation. *Southwestern Journal of Anthropology* 17:317–321.

Atkin, Ronald

1974 *Mathematical Structure in Human Affairs.* Heinemann Educational Books, London.

1975 *Q-Analysis: Theory and Practice.* Department of Mathematics, University of Essex, Colchester.

1977 *Combinatorial Connectivities in Social Systems.* Birkhäuser Verlag, Basel.

1978 Hard Language for the Soft Sciences. *Futures* 10:492–499.

1981 *Multidimensional Man.* Penguin Books, Harmondsworth, England.

Atkin, Ronald, and I. Witten

1975 A Multidimensional Approach to Positional Chess. *International Journal of Man-Machine Studies* 7:727–750.

Baerreis, David A.

1983 A Quantitative Approach to Culture Change: The Delaware Indians as an Ethnohistoric Case Study. In *Lulu Linear Punctated: Essays in Honor of George Irving Quimby,* edited by Robert C. Dunnell and Donald K. Grayson, pp. 185–207. University of Michigan, Museum of Anthropology, Anthropological Papers 72. Ann Arbor.

Bailey, Alfred G.

1937 *The Conflict of European and Eastern Algonkian Cultures, 1504–1700: A Study in Canadian Civilization.* New Brunswick Museum, Monographic Series 2. New Brunswick.

Bass, William M.

1965 The Physical Anthropology of the Sully Site, 39SL4. Manuscript on file, Department of Anthropology, University of Tennessee, Knoxville.

Bass, William M., David R. Evans, and Richard L. Jantz

1971 *The Leavenworth Site Cemetery: Archaeology and Physical Anthropology.* University of Kansas, Publications in Anthropology 2. Lawrence.

Bateson, Gregory

1935 Culture Contact and Schismogenesis. *Man* 35:178–183.

Beauregard, H. T. (editor)

1912 Journal of Jean Baptiste Trudeau Among the Arikara Indians in 1795. *Missouri Historical Society Collections* 4:9–48.

Berkhofer, Robert F.

1978 *The White Man's Indian: Images of the American Indian from Columbus to the Present.* Random House, New York.

REFERENCES CITED

Bernheimer, Richard

1952 *Wild Men in the Middle Ages: A Study in Art, Sentiment, and Demonology.* Harvard University Press, Cambridge.

Berry, James J.

1978 *Arikara Middlemen: The Effects of Trade on an Upper Missouri Society.* Ph.D. dissertation, Indiana University. University Microfilms, Ann Arbor.

Biglow, William

1830 *History of the Town of Natick, Massachusetts.* N.p., Boston.

Binford, Lewis R.

1967 Smudge Pits and Hide Smoking: The Use of Analogy in Archaeological Reasoning. *American Antiquity* 32:1–11.

Blakesley, Donald

1975 *The Plains Interband Trade System: An Ethnohistorical and Archaeological Investigation.* Ph.D. dissertation, University of Wisconsin-Milwaukee. University Microfilms, Ann Arbor.

1981 Toward a Cultural Understanding of Human Microevolution on the Great Plains. In *Progress in Skeletal Biology of Plains Populations,* edited by Richard L. Jantz and Douglas H. Ubelaker. Plains Anthropologist, Memoir 17. Lincoln, Nebraska.

Boller, Henry A.

1959 *Among the Indians Eight Years in the Far West, 1858–1866.* Lakeside Press, Chicago.

Bowers, Alfred W.

1950 *Mandan Social and Ceremonial Organization.* University of Chicago Press, Chicago.

Brackenridge, H. M.

1962 *Views of Louisiana Together with a Journal of a Voyage Up the Missouri in 1811.* Quadrangle Books, Chicago.

Brooks, Robert L.

1984 Planned vs. Unplanned Abandonment of Structures: Impacts on the Context of Living Surfaces. Paper presented at the Annual Plains Anthropological Conference, Lincoln, Nebraska.

Brown, Lionel A.

1974 The Archaeology of the Breeden Site. *Plains Anthropologist* 19(2).

Brown, Margaret K.

1979 *Cultural Transformations Among the Illinois: An Application of a Sys-*

tems Model. Publications of the Museum, Michigan State University, Anthropological Series 1(3). Lansing.

Bruner, Edward M.
1961 Mandan. In *Perspectives in American Indian Culture Change,* edited by Edward H. Spicer, pp. 187–277. University of Chicago Press, Chicago.

1973 The Missing Tins of Chicken: A Symbolic Interactionist Approach to Culture Change. *Ethos* 1:219–238.

Bruner, Jerome S., J. J. Goodnow, and G. A. Austin
1956 *A Study of Thinking.* Wiley, New York.

Burpee, L. J. (editor)
1927 *Journals and Letters of Pierre Gaultier de Varennes de la Verendrye and His Sons.* The Champlain Society, Toronto.

Cannon, Aubrey
1983 The Quantification of Artifactual Assemblages: Some Implications for Behavioral Inferences. *American Antiquity* 48:785–792.

Carrier, Lyman
1957 *Agriculture in Virginia, 1607–1699.* Jamestown 350th Anniversary Historical Booklet 14. Jamestown.

Catlin, George
1842 *Letters and Notes on the Manners, Customs, and Conditions of the North American Indians.* Tosswill, London.

Caldwell, Warren W.
1966 *The Black Partizan Site.* Smithsonian Institution River Basin Surveys, Publications in Salvage Archeology 2. Washington, D.C.

Chafe, Wallace L.
1973 Siouan, Iroquoian, and Caddoan. In *Current Trends in Linguistics,* edited by Thomas A. Sebeok, pp. 1164–1209. Mouton, The Hague.

Chalfant, Stuart A.
1951 *A Comparative Analysis of Arikara and Mandan Religious and Ceremonial Organization.* Unpublished M.A. thesis, Department of Anthropology, Columbia University, New York.

Chamberlain, M. Anne
1976 A Study of Behcet's Disease by Q-Analysis. *International Journal of Man-Machine Studies* 8:549–565.

Champagne, Duane
1985 *Strategies and Conditions of Political and Cultural Survival in American Indian Societies.* Cultural Survival, Occasional Papers 21. Cultural Survival, Cambridge, Massachusetts.

Chapin, Howard M.
1927 Indian Graves: A Survey of the Indian Graves That Have Been Discovered in Rhode Island. *Rhode Island Historical Society, Collections* 20:18–19.

Chapman, G. P.
1984 A Structural Analysis of Two Farms in Bangladesh. In *Understanding Green Revolutions,* edited by T. Bayliss-Smith and S. Wanmali, pp. 212–248. Cambridge University Press, Cambridge.

Charlton, Thomas H.
1976 Contemporary Central Mexican Ceramics: A View from the Past. *Man* 11:517–525.

Chiapelli, Fredi, Michael J. B. Allen, and Robert L. Benson (editors)
1976 *First Images of America: The Impact of the New World on the Old.* 2 vols. University of California Press, Berkeley.

Childe, V. Gordon
1956 *Piecing Together the Past.* Routledge and Kegan Paul, London.

Clark, J. G. D.
1953 Archaeological Theories and Interpretations: Old World. In *Anthropology Today,* edited by A. L. Kroeber, pp. 343–360. Aldine, Chicago.

Cohn, Bernard S.
1981 Anthropology and History in the 1980s. *Journal of Interdisciplinary History* 12:227–252.

Conkey, Margaret W.
1980 The Identification of Prehistoric Hunter-Gatherer Aggregation Sites: The Case of Altamira. *Current Anthropology* 21:609–630.

Cooper, P. L.
1953 Appraisal of the Archeological Resources of Oahe Reservoir, North and South Dakota. Manuscript on file, National Park Service, Midwest Archaeological Center, Lincoln, Nebraska.

Coues, Elliott (editor)
1893 *History of the Expedition Under the Command of Captains Lewis and Clark.* 4 vols. F. P. Harper, New York.

Csikszentmihalyi, Mihaly, and Eugene Rochberg-Halton

1981 *The Meaning of Things: Domestic Symbols and the Self.* Cambridge University Press, Cambridge.

Culbertson, Thaddeus A.

1851 Journal of an Expedition to the Mauvaises Terres and the Upper Missouri in 1850, edited by John F. McDermott. *Annual Report of the Smithsonian Institution* 5:84–145. Washington, D.C.

Cunningham, Clark E.

1973 Order in the Atoni House. In *Right and Left: Essays on Dual Symbolic Classification,* edited by Rodney Needham, pp. 204–238. University of Chicago Press, Chicago.

Curtis, Edward S.

1970 *The North American Indians.* Vol. 5. Johnson Reprint Company, London.

Cuthbertson, Stuart, and John C. Ewers

1939 *A Preliminary Bibliography on the American Fur Trade.* United States Department of the Interior, National Park Service, Jefferson National Expansion Memorial. St. Louis.

Dale, Harrison C.

1918 *The Ashley-Smith Explorations, 1822–1829.* N.p., Glendale, California.

David, Nicholas

1972 On the Life Span of Pottery, Type Frequencies, and Archaeological Inference. *American Antiquity* 37:141–142.

Dawson, John W.

1880 *Fossil Men and Their Modern Representatives.* Dawson Brothers, Montreal.

Deetz, James

1965 *The Dynamics of Stylistic Change in Arikara Ceramics.* Illinois Studies in Anthropology 4. Urbana.

De Land, Edmund (editor)

1918 Fort Tecumseh and Fort Pierre Journal and Letter Books. *South Dakota State Historical Society, Historical Collections* 9:69–239.

Denig, Edwin T.

1961 *Five Indian Tribes of the Upper Missouri: Sioux, Arikaras, Assiniboines, Crees, Crows,* edited by John C. Ewers. University of Oklahoma Press, Norman.

De Smet, Pierre Jean
1905 *Life, Letters, and Travels of Father Pierre Jean De Smet.* 3 vols., edited by H. M. Chittenden and A. T. Richardson. F. P. Harper, New York.

Donley, Linda W.
1982 House Power: Swahili Space and Symbolic Markers. In *Symbolic and Structural Archaeology,* edited by Ian Hodder, pp. 63–73. Cambridge University Press, Cambridge.

Doran, J. E., and F. R. Hodson
1975 *Mathematics and Computers in Archaeology.* Edinburgh University Press, Edinburgh.

Dorsey, George A.
1904a *Traditions of the Arikara.* Carnegie Institution, Publication 17. Washington, D.C.

1904b *Traditions of the Skidi Pawnee.* American Folklore Society, Boston.

Douglas, Mary
1970 *Natural Symbols.* Penguin, New York.

1972 Symbolic Orders in the Use of Domestic Space. In *Man, Settlement, and Urbanism,* edited by Peter J.Ucko, Ruth Tringham, and G. W. Dimbleby, pp. 513–521. Duckworth, London.

Douglas, Mary, and Baron Isherwood
1979 *The World of Goods: Towards an Anthropology of Consumption.* W. W. Norton, New York.

Eggan, Fred (editor)
1955 *Social Anthropology of North American Tribes.* University of Chicago Press, Chicago.

Elkin, A. P.
1951 Reaction and Interaction: A Food Gathering People and European Settlement in Australia. *American Anthropologist* 53:164–186.

Ellen, Roy F.
1979 Introductory Essay. In *Classifications in Their Social Context,* edited by Roy F. Ellen and David Reason, pp. 1–32. Academic Press, New York.

Elliot, J. H.
1970 *The Old World and the New, 1492–1650.* Cambridge University Press, Cambridge.

Evans, S.

1978 A Structural Analysis of the Central Place Hierarchy of the Valley of Mexico. Paper presented at the Annual Meeting of the Society for American Archaeology, Tucson.

Evans-Pritchard, E.

1940 *The Nuer.* Oxford University Press, London.

Ewers, John C.

1954 The Indian Trade of the Upper Missouri Before Lewis and Clark. *Missouri Historical Society Bulletin* 10:429–446.

1955 *The Horse in Blackfoot Indian Culture.* Bureau of American Ethnology, Bulletin 159. Washington, D.C.

1959 *Adventures of Zenas Leonard, Fur Trader.* University of Oklahoma Press, Norman.

1968 *Indian Life on the Upper Missouri.* University of Oklahoma Press, Norman.

Fairbanks, Charles H.

1962 Excavations at Horseshoe Bend, Alabama. *Florida Anthropologist* 15:41–56.

Fisher, Robin

1977 *Contact and Conflict: Indian-European Relations in British Columbia, 1774–1890.* University of British Columbia Press, Vancouver.

Fitting, James

1976 Patterns of Acculturation at the Straits of Mackinac. In *Cultural Change and Continuity: Essays in Honor of James Bennett Griffin,* edited by Charles Cleland, pp. 321–334. Academic Press, New York.

Fitzgerald, William R.

1986 The Introduction of European Goods into Neutral Iroquoian Society. Paper presented at the 51st Annual Meeting of the Society for American Archaeology, New Orleans.

Fitzhugh, William W.

1985 Introduction. In *Cultures in Contact: The European Impact on Native Cultural Institutions in Eastern North America, A.D.* 1000–1800, edited by William W. Fitzhugh, pp. 1–15. Smithsonian Institution Press, Washington, D.C.

Fletcher, A.

1906 The Arikara. In *Handbook of American Indians North of Mexico,* edited by F. W. Hodge, pp. 83–86. Bureau of American Ethnology, Bulletin 30(1). Washington, D.C.

Frake, Charles O.
1969 The Ethnographic Study of Cognitive Systems. In *Cognitive Anthropology,* edited by Stephen Tyler, pp. 28–41. Holt, Rinehart and Winston, New York.

Frantz, Wendell
1962 Crazy Bull site (39LM220), Big Bend Reservoir, South Dakota. *Plains Anthropologist* 7:36–42.

Fritz, John M.
1978 Paleopsychology Today: Ideational Systems and Human Adaptation in Prehistory. In *Social Archaeology: Beyond Subsistence and Dating,* edited by Charles L. Redman et al., pp. 37–59. Academic Press, New York.

Gass, Patrick
1958 *A Journal of the Voyages and Travels of a Corps of Discovery Under the Command of Capt. Lewis and Clarke.* Ross and Haines, Minneapolis.

Gatrell, Anthony C.
1983 *Distance and Space: A Geographical Perspective.* Clarendon Press, Oxford.

Gelburd, Diane E.
1978 *Indicators of Culture Change Among the Dobe !Kung San.* Unpublished M.A. thesis, Department of Anthropology, George Washington University, Washington, D.C.

Gilbert, B. Miles, and William M. Bass
1967 Seasonal Dating of Burials from the Presence of Fly Pupae. *American Antiquity* 32:534–535.

Gilmore, Melvin R.
1919 *Uses of Plants by the Indians of the Missouri River Region.* Bureau of American Ethnology, Annual Report 33. Washington, D.C.

1924a Glass Bead Making by the Arikara. *Indian Notes* 1:20–21.

1924b Arikara Fish Trap. *Indian Notes* 1:120–134.

1925 Arikara Household Shrine to Mother Corn. *Indian Notes* 2:31–34.

1926a The Arikara Consolation Ceremony. *Indian Notes* 3:256–274.

1926b Arikara Genesis and Its Teachings. *Indian Notes* 3:188–193.

1926c Arikara Commerce. *Indian Notes* 3:13–18.

1926d Indian Custom of 'Carrying the Pipe.' *Indian Notes* 3:89–95.

1927 Notes on Arikara Tribal Organization. *Indian Notes* 4:332–350.

1928 The Making of a New Head Chief by the Arikara. *Indian Notes* 5:411–418.

1929 The Arikara Book of Genesis. *Michigan Academy of Science, Arts and Letters, Papers* 12:95–120.

1930 The Arikara Tribal Temple. *Michigan Academy of Science, Arts and Letters, Papers* 14:47–70.

1931 The Sacred Bundles of the Arikara. *Michigan Academy of Science, Arts and Letters, Papers* 16:33–50.

Giraud, M.

1953 *Histoire de la Louisiane Française, 1698–1715.* Vol. 1. Presses Universitaires de France, Paris.

Goodenough, Ward H.

1957 Cultural Anthropology and Linguistics. *Georgetown University Monograph Series on Language and Linguistics* 9:167–173.

1963 *Cooperation in Change: An Anthropological Approach to Community Development.* Russell Sage Foundation, New York.

Gorenflo, Larry

1980 Q-Analysis and the Structure of Mortuary Data. Manuscript on file, Department of Geography, University of California, Santa Barbara.

Gould, Peter

1980 Q-Analysis, or a Language of Structure: An Introduction for Social Scientists, Geographers, and Planners. *International Journal of Man-Machine Studies* 13:169–199.

1981 Structural Language of Relations. In *Future Trends in Geomathematics,* edited by Richard G. Craig and M. Labovitz, pp. 312–321. Pion, London.

Gould, Richard A. (editor)

1978 *Explorations in Ethnoarchaeology.* University of New Mexico Press, Albuquerque.

1980 *Living Archaeology.* Cambridge University Press, Cambridge.

Grinnell, G. B.

1891 Marriage Among the Pawnee. *American Anthropologist* 4:275–281.

Gunther, Erna

1972 *Indian Life on the Northwest Coast of North America as Seen by the Early Explorers and Fur Traders During the Last Decades of the Eighteenth Century.* University of Chicago Press, Chicago.

Hall, C. L.

1879 A Little Ree Theology. In Records of the Mission of the American Board of Commissioners for Foreign Missions, at Ft. Berthold, Dakota Territory. Manuscript on file, North Dakota State Historical Society, Bismarck, North Dakota.

Hamell, George R.

1983 Trading in Metaphors: The Magic of Beads. In *Proceedings of the 1982 Glass Trade Bead Conference,* edited by Charles F. Hayes, III, pp. 5–28. Rochester Museum and Science Center, Research Records 16.

Hayden, Brian, and Aubrey Cannon

1984 *The Structure of Material Systems: Ethnoarchaeology in the Maya Highlands.* Society for American Archaeology, Papers 3. Washington, D.C.

Helgevold, Mary K.

1981 *A History of South Dakota Archaeology.* South Dakota Archaeological Society, Special Publications 3. Washington, D.C.

Hewitt, J. N. B. (editor)

1937 *Journal of Rudolph Friederich Kurz.* Bureau of American Ethnology, Bulletin 115. Washington, D.C.

Hill, James N.

1970 Prehistoric Social Organization in the American Southwest: Theory and Method. In *Reconstructing Prehistoric Pueblo Societies,* edited by William A. Longacre, pp. 11–58. University of New Mexico Press, Albuquerque.

Hodder, Ian

1978 Simple Correlations Between Material Culture and Society: A Review. In *The Spatial Organisation of Culture,* edited by Ian Hodder, pp. 3–24. Duckworth, London.

Hoffman, Bernard G.

1961 *Cabot to Cartier.* University of Toronto Press, Toronto.

Hoffman, J. J.

1967 *Molstad Village.* Smithsonian Institution River Basin Surveys, Publications in Salvage Archeology 4. Washington, D.C.

1968 *The La Roche Site.* Smithsonian Institution River Basin Surveys, Publications in Salvage Archeology 11. Washington, D.C.

1970 Two Arikara Villages: A Study in Bad River Phase Material Culture. Manuscript on file, National Park Service, Midwest Archeological Center, Lincoln, Nebraska.

Hoffman, W. J.

1884 La Fête Annuelle des Indiens Arikaris. *Societe d'Anthropologie de Paris, Bulletin* 3:526–532.

Holder, Preston

1958 Social Stratification Among the Arikara. *Ethnohistory* 5:210–218.

1967 The Fur Trade as Seen From the Indian Point of View. In *The Frontier Re-Examined,* edited by John F. McDermott, pp. 129–139. University of Illinois Press, Urbana.

1970 *The Hoe and the Horse on the Plains: A Study of Cultural Development Among North American Indians.* University of Nebraska Press, Lincoln.

Hollow, Robert C., and Douglas R. Parks

1980 Studies in Plains Linguistics: A Review. In *Anthropology on the Great Plains,* edited by W. Raymond Wood and Margot Liberty, pp. 68–97. University of Nebraska Press, Lincoln.

Howard, James H.

1972 Arikara Native-Made Glass Pendants: Their Probable Function. *American Antiquity* 37:93–97.

1974 The Arikara Buffalo Society Medicine Bundle. *Plains Anthropologist* 19:241–271.

Howard, James H., and Alan Woolworth

1954 An Arikara Bear Society Initiation Ceremony. *North Dakota History* 21:168–179.

Howson, Joan

1941 *A Protohistoric Arikara Village: The Buffalo Pasture Site.* Unpublished M.A. thesis, Department of Anthropology, Columbia University, New York.

Hugill, Peter J., and D. Bruce Dickson (editors)

1988 *The Transfer and Transformation of Ideas and Material Culture.* Texas A and M University Press, College Station.

Hurt, Wesley R., Jr.

1954 *Report of the Investigation of the Spotted Bear Site, 39HU26, and the Cottonwood Site, 39HU43, Hughes County, South Dakota, 1953.* South Dakota Archaeological Commission, Archaeological Studies, Circular 6.

1957 *Report of the Investigation of the Swan Creek Site, 39WW7, Walworth County, South Dakota, 1954–1956.* South Dakota Archaeological Commission, Archaeological Studies, Circular 7.

Hyde, George E.
1952 The Mystery of the Arikaras. *North Dakota History* 19:25–58.

Innis, Harold A.
1970 *The Fur Trade in Canada: An Introduction to Canadian Economic History.* Revised edition. University of Toronto Press, Toronto.

Isbell, W. H.
1976 Cosmological Order Expressed in Prehistoric Ceremonial Centers. Paper presented at the International Congress of Americanists, Paris.

Jablow, J.
1951 *The Cheyenne in Plains Indian Trade Relations, 1795–1840.* American Ethnological Society, Monographs 19. Washington, D.C.

Jackson, Donald D. (editor)
1962 *Letters of the Lewis and Clark Expedition with Related Documents, 1783–1854.* University of Illinois Press, Urbana.

Jaenen, Cornelius J.
1976 *Friend and Foe: Aspects of French-Amerindian Cultural Contact in the Sixteenth and Seventeenth Centuries.* Columbia University Press, New York.

Jantz, Richard L., Douglas W. Owsley, and Patric Willey
1978 Craniometric Relationships of Central Plains Populations. In *The Central Plains Tradition: Internal Development and External Relationships,* edited by Donald J. Blakeslee, pp. 144–156. Office of the State Archaeologist, University of Iowa, Report 11. Iowa City.

Jennings, Jesse D.
1985 River Basin Surveys: Origins, Operations, and Results, 1945–1969. *American Antiquity* 50:281–296.

Jensen, R. E.
1966 *The Peterson Site (39LM215), an Earthlodge Village in the Big Bend Reservoir, South Dakota.* Plains Anthropologist, Memoir 3. Lincoln.

Johnson, J.
1976 The Q-Analysis of Road Intersections. *International Journal of Man-Machine Studies* 8:531–548.

Johnson, J., and S. Wanmali
1981 A Q-Analysis of Periodic Market Systems. *Geographical Analysis* 13:262–275.

Johnson, Richard B.
1967 *The Hitchell Site*. Smithsonian Institution, River Basin Surveys, Publications in Salvage Archeology 3. Washington, D.C.

Kintigh, Keith W.
1984 Measuring Archaeological Diversity by Comparison with Simulated Assemblages. *American Antiquity* 49:44–54.

Kivett, Marvin F.
1958 The Oacoma Sites, 39LM26 and 39LM27, Lyman County, South Dakota. Manuscript on file, National Park Service, Midwest Archeological Center. Lincoln, Nebraska.

Knight, Vernon J.
1981 *Mississippian Ritual*. Ph.D. dissertation, University of Florida. University Microfilms, Ann Arbor.

Korn, Sheila M.
1978 The Formal Analysis of Visual Systems as Exemplified by a Study of Abelam (Papua New Guinea) Paintings. In *Art in Society*, edited by Michael Greenhalgh and Vincent Megaw, pp. 161–173. Brown and Little, New York.

Kramer, Carol (editor)
1979 *Ethnoarchaeology: Implications of Ethnography for Archaeology*. Columbia University Press, New York.

1982 *Village Ethnoarchaeology: Rural Iran in Archaeological Perspective*. Academic Press, New York.

Krause, Richard A.
1967 *Arikara Ceramic Change: A Study of the Factors Affecting Stylistic Change in Late 18th and Early 19th Century Arikara Pottery*. Ph.D. dissertation, Yale University. University Microfilms, Ann Arbor.

1972 *The Leavenworth Site: Archaeology of an Historic Arikara Community*. University of Kansas Publications in Anthropology 3. Lawrence.

Kuper, Adam
1980 Symbolic Dimensions of the Southern Bantu Homestead. *Africa* 50:8–23.

Lamarck, B. P.
1963 *Zoological Philosophy, an Exposition with Regard to the Natural History of Animals*. Translated by H. Eliot. Hafner, New York.

Larocque, François A.
1910 *Journal of Larocque from the Assiniboine to the Yellowstone, 1805.* Publications of the Canadian Archives 3. Toronto.

Larpenteur, Charles
1933 *Forty Years a Fur Trader on the Upper Missouri: The Personal Narrative of Charles Larpenteur, 1833–1872.* Lakeside Press, Chicago.

Leach, Edmund
1977 A View From the Bridge. In *Archaeology and Anthropology: Areas of Mutual Interest,* edited by M. Spriggs, pp. 161–176. British Archaeological Reports, Supplementary Series 19. Oxford.

Lehmer, Donald J.
1954a *Archaeological Investigations in the Oahe Dam Area, South Dakota, 1950–51.* Bureau of American Ethnology, Bulletin 158, River Basin Survey Papers 7. Washington, D.C.

1954b The Sedentary Horizon of the Northern Plains. *Southwestern Journal of Anthropology* 10:139–159.

1965 Salvage Archaeology in the Middle Missouri. Manuscript on file, National Park Service, Midwest Archaeological Center. Lincoln, Nebraska.

1971 *Introduction to Middle Missouri Archaeology.* National Park Service, Anthropological Papers 1. Lincoln, Nebraska.

Lehmer, Donald J., and Warren W. Caldwell
1966 Horizon and Tradition in the Northern Plains. *American Antiquity* 31:511–516.

Lehmer, Donald J., and David T. Jones
1968 *Arikara Archeology: The Bad River Phase.* Smithsonian Institution, River Basin Surveys, Publications in Salvage Archeology 7. Washington, D.C.

Le Raye, Charles
1908 Journal of Charles Le Raye, 1802. *South Dakota Historical Collections* 4:159–169.

Lévi-Strauss, Claude
1963 *Structural Anthropology.* Basic Books, New York.

Lewis, Kenneth E.
1975 *The Jamestown Frontier: An Archaeological Study of Colonization.* Ph.D. dissertation, University of Oklahoma. University Microfilms, Ann Arbor.

1977 An Archaeological Perspective on Social Change—The Virginia Frontier. In *The Frontier: Comparative Studies,* vol. 1, edited by D. H. Miller and J. O. Steffen, pp. 139–159. University of Oklahoma Press, Norman.

Linton, Ralph (editor)
1940 *Acculturation in Seven American Indian Tribes.* Appleton-Century-Crofts, New York.

Lowie, R. H.
1915 Societies of the Arikara Indians. *American Museum of Natural History, Anthropological Papers* 11:647–678. New York.

Luttig, John C.
1920 *Journal of a Fur Trading Expedition to the Upper Missouri, 1812–1813,* edited by Stella M. Drumm. Missouri Historical Society, St. Louis.

Mackenzie, Charles
1960 The Missouri Indians: A Narrative of Four Trading Expeditions to the Missouri, 1804–1805–1806. In *Les Bourgeois de la Compagnie du Nord-Ouest,* 2 vols., edited by Louis F. R. Masson, pp. 315–393. Antiquarian Press, New York.

Mandelbaum, David G.
1940 The Plains Cree. *American Museum of Natural History, Anthropological Papers* 37:155–315. New York.

Margry, Pierre (editor)
1876–1886 *Découvertes et Établissements des Français dans l'Ouest at dans le Sud de l'Amérique Septentrionale, 1614–1754.* 6 vols. D. Jouaust, Paris.

Martin, Calvin
1978 *Keepers of the Game: Indian-Animal Relationships and the Fur Trade.* University of California Press, Berkeley.

Masson, Louis François Rodrigue (editor)
1960 *Les Bourgeois de la Compagnie du Nord Ouest.* 2 vols. Antiquarian Press, New York.

Matthews, Washington
1877 *Ethnography and Philology of the Hidatsa Indians.* United States Geological and Geographical Survey, Miscellaneous Publications 7. Washington, D.C.

Mattison, Ray H.
1966 The Letters of Henry A. Boller: Upper Missouri Fur Trader. *North Dakota History* 33(1).

Metcalf, George

1963 Star Village: A Fortified Historic Arikara Site in Mercer County, North Dakota. *Bureau of American Ethnology, Bulletin* 185:57–122. Washington, D.C.

Meyer, Roy W.

1977 *The Village Indians of the Upper Missouri: The Mandans, Hidatsas, and Arikaras.* University of Nebraska Press, Lincoln.

Milanich, Jerald T.

1978 The Western Timucua: Patterns of Acculturation and Change. In *Tacachale: Essays on the Indians of Florida and Southeastern Georgia During the Historic Period,* edited by Jerald Milanich and Samuel Proctor, pp. 59–88. University Presses of Florida, Gainesville.

Miller, D.

1982 Artefacts as Products of Human Categorisation Processes. In *Symbolic and Structural Archaeology,* edited by Ian Hodder, pp. 17–25. Cambridge University Press, Cambridge.

Missouri Historical Society

1819 Letter from Thomas Biddle to Col. Henry Atkinson, Camp Missouri on the Missouri River. In Indian Trade Papers. Manuscript on file, Missouri Historical Society, St. Louis.

1822 Inventory of Goods, Wares, and Merchandise Taken at St. Louis the 4th of August, 1822 Being the Remains of Russell Farnham's Outfit 1821. In Pierre Chouteau Papers, Inventory Book. Manuscript on file, Missouri Historical Society, St. Louis.

1826 Prices at Which Some of the Articles of Merchandise are to be Furnished, October 14. In William Ashley Papers. Manuscript on file, Missouri Historical Society, St. Louis.

1829 Inventory of Goods, etc. Remaining on Hand at Fort Clark, Mandan village, April 17. In Chouteau-Papin Collection. Manuscript on file, Missouri Historical Society, St. Louis.

1831a A List of Merchandise with Quantities and Prices, Ree Outfit Under Charge of Dominique Lachapelle, October 17th. In American Fur Company Ledger, vol. 5. Microfilm edition, reel 6. Manuscript on file, Missouri Historical Society, St. Louis.

1831b Letter from William Gordon to Lewis Cass, October 8. In Fur Trade Envelope. Manuscript on file, Missouri Historical Society, St. Louis.

1849 A List of Merchandise with Quantities and Prices, Upper Missouri Outfit, Fort Clark. In American Fur Company Ledger, Book oo. Microfilm edition, reel 14. Manuscript on file, Missouri Historical Society, St. Louis.

Missouri Intelligencer
1822 Newspaper, September 17. St. Louis.

Moore, H. L.
1982 The Interpretation of Spatial Patterning in Settlement Residues. In *Symbolic and Structural Archaeology,* edited by Ian Hodder, pp. 74–79. Cambridge University Press, Cambridge.

Morgan, Dale L.
1953 *Jedediah Smith and the Opening of the West.* University of Nebraska Press, Lincoln.

1964 *The West of William H. Ashley.* The Old West Publishing Company, Denver.

Morgan, Lewis Henry
1959 *The Indian Journals, 1859–62,* edited by Leslie A. White. University of Michigan Press, Ann Arbor.

Munn, Nancy D.
1974 Symbolism in a Ritual Context: Aspects of Symbolic Action. In *Handbook of Social and Cultural Anthropology,* edited by John J. Honigmann, pp. 579–612. Rand McNally, New York.

Nasatir, Abraham P. (editor)
1952 *Before Lewis and Clark.* 2 vols. St. Louis Historical Documents Foundation, St. Louis.

Nicklin, Keith
1971 Stability and Innovation in Pottery Manufacture. *World Archaeology* 3:13–48.

Oglesby, Richard E.
1963 *Manuel Lisa and the Opening of the Missouri Fur Trade.* University of Oklahoma Press, Norman.

Orser, Charles E., Jr.
1980a *An Archaeological and Historical Socioeconomic Analysis of Arikara Mortuary Practice.* Ph.D. dissertation, Department of Anthropology, Southern Illinois University. University Microfilms, Ann Arbor.

1980b Toward a Partial Understanding of Complexity in Arikara Mortuary Practice. *Plains Anthropologist* 25:113–120.

1984a Trade Good Flow in Arikara Villages: Expanding Ray's "Middleman Hypothesis." *Plains Anthropologist* 29:1–12.

1984b Understanding Arikara Trading Behavior: A Cultural Case Study of the Ashley-Leavenworth Episodes of 1823. In *Selected Papers from the Fourth North American Fur Trade Conference, 1981,* edited by Thomas C. Buckley, pp. 191–107. North American Fur Trade Conference, St. Paul.

Orser, Charles E., Jr., and Larry J. Zimmerman

1984 A Computer Simulation of Euro-American Trade Good Flow to the Arikara. *Plains Anthropologist* 29:199–210.

Osborn, Alan J.

1988 Limitations of the Diffusionist Approach: Evolutionary Ecology and Shell-Tempered Ceramics. In *The Transfer and Transformation of Ideas and Material Culture,* edited by Peter J Hugill and D. Bruce Dickson, pp. 23–44. Texas A and M University Press, College Station.

Osgood, Ernest S. (editor)

1964 *The Field Notes of Captain William Clark, 1803–1805.* Yale University Press, New Haven.

O'Shea, John M.

1978 *Mortuary Variability: An Archaeological Investigation with Case Studies from the Nineteenth Century Central Plains of North America and the Early Bronze Age of Southern Hungary.* Unpublished Ph.D. dissertation, University of Cambridge.

1984 *Mortuary Variability: An Archaeological Investigation.* Academic Press, New York.

Oswalt, Wendell H.

1976 *An Anthropological Analysis of Food-Getting Technology.* John Wiley and Sons, New York.

Parks, Douglas R. (editor)

1981 *Ceremonies of the Pawnee, Part I: The Skiri, Part II: The South Bands,* by James R. Murie. Smithsonian Contributions to Anthropology 27. Washington, D.C.

Parmalee, Paul W.

1979 Inferred Arikara Subsistence Patterns Based on a Selected Faunal Assemblage from the Mobridge Site, South Dakota. *The Kiva* 44:191–218.

Parmentier, Richard J.

1985 Diagrammatic Icons and Historical Process in Belau. *American Anthropologist* 87:840–852.

Peterson, Nicolas

1971 Open Sites and the Ethnographic Approach to the Archaeology of Hunter-Gatherers. In *Aboriginal Man and Environment in Australia,* edited by D. J. Mulvaney and J. Golson, pp. 14–29. Australian National University Press, Canberra.

1973 Camp Site Location Amongst Australian Hunter-Gatherers: Archaeological and Ethnographic Evidence for a Key Determinant. *Archaeology and Physical Anthropology in Oceania* 8:173–193.

Phillips, Paul Chrisler

1961 *The Fur Trade.* 2 vols. University of Oklahoma Press, Norman.

Peirce, Charles Sanders

1931–1935 *Collected Papers of Charles Sanders Peirce.* 8 vols., edited by C. Hartshorne and P. Weiss. Harvard University Press, Cambridge.

Pollack, David, and A. Gwynn Henderson

1983 Contact Period Developments in the Middle Ohio Valley. Paper presented at the 48th Annual Meeting of the Society for American Archaeology, Pittsburgh.

Quimby, George I.

1966 *Indian Culture and European Trade Goods.* University of Wisconsin Press, Madison.

Ramenofsky, Ann F.

1987 *Vectors of Death: The Archaeology of European Contact.* University of New Mexico Press, Albuquerque.

Ray, Arthur J.

1974 *Indians in the Fur Trade: Their Role as Trappers, Hunters, and Middlemen in the Lands Southwest of Hudson Bay, 1660–1870.* University of Toronto Press, Toronto.

1978 History and Archaeology of the Northern Fur Trade. *American Antiquity* 43:26–34.

1979 A Reply to Tracy. *American Antiquity* 44:595–596.

Reid, Russell

1930 The Earth Lodge. *North Dakota Historical Quarterly* 4(3).

Robbins, Michael C., and Richard B. Pollnac

1977 A Multivariate Analysis of the Relationship of Artifactual to Cultural Modernity in Rural Buganda. In *Experimental Archaeology*, edited by A. Ingersoll, J. Yellen and P. MacDonald, pp. 332–351. Columbia University Press, New York.

Roberts, Frank H. H., Jr.

1952 River Basin Surveys: The First Five Years of the Inter-Agency Archeological and Paleontological Salvage Program. *Bureau of American Ethnology, Annual Report.* Washington, D.C.

Robinson, Doane (editor)

1902 Official Correspondence Pertaining to the Leavenworth Expedition of 1823 into South Dakota for the Conquest of the Ree Indians. *South Dakota Historical Collections* 1:179–256.

Rodriguez, William, and William M. Bass

1985 Decomposition of Buried Bodies and Methods That May Aid in Their Detection. *Journal of Forensic Sciences* 30:836–852.

Rogers, Everett M.

1983 *Diffusion of Innovations.* 3rd edition. Free Press, New York.

Rogers, Garry F.

1979 A Computer Program for Calculating the Information Theory Diversity Index. Manuscript on file, Department of Geography, Columbia University, New York.

Rogers, J. Daniel.

1987 *Culture Contact and Material Change: Arikara and Euro-American Interactions in the Eighteenth and Nineteenth Centuries.* Ph.D. dissertation, University of Chicago. University Microfilms, Ann Arbor.

Russell, B.

1956 Mathematical Knowledge as Based on a Theory of Types. In *Logic and Knowledge: Essays 1901–1950,* edited by R. Marsh, pp. 57–102. George Allen and Unwin, London.

Russell, Osborne

1965 *Journal of a Trapper, 1834–1843.* University of Nebraska Press, Lincoln.

Sahlins, Marshall

1981 *Historical Metaphors and Mythical Realities: Structure in the Early History of the Sandwich Islands Kingdom.* Association for Social Anthropology in Oceania, Special Publications 1. Ann Arbor.

1985 *Islands of History.* University of Chicago Press, Chicago.

Schiffer, Michael B.

1983 Toward the Identification of Formation Processes. *American Antiquity* 48:675–706.

Sharp, Lauriston

1934a The Social Organization of the Yir Yoront Tribe, Cape York Peninsula. *Oceania* 4:404–431.

1934b Ritual Life and Economics of the Yir Yoront. *Oceania* 5:19–42.

1939 Tribes and Totemism in Northeast Australia. *Oceania* 9:254–275, 439–461.

1952 Steel Axes for Stone Age Australians. In *Human Problems in Technological Change: A Casebook,* edited by Edward H. Spicer, pp. 69–90. Russell Sage Foundation, New York.

Smith, Carlyle S., and Alfred E. Johnson

1968 *The Two Teeth Site.* Smithsonian Institution River Basin Surveys, Publications in Salvage Archeology 8. Washington, D.C.

Smith, G. Hubert

1972 *Like-A-Fishhook Village and Fort Berthold, Garrison Reservoir, North Dakota.* National Park Service, Anthropological Papers 2. Lincoln, Nebraska.

Smith, G. Hubert, and John Ludwickson

1981 *Fort Manuel: The Archeology of an Upper Missouri Trading Post of 1812–1813.* Special Publications of the South Dakota Archaeological Society 7.

Spaulding, Albert C.

1956 *The Arzberger Site, Hughes County, South Dakota.* Museum of Anthropology, University of Michigan, Occasional Contributions 16. Ann Arbor.

1982 Structure in Archaeological Data: Nominal Variables. In *Essays in Archeological Typology,* edited by Robert Whallon and James A. Brown, pp. 1–20. Center for American Archeology Press, Evanston, Illinois.

Sperber, Dan

1975 *Rethinking Symbolism.* Translated by Alice L. Morton. Cambridge University Press, Cambridge.

Spicer, Edward H. (editor)

1961 *Perspectives in American Indian Culture Change.* University of Chicago Press, Chicago.

Stearn, E. Wagner, and Allen E. Stearn
1945 *The Effect of Smallpox on the Destiny of the Amerindian.* Bruce Humphries, Boston.

Stephenson, Robert L.
1954 Taxonomy and Chronology in the Central Plains-Middle Missouri River Area. *Plains Anthropologist* 1:15–21.

Stirling, M. W.
1924 Archaeological Investigations in South Dakota. *Explorations and Field-Work of the Smithsonian Institution, 1923,* pp. 66–71. Washington, D.C.

Strong, William D.
1935 *An Introduction to Nebraska Archeology.* Smithsonian, Miscellaneous Collections 63(10). Washington, D.C.

Sunder, John Edward
1965 *The Fur Trade on the Upper Missouri, 1840–1865.* University of Oklahoma Press, Norman.

Swanton, John R.
1942 *Source Material on the History and Ethnology of the Caddo Indians.* Bureau of American Ethnology, Bulletin 132. Washington, D.C.

Thomas, David H.
1978 The Awful Truth About Statistics in Archaeology. *American Antiquity* 43:231–244.

1983 *The Archaeology of Monitor Valley, 2: Gatecliff Shelter.* Anthropological Papers of the American Museum of Natural History 59, Part 1. New York.

Thwaites, Reuben Gold (editor)
1896–1901 *The Jesuit Relations and Allied Documents,* vol. 10. Burrows Brothers, Cleveland.

1904a Travels in the Interior of America, 1809–1811 by John Bradbury. In *Early Western Travels, 1748–1846,* vol. 5. Arthur H. Clark, Cleveland.

1904b Journal Up the Missouri, 1811 by Henry Marie Brackenridge. In *Early Western Travels, 1748–1846,* vol. 6. Arthur H. Clark, Cleveland.

1904–1905 *Original Journals of the Lewis and Clark Expedition, 1804–06,* vols. 6 and 7. Dodd and Mead, New York.

1906a Travels in the Interior of North America by Maximilian, Prince of Weid. In *Early Western Travels, 1748–1846,* vols. 22–24. Arthur H. Clark, Cleveland.

1906b Letters and Sketches of Father Pierre Jean De Smet. In *Early Western Travels, 1748–1846,* vol. 27. Arthur H. Clark, Cleveland.

Toom, Dennis L.
1979 *The Middle Missouri Villagers and the Early Fur Trade: Implications for Archaeological Interpretation.* Unpublished M.A. thesis, Department of Anthropology, University of Nebraska, Lincoln.

Tracy, William A.
1979 A Reconsideration of the Archaeological Significance of the Role of the Middleman in the Fur Trade. *American Antiquity* 44:594–595.

Trimble, Michael K.
1986 *An Ethnohistorical Interpretation of the Spread of Smallpox in the Northern Plains Utilizing Concepts of Disease Ecology.* Reprints in Anthropology 33. Lincoln, Nebraska.

Trobriand, Philippe Regis Denis de Keredern de
1941 *Army Life in Dakota: Selections from the Journal of Philippe Regis Denis de Keredern de Trobriand.* Lakeside Press, Chicago.

Tschopik, Harry, Jr.
1950 An Andean Ceramic Tradition in Historical Perspective. *American Antiquity* 15:196–218.

Turner, Terance
1969 A Central Brazilian Tribe and Its Symbolic Language of Bodily Adornment. *Natural History* 78:1–8.

Turner, Victor W.
1977 Symbols in African Ritual. In *Symbolic Anthropology,* edited by Janet L. Dolgin, David S. Kemnitzer, and David M. Schneider, pp. 183–194. Columbia University Press, New York.

Ubelaker, Douglas H.
1966 Arikara-Made Glass Pendants. *Plains Anthropologist* 32:172–173.

Ubelaker, Douglas H., and William Bass
1970 Arikara Glassworking Techniques at Leavenworth and Sully Sites. *American Antiquity* 35:467–475.

Ubelaker, Douglas H., and Richard L. Jantz
1979 Plains Caddoan Relationships: The View from Craniometry and Mortuary Analysis. *Nebraska History* 60:249–259.

Ubelaker, Douglas H., and Patrick Willey
1978 Complexity in Arikara Mortuary Practice. *Plains Anthropologist* 23:69–74.

United States
1829 *20th Congress, Second Session, Senate Document 72 (Serial 181).* U.S. Government Printing Office, Washington, D.C.

1836 *24th Congress, First Session, Senate Document 1 (Serial 278).* U.S. Government Printing Office, Washington, D.C.

1837a *Annual Report, Commissioner of Indian Affairs.* U.S. Government Printing Office, Washington, D.C.

1837b *24th Congress, Second Session, Senate Document 1 (Serial 297).* U.S. Government Printing Office, Washington, D.C.

1838 *25th Congress, Second Session, Senate Document 1 (Serial 314).* U.S. Government Printing Office, Washington, D.C.

1842 *27th Congress, Second Session, Senate Document 1 (Serial 395).* U.S. Government Printing Office, Washington, D.C.

1847 *29th Congress, Second Session, Senate Document 1 (Serial 493).* U.S. Government Printing Office, Washington, D.C.

1849 *Annual Report, Commissioner of Indian Affairs.* U.S. Government Printing Office, Washington, D.C.

1857 *Annual Report, Commissioner of Indian Affairs.* U.S. Government Printing Office, Washington, D.C.

1863 *Annual Report, Commissioner of Indian Affairs.* U.S. Government Printing Office, Washington, D.C.

1874 *Annual Report, Commissioner of Indian Affairs.* U.S. Government Printing Office, Washington, D.C.

1878 *Annual Report, Commissioner of Indian Affairs.* U.S. Government Printing Office, Washington, D.C.

Villiers, Baron Marc de
1925 *La Decouverte du Missouri et l'Histoire du Fort d'Orleans (1673–1728).* Libraire de la Société de L'Histoire de France, Paris.

Washburn, Wilcomb E.

1967 Symbol, Utility, and Aesthetics in the Indian Fur Trade. In *Aspects of the Fur Trade: Selected Papers of the 1965 North American Fur Trade Conference,* edited by Russell W. Fridley, pp. 50–54. Minnesota Historical Society, St. Paul.

Waselkov, Gregory A., and R. Eli Paul

1981 Frontiers and Archaeology. *North American Archaeologist* 2:309–329.

Wedel, Waldo R.

1938 *The Direct-Historical Approach in Pawnee Archaeology.* Smithsonian Miscellaneous Collections 97(7). Washington, D.C.

1961 *Prehistoric Man on the Great Plains.* University of Oklahoma Press, Norman.

1967 Salvage Archaeology in the Missouri River Basin. *Science* 196:589–597.

Weltfish, Gene

1965 *The Lost Universe.* Basic Books, New York.

Whallon, Robert, and James A. Brown (editors)

1982 *Essays in Archaeological Typology.* Center for American Archeology Press, Evanston, Illinois.

White, J. Peter

1967 Ethno-Archaeology in New Guinea: Two Examples. *Mankind* 6:409–414.

White, Richard

1983 *The Roots of Dependency: Subsistence, Environment and Social Change Among the Choctaws, Pawnees, and Navajos.* University of Nebraska Press, Lincoln.

Will, George F.

1928 Magical and Sleight of Hand Performances by the Arikara. *North Dakota Historical Quarterly* 3:50–65.

1930 Arikara Ceremonials. *North Dakota Historical Quarterly* 4:247–265.

Will, George F., and George E. Hyde

1964 *Corn Among the Indians of the Upper Missouri.* University of Nebraska Press, Lincoln.

Wilson, Gilbert L.

1917 *Agriculture of the Hidatsa Indians: An Indian Interpretation.* University of Minnesota Studies in the Social Sciences 9. Minneapolis.

1934 The Hidatsa Earthlodge, edited by Bella Weitzner. *Anthropological Papers of the American Museum of Natural History* 33:341–420. New York.

Wilson, Samuel M.

1986 *The Conquest of the Caribbean Chiefdoms.* Ph.D. dissertation, University of Chicago. University Microfilms, Ann Arbor.

Wishart, David

1975 Images of the Northern Great Plains from the Fur Trade, 1807–1843. In *Images of the Plains: The Role of Human Nature in Settlement,* edited by Brian W. Blouet and M. P. Lawson, pp. 45–55. University of Nebraska Press, Lincoln.

1979 *The Fur Trade of the American West, 1807–1840: A Geographic Synthesis.* University of Nebraska Press, Lincoln.

Witt, Shirley H.

1968 Nationalistic Trends Among American Indians. In *The American Indian Today,* edited by S. Levine and Nancy O. Lurie, pp. 93–127. Everett Edwards, New York.

Wolf, Eric R.

1982 *Europe and the People Without History.* University of California Press, Berkeley.

Wood, W. Raymond

1972 *Contrastive Features of Native North American Trade Systems,* pp. 153–169. University of Oregon Anthropological Papers 4. Eugene.

1974 Northern Plains Village Cultures: Internal Stability and External Relationships. *Journal of Anthropological Research* 30:1–16.

Yellen, John

1977 *Archaeological Approaches to the Present.* Academic Press, New York.

INDEX